Beyond the Corporation
HUMANITY WORKING

DAVID ERDAL

THE BODLEY HEAD
LONDON

Published by The Bodley Head 2011

2 4 6 8 10 9 7 5 3 1

First published in Great Britain in 2011 by
The Bodley Head
Random House, 20 Vauxhall Bridge Road,
London SW1V 2SA

www.bodleyhead.co.uk
www.rbooks.co.uk

Addresses for companies within The Random House Group Limited can be found at:
www.randomhouse.co.uk/offices.htm

The Random House Group Limited Reg. No. 954009

A CIP catalogue record for this book
is available from the British Library

ISBN 9781847921093

The Random House Group Limited supports The Forest Stewardship
Council (FSC), the leading international forest certification organisation. All our titles
that are printed on Greenpeace approved FSC certified paper carry the FSC logo. Our
paper procurement policy can be found at www.rbooks.co.uk/environment

Mixed Sources
Product group from well-managed
forests and other controlled sources
www.fsc.org Cert no. TT-COC-2139
© 1996 Forest Stewardship Council
FSC

Typeset in Dante MT by Palimpsest Book Production Limited, Falkirk, Stirlingshire

Printed and bound in Great Britain by
Clays Ltd, St Ives PLC

For Robert Oakeshott
inspiration to so many

and for Jennie
without whom

Contents

Introduction

We are reasonable people. If our ideas are shown to be wrong, if the case against them is cogent and backed with evidence, then we change our ideas. That, at least, is the ideal, the intelligent way for human beings to behave – and especially for those who aspire to use the scientific method.

In the real world, however, when people are playing for high stakes, this does not quite capture what goes on. We fall short of our ideal. We become committed to our own particular views. We see clearly how contemptible are those who disagree with us. If possible, we ignore them; if they get attention anyway, then we dismiss their ideas as nonsense. We predict that they will fail, and explain away all their successes as aberrations.

This is true even in science. The great physicist Max Planck observed that new, better theories only really flourish after those who hold the old ones have died. When you have built a career by working with a particular theory, it is hard to give it up, no matter what the evidence against it. Furthermore the old, established people hold the power. The theories of Alfred Wegener, the man whose work led eventually to our understanding of how continents shift on tectonic plates, were ridiculed by orthodox geologists until long after his death; Arthur Holmes, a key supporter, found it extremely hard to obtain university posts. Charles Darwin worked for years on barnacles, to establish his credentials as a serious scholar worthy of acceptance by the scientific establishment, partly in order to outflank what he knew would be powerful opposition to the idea of evolution by natural selection.

Where the subject of study is the behaviour of human beings, resistance to new ideas is even more characteristic. Evidence is less clear-cut, theories are harder to disprove, and the behaviour that is being studied can actually be shaped by the theory itself. In a famous study Robert Frank showed that students of economics tend to give no less to charity in their first year at university than the first-year students of astronomy. But after studying economics for some years, during which time they have been told repeatedly that human beings are monomaniacally selfish and that it is irrational to behave in any other way, they donate significantly less than their peers.[1]

For the last 200 years and more we have been working with a particular standard theory about the rights of owners of corporations and their relationship with their employees. Being told by experts that there is no alternative, people have tended to act as though there really is none. Economists have then seen confirmation for their claims in a world they have in part created. This book is about what happens when the model changes, when the employees – all the employees – of a company come to own the business where they work. Instead of toiling as the servants of people who make all the decisions and take all of the profits, the employee-owners become active partners in their business, sharing information, influence and profits together. They share the effort and they share the wealth. Productivity and happiness are the result.

This book sets out to challenge traditional economists, whose theories have provided ideological justification for small coteries of business executives and financiers to plunder the economy even as they led it into near collapse. These same economists have predicted nothing but problems and failure for employee-owned companies. From their dominant position, with their theoretical models that justify the current ownership structure, they have for too long ignored the facts and rubbished the evidence – painstakingly gathered by diligent researchers over the course of their careers – that employee-owned companies work very well.

It is time to acknowledge this evidence, and to hear the voices of the employee-owners. What the available information shows is that in fact employee-owned companies do well – as long as the employees are treated as partners. With the right leadership they do *very* well, both economically and for the people in them.

While drawing on academic studies, this book is mainly about arguments, illustrated with accounts of individual experience. In the end what makes people tick is seen most clearly from the stories they tell about their lives. An understanding of employee ownership is best achieved through accounts of what actually happens, in the real world, to real people, when they are engaged partners in their own shared business. Such an understanding shows that the economic orthodoxy is mistaken.

Humanity working in the traditional corporate and financial structures is humanity undermined and betrayed; humanity working with shared ownership becomes happier and wealthier and wiser than the defenders of the current system can imagine. Only a few years ago those who claimed that mainstream economic theory overlooked key aspects of reality would have faced ridicule from a self-confident and well-rewarded establishment. Now, perhaps, after the financial crisis of 2008–9, the facts of the matter will become a little more conspicuous, a little more difficult to ignore or explain away. Economists were wrong about finance. What follows aims to convince you that they are wrong about the business enterprise too.

This book is in four parts. Part One sets out the traditional model, before telling the stories of some employee-owned businesses and contrasting the experience of those who work there with some of the predictions made by traditional economists. Part Two tells stories of traditional employment, which removes key natural rights from people, and of its history. Part Three examines how and why employee ownership works so well. And Part Four deals with human nature, some of the wider effects of employee ownership, and some ideas on the way forward.

PART ONE

PREDICTIONS AND REALITY

... the ideas of economists and political philosophers, both when they are right and when they are wrong, are more powerful than is commonly understood. Indeed the world is ruled by little else. Practical men, who believe themselves to be quite exempt from any intellectual influences, are usually the slaves of some defunct economist.

John Maynard Keynes, 1936

'Things cannot be otherwise than as they are.'

Dr Pangloss, in Voltaire's *Candide*, 1759

'I've found a flaw.'

Alan Greenspan to Congress, 23 October 2008

1

Owning a Business, and Making It Perform

I was born into a family that owned a papermill. It had been in the family for nearly a century and a half: the father-in-law of my great-grandfather's sister had started the business with a £6,000 invest-ment* in 1809, the year in which Tom Paine died and Charles Darwin was born. Tom Paine's great contribution to the world had been to help inspire the Americans to do three things: to declare independ-ence from Britain, to found a republic and eventually to install demo-cratic government. Charles Darwin's was to work out how we and all living things actually got here, thereby bringing light into the darkness of archaic religious notions. My ancestral relative's achieve-ment was not quite in the same league, but it was still significant: he started a business that for generations has given jobs to hundreds of people – some 1,500 worked in the mill at the point when I joined in 1977.

It is now over 200 years since the founding of the business, and still day after day and night after night hundreds of employees flock to the mill, to take up their roles in the service of the great machines that churn out the paper twenty-four hours a day, seven days a week. You can fall in love with the machines, and many do – in fact it is hard not to: such scale, such pace, such subtle control, such massive, beautiful engineering. Even the smell in the moisture-laden air becomes fragrant after a year or two working there.

My ancestor's achievement made him rich, and also brought wealth

* The equivalent of about £360,000 in 2009.

to his descendants. People who own papermills are well off, and during my childhood we did not lack for money. If you own the mill, you and your children and your children's children will receive all the wealth created by the endless hard work of the employees. You don't have to do anything: it is simply given to you, it is yours by legal right, even if you have nothing to do with the mill and have never contributed anything to its success, and even if for generations your family has invested no new money in the business, other than some of what the business itself generates through the work of the employees.

In the generally accepted version of the world, this is the way that things are supposed to be. The world of work is divided into the owners and their employees. The owners call the shots; the employees do what they are told. The employees get paid for their time; the owners get all the profits. If there are losses, then the owners suffer from the effects of the losses, but only up to the limited amount of money that they have invested. If the losses are greater than that, then the business goes bust, and the people to whom money is owed suffer the rest of the losses.

According to the theory, this produces the healthiest possible economy. Entrepreneurial people like my ancestor are encouraged to start businesses in the hope that they will make lots of money, since they and their descendants will pocket all the profits. If those descendants make a success of it, the company stays a 'family business'. In Europe the proportion of enterprises classified as family businesses ranges from about 60 per cent in Germany and France to over 80 per cent in Italy. A 2008 report on the family businesses in the UK estimated that they produce about 38 per cent of private sector turnover – a little over £1,000bn – and employ around 42 per cent of all employees in the private sector.

When the entrepreneurs or their descendants decide to sell a business, there are usually two options: they can sell to a larger corporation (a 'trade sale') or they can float the shares on the Stock Exchange (an 'initial public offering,' or IPO). Either way, the position of the employees does not change: they are still working for the owners. The new owners may change things. They have a perfect right to do so: they have the rights to all the information about the business, and to appoint the directors, and to make all the major decisions. Without those rights the owners could not ensure that they get the best possible profit.

There can, however, be a third option. If the original owners have taken this and sold to private equity investors, then there will certainly be changes, as we shall see in the course of this book. In the UK in 2007 the turnover of private-equity-owned companies was in total nearly half of the turnover of family companies.

It is hard to find statistics about how much of the economy is created by private companies, that is, companies whose shares are not traded publicly on the Stock Exchange (including the family companies, the private-equity-owned companies and others) as opposed to those whose shares are traded. But it seems a reasonable estimate that in the UK and USA somewhat over half of the non-government economy is in the private company category. In the USA around 6,000 corporations have their shares traded publicly. Those companies tend to be larger than the private companies. For example, the largest private company in 2007 was Koch, with a turnover of just under $100bn, but there were thirteen quoted companies with greater turnover. Mars, the tenth-largest private company, with a turnover of $25bn, was topped by eighty-eight quoted companies. On the other hand, at the small-company end, the vast majority are private, and do not have their shares traded.

According to the consensus, it is a very healthy thing to have a company's shares traded on the Stock Exchange. It means that the actions of the managers are constantly under scrutiny. If they do not do well, then the price of that company's shares falls, until eventually it is worthwhile for someone to buy the whole company and turn it round. That is called capital market discipline. It is a form of supervision, a constant prod for the managers to do better.

The other great advantage attributed to having the shares traded is access to capital. For example, a company can put together a proposal for a new project, present the idea to the financial institutions and in a short time raise a large amount of capital for that project. In the case of the great majority of companies, this advantage remains simply theoretical: most quoted companies do not raise money in this way. But the raising of capital for large new projects is a very important function, which must be solved if any economy is to thrive.

The problems of the system are widely recognised, in particular the pressure on the managers in every company to produce short-term profit rather than strategically to build a strong business. Most shares are owned by institutional shareholders such as pension funds, whose managers are themselves judged from quarter to quarter. They pass on that pressure to the companies whose shares they hold. A second and growing problem is the way that chief executives, especially in the UK and USA, have managed to increase the rewards they extract from the companies to levels that are truly extraordinary. But no solution to these problems has been found, and the situation is accepted. Everyone believes that this is the best system, so the problems are simply tolerated as unfortunate necessities.

In 1985, when I took over as executive chairman and de facto CEO of the papermill, the ownership of the company was rather dispersed, and I could see that many of my cousins and other relatives would be delighted to sell their shares. I approached private equity providers and was horrified at what they proposed: essentially they would have bought family members' shares and put some new money into the company, but only if we gave them a virtually guaranteed return of 30 per cent a year. The merchant banker I subsequently approached recommended an IPO or a trade sale. But I felt deeply uneasy about that. It would have meant passing the future of the business and all its employees into the hands of people whose only concern might be to extract cash from the business, not to build it. There was no way of telling what they would do: I knew enough to be aware that the promises of acquirers were not to be trusted.

My concern about the powerlessness of the employees was not a paternalistic affectation, driven by a sense of privilege. After getting a degree in Chinese I had decided, following advice gleaned from Chairman Mao's Little Red Book, to go and learn from the workers. I got a job as an unskilled labourer on a building site in London and indeed learned a great deal, gradually coming to understand what it was to be employed. We would work hard enough to keep our jobs, but no harder. Since it was tough to survive on the meagre base pay, most of us would take overtime if it was offered – after which we'd be too exhausted to do much else. There was an automatic fellow feeling among us and an unenthusiastic obedience of the foreman's instructions. During the tea breaks, which we stretched out as long as we could, I did my best to 'learn from the workers' by quizzing them about their lives. As a result they elected me shop steward. In trying to sort out problems – for example, negotiating bonus rates, or making an unrealistic bid to have a man reinstated after he'd come to work drunk – I got to know the site manager a little. He was decent enough, but we both knew that the gulf between us was unbridgeable. He represented the corporation, I the workers. But he held most of the cards: as employees we could accept his terms or go on strike. I then played an active role in the national building workers' strike of 1972. It felt good to fight back, aware of all the thousands of others battling in the same cause all over the country. It wasn't about the money: in purely financial terms we would never get back what we'd lost by standing on the picket lines for thirteen weeks. It was about dignity and pride and standing tall together on the earth. We could not get these from our working lives, which gave us no way to be participants beyond just obeying instructions. When, many years later, I took over as chairman of the paper company, I had still not solved the basic problem that had haunted me from my childhood visits to the paper-mill and my brief stint in the building trade, unanswered even after obtaining an MBA at Harvard. Why should the employees bother to do anything other than the absolute minimum to keep their jobs?

Yes, they had to make a living. It followed that they had to do enough to get paid – they had no choice. And yes, in their shoes, and under the active supervision that was the practice in the mill, I too would have worked, to an extent. But where was the incentive for the great majority of them to do anything more than just enough? It was already clear from the paper industry trends that competitive pressure could only get more intense,[2] and I knew that the secrets of success would include getting as many people as possible to commit themselves to making the business work well. But really, when you looked at it, why should they bother?

Conventional wisdom has it that there is nothing more beneficial than having a job. It is the earnest wish of parents for their children that they will get jobs, and not just because that lets them stand on their own feet, without parental subsidy. A job connects you to other people, gives you a role in life, is fulfilling. The long-term unemployed are subject to loss of self-esteem, depression, abuse of drugs and alcohol, marriage breakdown. A job makes your life a thousand times better. It makes you autonomous, empowers you. That, at least, is the theory. But, in reality, the only truthful message I could give to young people on the shop floor was that they were working *to make my family rich*. They may indeed have been lucky to have their jobs, but not because it would let them have a share of the wealth they were helping to create, nor because it was empowering: only because the alternative was to be unemployed.

'Empowerment' is a word much evident in the PR statements of corporations with conventionally structured ownership, their shares traded on the Stock Exchange and their chief executives 'incentivised' with millions in share options. What empowerment actually means, however, turns out to be something of a will o' the wisp – in reality it has very little substance. And to the extent that any company succeeds in making it real, it can be ended in an instant, by fiat of the owners.

This happens often, for example, when a company is taken over by a group of private equity investors. Inside the corporation, owners hold far-reaching powers, and private equity thrives by using those powers to the limit. I was unable to find insiders willing to talk on the record about their experiences in companies taken over by private equity. It would appear that telling a critical truth in public is no easier in the case of a big, litigious Western corporation than it is under any authoritarian regime anywhere in the world. But a distillation of stories, without disclosing the companies or the people involved, runs as follows.[3]

A large corporation decides to sell one of its subsidiaries. The executive directors of the subsidiary welcome the opportunity: instead of leading a business that is a neglected and non-strategic backwater in a huge corporation, they look forward to being independent – at last they will have a chance to build the business in the way they have long hoped for. The private equity investors who acquire the company assure them before the deal is done that capital will be made available to invest in developing the business, and that the new owners will be delighted to work with the existing team of executive directors. These directors will be given the opportunity to acquire significant quantities of shares on favourable terms. Soon after the acquisition has been completed, however, a new chairman is appointed, a man famous for cutting costs rather than building businesses; the CEO departs and no one is told why; the board is reduced in size, so that only new people appointed by the new owners sit on it; the allocations of shares to the now demoted ex-directors turn out to be much lower than originally indicated.

At this point communication from the board is reduced to virtually nothing: not even the executives, until recently on the board, are told what is going on. In direct contradiction of earlier promises, no significant capital is made available for investment. And people start to disappear without warning or explanation: from time to time when employees arrive at work, they find that the desk of someone they have worked with for years has been cleared overnight. Even with the previous, neglectful owners, the human resource (HR) function will have been aimed at creating a good and well-run organisation. The new HR director's role is simply to minimise the chance of any of these disappearances ending up in court. But for the employees, right up to ex-director level, there is nothing to be done. Even the executives have no rights or powers: they have no right to be heard, no right to influence anything, no right to know anything. They are merely employees. The investors are the owners and can do as they wish. What they wish is usually to squeeze as much cash out of the business as quickly as possible. The fact that the feedback from customers slides more or less rapidly from good to poor is a matter of low priority.

The point is not whether the people involved are good or bad people. The point is that the distribution of power – the owners' power and the employees' lack of it – enables owners to treat people in this way. Any way in which employees actually are empowered is by grace and favour of the owners, and can be removed without warning.

In normal – that is, non-working – life, in a democratic country with a more or less free press, human beings are indeed empowered, able to exercise their autonomy. They can get most of the information they want. They can express their opinions. They can join any group or movement they please. They are active in their lives, to the extent that they wish, and to the extent that they have the money. If they create something, it belongs to them and they can consume it or dispose of it as they wish. If they combine with others to create things – a school picnic or a sailing regatta or a political group – then the decisions will be jointly made, and they will all have their say, if they wish.

In the workplace, however, those rights, that autonomy and that empowerment are theirs no longer. They are removed by the employment contract. Employees have no right to receive any information; they can ask, but the employer is not obliged to reply. They have no right to have their opinions heeded on anything. Indeed, the managers are perfectly entitled to remain deaf to their views, in that way preserving for themselves their 'right to manage'. The managers are appointed by others, with nobody paying any attention to what the employees think. In fact the employees have no right to influence in any way any decision that the company takes.

Why should those who work in a business have no right to obtain information, no right to be listened to, and no right to influence the choice of managers or the business decisions, large or small? The answer is that those rights belong to the owners of the shares. Shareholders' rights must not be diluted by giving mere employees any part of them – so the mainstream thinking goes.

And it does not end there. The employees' work creates wealth. That wealth is used to pay their salaries, and if the company is well run, and if pillager-bankers have not caused an implosion of the economy, then there may be quite a bit of profit left over at the end. The employees have been involved in creating that profit – it is because of the efforts made by all of them that there is *any* wealth. But are they allowed to participate in this wealth that they have helped create?

No.

Is this the best we can do, for the great majority of people in the world – all those who are employed?

There exists a whole ideology to justify this mistreatment of people at work. It is based ultimately on the mathematical models of traditional mainstream economists, whose conclusions bear a striking resemblance to the philosophy of Voltaire's famous optimist, Dr Pangloss.

In 1755 Dr Pangloss, the hero's tutor and companion in *Candide,* sat dejected amid the ruins of a beautiful capital city – Lisbon – which had been utterly destroyed by an enormous earthquake and tsunami. Things had not gone well for him. The castle where he had been employed as a tutor had been sacked by the Bulgarians and nearly everyone killed. He had lost an eye and an ear to syphilis contracted from a serving girl, and he had been reduced to beggary. On top of all that, he was dripping wet, having nearly drowned after being ship-wrecked.

But Dr Pangloss had spent his adult life profitably selling positive thinking, and he was not going to let these little difficulties make him doubt the convictions that had served him so well.

'All that is, is for the best,' he preached to a small group of survivors. 'It is impossible that things should be other than as they are. For every-thing is right.'

Today the global financial tsunami of 2008 has brought real misery to untold numbers of people. But traditional mainstream economists and their followers on the commanding heights of the economy are in essentially the same position as Dr Pangloss. Their lifelong convic-tion is that whatever the Market ordains is right. This is coupled with the belief that what exists now has been ordained by the Market. It follows that what exists now is right. We live in the best of all possible worlds.

The idea that what the Market produces cannot be bettered goes back to a phrase of Adam Smith's. In 1776 he famously wrote of the average businessman that:

by directing [his] industry in such a manner as its produce may be of the greatest value, he intends only his own gain; and he is in this, as in many other cases, led by an invisible hand to promote an end which was no part of his intention ... By pursuing his own interest, he frequently promotes that of the society more effectually than when he really intends to promote it.

Adam Smith was talking about people who build businesses selling useful products and services. Building up a business which serves an unmet need undoubtedly benefits the community and increases GDP – it serves society well.

Alas, the concept did not stay limited to that arena. From the first, the notion of the invisible hand moved rapidly out across the world, eventually spreading its digits into the markets and leaving its prints on the legislation of all developed countries. It is not hard to see why. It is a concept that releases business leaders from any need to consider the wider effects of what they do.

Don't worry about that – the invisible hand will take care of it. Just get on and make money to the greatest possible extent, in whatever way you can, and the invisible hand will see to it that all will be well.

This is also a great comfort to politicians, who are often mightily impressed by the wealthy, and by their large donations to party funds.

The comment 'The markets would not like it!' is enough to dampen many a proposal for reform. In this context 'the markets' always refers to the capital markets, or, more accurately, to the people who run them. The product markets such as those for food and clothing are not seen as having any opinions, or indeed any power. The labour market is not deemed to like or dislike anything. But the capital markets – that is, the people who run them – have a huge amount of power, as well as strong opinions. When they phone the President or the Prime Minister, the call is put through. What they like and dislike counts.

Even in Adam Smith's day, when powerful corporations did not yet exist, let alone capital market players who speculate in thousands of billions on a capital base of a tiny fraction of those sums, he refrained from saying that self-interest would *always* produce socially beneficial results. His followers were less cautious. More recently the ideology of the all-good, all-powerful Market increasingly took hold from the 1980s onwards, especially in the USA led by Ronald Reagan and the UK led by Margaret Thatcher. In the twenty-first century Alan Greenspan, who as chairman of the Federal Reserve in America had greater influence on the finances of the world, and for longer, than anyone else in history so far, was reported as telling Brooksley Born, a highly reputable lawyer proposing to regulate derivatives: 'Well, you probably will always believe there should be laws against fraud, and I don't think there is any need for a law against fraud.' Greenspan, Born says, believed the market would take care of itself. Greenspan said that the alleged statement ran against his long-held view that rooting out fraud was, as expressed in his 2007 book *The Age of Turbulence*, an 'area in which more rather than less government involvement is needed'. However, also in that book he wrote that 'I concluded, and I suspect most regulators agree, that the first and most effective line of defense against fraud and insolvency is counterparties' surveillance.' He was justly tagged a market fundamentalist. His testimony to Congress in October 2008 admitted that 'those of us who have looked to the self-interest of lending institutions to protect shareholder's equity (myself especially) are in a state of shocked disbelief. Such counterparty surveillance is a central pillar of our financial markets' state of balance . . . There are additional regulatory changes that this breakdown of the central pillar of competitive markets requires in order to return to stability, particularly in the areas of fraud, settlement, and securitization.'[4]

One of the reasons why the markets in the developed countries are successful is that they are strictly regulated. This doesn't fit the market fundamentalist account of the world so it is largely ignored. America is one of the most intensely and effectively regulated market systems in the world – and that is a large part of the reason why the American markets generally work well. Trust is essential if markets are to be effective, and trustworthy behaviour has to be enforced, through legislation and regulation. For example, regulations require corporations to file financial accounts. Those accounts have to be accurate. There are significant penalties both for the company and for the accountants if this rule is breached. Arthur Andersen, one of the largest accountancy firms in the world, was in effect obliterated after the Enron scandal appeared to implicate it in allowing inadequate accounts to be produced. A similar degree of supervision applies at many levels. For example, if companies conspire together to keep prices up, there are again serious penalties for doing so. Without that supervision, the markets would not work – they would simply be open to abuse by the powerful and the ruthless. Deregulation in the financial market showed how the invisible hand would soon pick the pockets of the unwary.

Yet when some of the most prestigious American economists went to Russia from 1989 onwards, to advise the government on how best to move the sclerotic Russian economy towards a free market system, somehow the fact of intensive institutional regulation was forgotten. The advice they gave the Russians can be summarised as 'let the Market rip'. Unfortunately for the Russians, their leaders took the advice, and the end result was essentially banditry. The state-owned economy was in essence looted by a few well-placed individuals, who became mega-billionaires. China learned from the shambles in Russia, and from the success of the Asian economies that ignored the market fundamentalists. The Chinese have moved step by step and bottom up towards a market economy, preserving the structure of their institutions even as they transformed their roles. The same Western advisers tried to sell their free market ideology to the Chinese and were politely rejected. Which was fortunate for the Chinese people – and for the world's economy.

This absolute faith in the Market is based on the faith of traditional economists in their mathematical models. The secret and not so secret dream of many economists has been to elevate their profession to the status of a real science – they do not mind the fact that economics is called 'the dismal science', as long as the word 'science' is included. But they face a drawback. Physicists and chemists and astronomers and biologists all deal with processes that are out there in the world – processes that are independent of the will of human beings. We humans may decide to use nuclear fission to make bombs or to generate electricity, but the nature of nuclear fission is not subject to our will.

The same is not true of the material studied by economists. For example, a share – a unit of stock in a corporation – has existed for only a couple of centuries, with only a few precursors going further back. And it is quite possible, even likely, that a share will not be part of the lives of our grandchildren's grandchildren. Certainly, in a thousand years the share may have been altered beyond recognition. It is designed by people, it can be changed by people and in time it will be utterly transformed by people. The same is true of the employment contract, on which the economists' models of the labour market depend. If we redesign the basic units – the share and the relationship between the owners and the employees – then the predictions made by economists must also change.

It is widely recognised that the laws of the Market in the economists' models depend on assumptions that are never found in the real world. One of the assumptions, for example, is that people are psychotically self-interested. This is not true. Most people are fair-minded, and will resist being treated unfairly, even if that costs them.[5] Furthermore people enjoy being part of something where they are active partners, rather than being pushed around and kept in the dark. A recent study in the US found that the majority of employee-owners who together control the companies where they work would not sell out to an investor even if someone offered them 50 per cent more than the current share price.[6]

Another assumption is that everyone in a market has full and accurate information. This is never true. For example, the people who sold the dodgy mortgages to poor people in America knew that the small print disclosed the fact that the poor people could not afford those mortgages. They did not tell the poor people this, and indeed made careful efforts to conceal that information from them. They then sold those mortgages on to investment banks, which were similarly unaware of just how flaky those deals had been. And the investment bankers then diced up the mortgages, mixed them together and sold them like hamburgers to other bankers, who were equally ignorant. The rating agencies, whose fees came from the investment banks that had diced the mortgages up in the first place, assured the investors that all would be well. When the crunch came, nobody knew which bits of beef were in which hamburger, so it was impossible to value them. It is impossible ever to meet the basic assumption normally made by economists: that people are equally well informed.

Joe Stiglitz, the Nobel Prize-winning economist (and thorn in the flesh for many traditionally minded mainstream economists), worked on this point – that conventional economics is based on the hypothesis of perfect markets, with each player having perfect information and with perfect competition between them. In this wholly unrealistic mathematical utopia the idea of an invisible hand might have some theoretical validity. The hope was that a world in which there were not too many imperfections would look approximately like the perfect world seen in the models. But the development of 'information economics' has shown that hope to be wrong. Stiglitz summarises the results of his research: 'Whenever information is imperfect – that is, *always* – the reason that the invisible hand seems invisible is that it is not there.'[7]

But, in the meantime, the invisible hand *is* there in the theory, the ideology that justifies the ownership arrangements of corporations, and the lack of rights of employees. In chapter 9 we will see how the theory was used 200 years ago to remove the protection provided by having a minimum wage, and to wipe out the right of employees even to talk about their pay. The Market in this case produced starvation in England, the most prosperous country in the world. It is appalling that today the same project – getting rid of the minimum wage – remains an ambition of neoconservatives, and the same ban on talking is found in major corporations. When Barbara Ehrenreich took a low-paying job in Wal-Mart, she was startled when a fellow worker she was talking to suddenly dived out of sight. On re-appearing, the fellow worker explained that a manager had walked past. 'Didn't you see him come by? We're not allowed to talk to each other, you know.'[8]

Wal-Mart denies that its management approach has anything to do with such allegations from employees, with a spokesman telling the BBC: 'Wal-Mart provides an environment of open communications and gives our associates every opportunity to express their ideas, comments and concerns.'

But the anti-union stance of the company is well known. Human Rights Watch issued a report in 2007 alleging that in the US: 'Wal-Mart managers receive explicit instructions on how to keep unions away and have to call a union hotline at headquarters if workers try to organize' and that Wal-Mart 'had sent managers to eavesdrop on employees, repositioned surveillance cameras to monitor union supporters and told workers that they would lose benefits if they organized'.

It was this report that brought the denial from Wal-Mart given above. Bob Ortega, a journalist on the Wall Street Journal, summed up Wal-Mart's approach: 'Of course, any worker who tries to organize, or who engages in such heresies as discussing his or her pay, finds, as have the thousands of workers who are part of a floating slush pile of temporaries, that you can be booted out of this "family" in the blink of an eye.'[9]

In theory, this is the Market at work. But anyone who has lived under an authoritarian regime would recognise it as something rather familiar: the naked exercise of power. It is the power of the owners flowing down through the corporation.

There is one group of employees, however, who have managed to corner some countervailing power. Those employees do rather well for themselves, albeit at the expense of the other employees as well as of the owners. They are the chief executives and their fellow directors. In chapter 8 we will look at the fatuous and hypocritical attempts at justifying their rewards, attempts which also hark back to the invisible hand of the market. And we will meet a worker in Oxford Street in London who expresses rather neatly what it is like to work under such chief executives. 'They're making mega, mega money, and the workers making the money for them are like ants – the top people can't see them. But I think they should concentrate on those people, because those people are at the forefront of the business.' It does not encourage high performance.

What are the ingredients of high performance? In sports from time to time the favourite team is defeated by a little-fancied one. A famous example was in the Olympics of 1980 – the defeat of the Soviet Union ice hockey team. They were professional in all but name and had barely lost a game for twenty years, but they were beaten by the American college amateurs, who won the gold medal. And, in war, highly motivated guerrilla armies have defeated among others the USA in Vietnam and the Soviet Union in Afghanistan. In both sports and war strong leadership undoubtedly plays a central role, but the key ingredient is commitment – widespread, deeply felt commitment that breeds passionate, creative teamwork by all, or nearly all, the players or troops on the ground.

In business, similar factors are in play. Leadership is vital. But effective leadership depends on the abilities and commitment of everyone in the organisation. A shared commitment to achieving success helps ensure that those making strategic decisions have the information and support they need. Leadership spreads through the organisation as individuals take responsibility for improving the processes that they understand. The more people identify with the business, and the more deeply committed they are to achieving success, the more likely it is that they will succeed. This is where employee ownership makes its most important difference to performance – when you and your colleagues own the company most of you tend to feel pretty committed to making it work well.

Employee ownership takes many specific forms, which vary from country to country and even from company to company.

In Spain, Italy and France the commonest form is the worker co-operative – a long-recognised corporate form. Here assets are held wholly or largely collectively; a democratic constitution is a given; and the cooperative is subject to special provisions in the tax system.

In America a group of researchers has established that around half of all employees are involved in some form of 'shared capitalism' – profit-sharing, gain-sharing, share options or various forms of share-holding.[10] The US has been quite serious about promoting employee ownership, and has done so for a long time. Since the mid-1970s three schemes have been given substantial tax breaks: broad-based option schemes and two forms of pension fund investment. By 2009 the larger of these latter schemes, the Employee Share Ownership Plan, or ESOP, as we shall see in chapter 2, covered over 11,000 companies, with nearly 14 million employees. These schemes range from companies that give out just a few non-voting shares right through to companies wholly owned by their employees, who have full governance rights. Because there is a substantial tax break for owners who sell 30 per cent of the ownership to an ESOP, a considerable proportion of the American companies have an employee holding at 30 per cent or above.

In Britain the great majority of large quoted companies have at least one tax-advantaged employee share distribution scheme. People are so used to being ignored and exploited, and are so willing to respond to the slightest sign of an improvement, that even this kind of give-the-workers-a-few-shares approach has been shown to be highly effective at increasing productivity.[11] But it transfers no real influence to the employees and can therefore easily be reversed.

At the more serious end of employee ownership – the kind discussed in this book – the Employee Ownership Association in the UK has over 100 member companies, each of them substantially owned by its employees, and most of them controlled by the employees. Their combined annual turnover totals some £25bn, which is substantially more than the total sales of the whole agricultural sector. The range runs from companies bought by their employees individually using their redundancy money through to companies wholly owned by trusts for the benefit of the employees, as in the case of the retailer John Lewis and the consulting engineers Arup. When ownership is held collectively, through a trust or cooperative structure, employee ownership tends to last longer; when the shares are held by individuals employee ownership is less likely to make it to the next generation.

Certain key principles can be discerned through the buzzing chaos of forms.

The most important is that the employees must *feel* like owners – they must from their day-to-day experience believe that their owner-ship is real. The creation of this feeling depends crucially on the approach of the managers. Since most people for most of their lives are used to being manipulated by managers to achieve ends that are not their own – the much vaunted shareholder value of the conventional corporation – it is not easy to convince them that a change of ownership is genuinely different, and not just a trick. But when that feeling, that belief, becomes widespread it makes a huge difference, to most people, for most of the time. This then feeds into their performance.

The behaviour of managers can in several ways foster – or under-mine – the sense of ownership. Most importantly, the managers must make information fully and openly available; they must listen to the views of the employees; and they must allow the employees to make contributions to improving the way things are done. In addition there must be a way in which the employees can influence the policies and major decisions – they must be able to be heard by the board.

Many companies set out to create among their employees a feeling of ownership, without any real ownership. This can be done through team-building techniques, systems for making continuous improve-ment and through participative management styles. Managers them-selves can be honest believers in these approaches. But the end result is deceitful: the employees feel like owners but have none of the rights and benefits of ownership. The psychological ownership that is induced is good for performance and good for the people involved, but it is false. It can be reversed overnight and the employees can do nothing to protect it.

In the final analysis, ownership means control. Employee-owners who together control their business have a powerful reason to iden-tify with their company and to work together to achieve the common aim – the success of the business. The reason is very simple: they all share the results, both good and bad. They are working for them-selves, together, and not being pushed around by someone else, for someone else.

Like great teams and great armies, employee-owners need leaders. But given the same quality of leadership, an employee-owned busi-ness will always outperform one owned by outsiders, and for the same reason: the people care about the business in a completely different way. It is theirs. They identify with it. They think about it. They want to help make it better. They want to do their best for it, not just because they have a career plan and want to show their bosses how good they are, with a view to building a good CV and moving on; but because they really do care, along with their colleagues, about the business that they own together. Over the last twenty-five years and more, study after study has shown that companies with employee ownership – even quite low levels of employee ownership – out-perform the competition. They are more productive. They survive better in the bad times. They last longer. Employee turnover is low. Absenteeism is low. They also give good service – their customers tend to rate them more highly than their conventionally structured competition. For example, the top-rated retailer in the USA and the top-rated retailer in the UK – both of them very large companies – are employee-owned.

When everyone who works in a company shares in the ownership, the interests of the leaders are aligned with those of all the employees. The leaders are not manipulating the employees for some other purpose, but giving leadership in everyone's shared interest. As a result, the flow of information both ways can be easier and faster. And leadership is diffused throughout the organisation: everyone can take initiatives to improve how things are done.

Not surprisingly, at the human level as well as economically, employee-owned businesses do better. Employees tend to learn more participation skills. They are better trained. They contribute more innovative ideas. They implement change quicker. And they are wealthier, because they have one of the key rights of owners: to participate in the profits they help produce. Their communities benefit not only from the flow of that wealth into the local economy, but also because the skills of participation learned at work can be deployed in community activities.

This is not to say that employee-owned companies are Shangri-la. They take hard work. Some people will never 'get it', never feel like real owners, never join in improving things on their own initiative. And employee ownership does not solve business problems: the companies need to be well led. If the directors make a strategic mistake, or the market turns against a company's product, then employee ownership may well help a company survive for longer, but it will not turn the tide. It is not a panacea for every problem. But it is highly effective in many important ways, both economically and for the people as people.

However, traditional economists never tire of predicting the opposite, usually from purely theoretical reasoning – they characteristically ignore the evidence. One famous paper[12] in particular is quoted again and again whenever employee ownership is discussed. This paper predicts that employees will not want to invest to build their businesses beyond the date of their own employment; that they will be likely to extract too much cash, even at the expense of carrying out necessary maintenance; that they will invest only if their incomes rise immediately as a result; that unlike companies supervised by stock market analysts they will be weakened by less active management; that they will suffer from lack of diversification; and that they will consume the assets of the business. Written in 1979, the predictions have been disproved by an overwhelming mass of empirical studies carried out in the subsequent decades. And yet it is still quoted and referenced in recent works, such as a 2008 paper claiming that when employees own 5 per cent or more of the stock in a company, the other shareholders will suffer from a decline in performance.[13] Other predictions have been added: employee-owned companies will be overwhelmed by free riders; decision-making will be impracticably slow; employee-owners will always be falling out with each other – about wages, for example; they will find it impossible to make 'difficult' decisions, that is, decisions against the immediate interests of any group of employee-owners; and finally employee ownership will stay rare because its governance is inefficient. These predictions will be examined in more depth later. Every single one of them is wrong. But they are part of the conventional model, justifying the existing order of things, and as a result they are not tested and thrown back into the sea of unexamined prejudice from which they come. Secure in the faith that it is the Market that has made things as they are, and that the Market is always right, traditional economists feel the need only to dream up just-so stories to explain why things are as they are, never testing them to see if the evidence points in another direction. Evidence couldn't conceivably point in another direction, because it is the Market that has made things as they are. A truly critical economics is not possible, by definition, unless those two crucial assumptions – that the Market is working as envisaged and that it is always right – are challenged. These challenges are being made, but they have not yet entered the mainstream.

As a result, even today those who want to foster employee owner-ship face pressure from the orthodox. In the early 1980s, when I started investigating the possibility of an employee buyout of my family paper-mill, Tullis Russell, the situation was worse. I was in any case worried that I might be heading down the wrong track, beguiled by utopian fantasy. What if the notion of employee ownership was just a hippy dream, more appropriate for idealistic candlemakers than serious, large-scale, blue-collar industry? Was I just being irresponsible? Our legal and financial advisers were highly sceptical. The merchant bankers I approached for help spent perhaps three years trying to convince me not to take that route. They had considerable standing: maybe they were right? But I had the cautious support of my uncle, still chairman at that time. In the 1970s he had investigated the possibility of an employee trust, and had talked to people from the John Lewis Partnership. He had been persuaded by his financial adviser not to pursue it: the argument was that it would never work with a unionised workforce. Behind this apparently logical reasoning rose the spectre of the destruction of the business by a rampant and irresponsible set of power-crazed blue-collar militants, given control of his beloved family business.

By a stroke of good fortune, in the *Financial Times* of 31 March 1983 I saw an article on the employee buyout of Baxi Partnership, a domestic-boiler manufacturer of a similar size to Tullis Russell, the papermakers. I called Philip Baxendale, the owner of the company and architect of the buyout, and we arranged to meet. A vital, energetic man, clearly on the ball, he had reached very similar conclusions to my own, but with greater conviction. He believed that employee ownership, prop-erly structured, was a highly effective way to organise manufacturing, and a fair one. He introduced me to a pioneer of worker cooperatives in Scotland, Cairns Campbell, who was in the midst of arranging a visit for senior bankers – one of them, George Matheson, later chief executive and then chairman of the Royal Bank of Scotland – to the Basque region of Spain. The destination seemed a bit unlikely, but given the assurance that the visit would show me what was possible in employee ownership I tagged along, a last-minute addition to the group. We visited Mondragón, and I never looked back.

When they are well led, and when they have well-designed governance systems, employee-owned companies do wonderfully well, and their employee-owners lead more productive and more satisfying lives than is possible in any other system. In the next chapter we will meet the founder of Mondragón, and four other early pioneers, each from a different country.

2

Founders

In every generation a handful of business owners, and sometimes groups of ordinary working people, have realised intuitively that there is more to humanity at work than is dreamt of in the economists' philosophy. This insight has led them to experiment with employee ownership in practice. In some cases employee ownership has not lasted for very long, and in others painful lessons have been learned about how not to do it, and about how wolves can disguise themselves as sheep. But in the main the results of these experiments have been startlingly good – the businesses characteristically outperforming conventional competitors, while proving hugely beneficial for the people involved and for their customers.

In most cases it is not the employees who establish employee ownership. In general, most transformative initiatives are taken by owners. This is not surprising: to take a major initiative you have to be confident, you have to see the company as a whole, you have to feel you have the right – or the desperate need – to change things. The people with those perceptions and qualities are most commonly owner-managers, rather than ordinary people going about their business in companies where employees are expected to obey and do their jobs as servants of the shareholders.

There have been notable exceptions: the American airline and steel industries, as well as the British coal-mining industry, have seen significant and successful employee ownership initiatives taken by union leaders. And the engineers who founded and built Mondragón in Spain were inspired by the local priest – there were no prior owners. But in the main the transformation of ownership in the thousands of companies that are employee-owned has been led by owners.

The individuals involved are often unusual. They have to be strong enough to stand against the prevailing orthodoxy and against their legal and financial advisers. Even today, when in the USA alone there are thousands of successful companies with substantial or controlling employee ownership, and where there are considerable tax advantages for any owner selling a company to its employees, the first recommendation of lawyers and accountants will most often be a trade sale – a sale to a competitor. Why not just sell out, make lots of money and forget about the employees? Nobody would blame a business owner for doing so – it is the normal thing to do. But the itch persists: notions of fairness, and gratitude to employees who have helped build a business, and the conviction that it ought to work better when everyone has a stake in the company – all these factors combine to animate their search for a new way. They reject orthodoxy and work with passion, in some cases for decades, to ensure that their companies are successfully transferred into the hands of their erstwhile employees.

Early leaders with particular genius stand out, partly because of the scale of their achievements and partly because it was tougher then, when there were so few models and those that existed were not well known. Five companies in five different countries provide early examples of long-lived, commercially-successful employee-owned companies. Among the originators of those five, three were owner-managers, one was a lawyer and one a priest. We will start in Mondragón, since it was there that my eyes were opened to what was possible.

SPAIN: FATHER JOSÉ MARÍA ARIZMENDIARRIETA

One of the great pioneers in the field of employee ownership and control did not start a company himself; nor did he convert one to employee ownership; nor was he ever employed by one. He lived as a parish priest in the Basque town of Arrasate (better known by its Spanish name of Mondragón), in the foothills of the Pyrenees, not far from where they meet the Atlantic. Father José María Arizmendiarrieta

(Arizmendi for short, pronounced 'Arithmendi') settled there in 1941 at the age of twenty-five. He went on to provide the inspiration behind the founding of the workers' co-ops now employing some 100,000 people with operations in every continent in the world – including over 100 businesses, two universities, numerous research institutes, a complete social security system, and, crucially, a multibillion-euro bank, which in 2008 remained highly solvent after writing off €40m against Lehman Brothers bonds.

Like so many Basques, Arizmendi had fought against the fascist-leaning General Franco in the civil war. He was captured and narrowly avoided execution. After the war the Basque economy was in ruins – it had been especially targeted by Franco in revenge for the near universal Basque resistance. The new priest embraced with enthusiasm his instruction from the bishop to address, in addition to their spiritual needs, the day-to-day concerns of the people. Indeed their spiritual needs, in the sense of church-related activities, seem to have taken second place throughout his long ministry. His view seems to have been that the spirit should be expressed through actions in daily life.

His first major venture was in 1943, when he founded a technical school to train young men in basic engineering. At the same time as giving them this training, and in spite of an unimpressive demeanour and opaque use of language that initially alienated his parishioners, Arizmendi passed on the values he had derived from Catholic social teaching. The essence was that employees should be active, auto-nomous participants, not passive servants, and that capital should serve the needs of people, not people the needs of capital.

However, when the members of the first graduating class obtained work in the only significant local business, a foundry, they soon discovered that the supervisors and managers did not share that attitude: when they asked for information and gave opinions they were told to shut up and get on with their work. But they kept in contact with Arizmendi, continued the training started with his help, and in 1956 five of them decided to leave the foundry to establish their own busi-ness. This business made simple paraffin stoves under licence from a German company – and at the same time aimed to embody Ariz-mendi's principles. It was established as an ordinary limited company, and only as a result of Arizmendi's research into corporate forms did they change it later to a cooperative.

In a favourable market, and with the determination of the founders, the company succeeded rapidly. They soon spun out a second business and then two more. At which point the money ran out. The businesses were growing fast, and had reached the limit of what the banks would lend them: after all, these were workers' cooperatives – whom could the bank hold to account if they failed to repay their debts?

In some despair they went to see the priest.

'Banks have money,' he said, according to the legend that still animates the cooperatives. 'Why not start a bank?'

The men were aghast. We are simple country folk, they said. Already Arizmendi had made them into engineers and now they were running businesses. But *bankers*! Ridiculous. And they stormed out.

At one of their regular meetings some months later Arizmendi turned up carrying a sheaf of papers, which he placed on the table in front of them.

'There,' he said. 'You are all directors of the Caja Laboral Popular – the Workers' Bank of the People.'

The bank went on to gather an enormous proportion of the savings made by the locals, partly because as a cooperative bank it could pay a slightly higher rate of interest on savings, and partly because it guaranteed to invest the money in supporting the development of the local workers' cooperatives. Conventional banks would have spirited their cash away to Madrid, doing nothing for the local economy. In Spanish that produced a highly effective rhyming slogan, *Libreta o maleta!* Literally, 'Bank book or suitcase!', meaning, 'Save with us or pack your bags' (because there won't be jobs round here).

For many years the bank's investments had a risk profile that would not be tolerated under modern banking rules: a large proportion of its lending was to new and recently started workers' cooperatives. A whole division within the bank was aimed at fostering new start-ups: the bank would identify an entrepreneur and pay him or her for a year to work on the business proposal, mentored by a 'godfather' within the bank, generally someone who had done it before. Each entrepreneur had to work up proposals for *two* businesses – one to make the product that had stimulated the original impulse and a second one. In the event that a start-up failed, there would then be a shelf-full of business plans in the bank, all of which had been through a full evaluation process and were ready to run. Over the succeeding decades well over 100 businesses were started, and virtually none failed. This record is unsurpassed by any entrepreneurial support mechanism anywhere in the world.

Arizmendi's genius did not stop at education and cooperative business, banking and entrepreneurial support. He inspired a complete social security system. People in workers' co-ops were classed by the authorities as self-employed, which put them outside the national social security system. Stimulated by Arizmendi, the co-ops developed their own system, which in short order gave better terms than the national scheme.

The man himself remains something of an enigma. Like his writings, his sermons are said to have been hard to understand, and his speeches boring. He showed no interest in profiting in any way from the numerous businesses and institutions for which he provided the animating spark. His views were rarely expressed in religious terms; rather than doctrine and theory, he was committed to 'practice' as the way to learn. Close to his heart was the traditional Basque value of 'solidarity', treated not as an ideal but as a practical way forward, with the ultimate aim of benefiting the individuals – the free autonomous individuals – in the group.

For me, solidarity is the key . . . even the atomic secret that will revolutionise all social life . . . It is not enough for the managers and bosses to perform good deeds, it is necessary that the workers participate; it is not enough that the workers dream of great reforms, it is necessary that the bosses and managers believe in them as well. It is necessary that the authorities become associated with the people.[14]

Like many others who have founded or converted companies to employee ownership, Arizmendi is regarded with awe and love by many of his successors. His practical determination was driven by the aim of benefiting every single individual. He was aware that the powerful can abuse their position, and he was therefore equally concerned to equip people at every level with the knowledge and confidence to participate fully. 'Our beloved democracy may degenerate into a dictatorship through the abuse of power by those at the top, but also by the renunciation of power by those at the bottom.'[15]

He recognised that employees are generally socialised into passive

roles, and, if employee ownership is to work, one of the great educational tasks is for employees to develop the knowledge, skills and confidence to become active participants.

BRITAIN: JOHN SPEDAN LEWIS

For my uncle, it had been the John Lewis Partnership that primed
him in favour of employee ownership. Again, this company has been
employee-owned for a considerable time – more than eighty years as
I write – and it has been hugely successful. Its conversion to being
employee-owned was achieved by John Spedan Lewis (known as
Spedan to distinguish him from his father, John Lewis).

In the spring of 1909, the 24-year-old Spedan was cantering through
Regent's Park in London. He was on his way from his parents' magnificent family home on the edge of Hampstead Heath to work in his
father's draper's shop in Oxford Street.

Riding a spirited horse is exhilarating, partly because of the adren-
aline that comes from not knowing quite what the horse will do next.
In this case, disaster happened: the horse threw him.

Lying in a hospital bed after two operations to repair a punctured
lung is not at all exhilarating, but it does allow time for contempla-
tion. Spedan's thoughts turned to his father – so assiduous in charming
the customers of his shop and so dictatorial towards his employees
and his two sons. Spedan had been prevented by his parents from
going to Oxford University, on the grounds that he was needed in the
family firm. In the manner of parents intent on their own ambitions,
they argued that he would also get his best education in the business.
Despite that intense disappointment, after five years working in the
company he was filled with admiration for what his father had achieved.

In 1850 John Lewis senior had been apprenticed at the age of fourteen to a draper in Somerset; in his early twenties he had become the
youngest silk-buyer in London; and at twenty-eight he had opened his
own small draper's shop on Oxford Street. In his son's view, he had
prospered largely because of his determination to give his customers
good service and value. To Spedan's surprise, the man he knew as a
rather withdrawn, severe father at home turned out to be warm and
charming to the many customers who came in search of haberdashery.

The man who was a dictator to his family was at work a model of willing service; he exuded care for the middle-aged ladies who made up most of his clientele. Towards his employees, however, the severity familiar to Spedan was uniformly applied.

In 1906, when Spedan reached the age of twenty-one, his birthday gift from his father was a quarter-share of the business. His spell in hospital now gave him time to study the accounts. He discovered that his father was receiving £26,000 annually from the business – the equivalent of £2m today. The pay of the 300 people who worked in the business totalled not much more than half that between them – in today's terms, an average yearly salary of a little over £4,000. Reflecting on this discovery some fifty years later, Spedan remarked that he had seen at the time that if his father had treated the employees with the same spirit that he showed towards his customers 'the business would have grown further and my father's life would have been much happier' – as would the lives of the employees. This combination of better business performance and greater happiness for working people is the core of the employee ownership project.

There is a mystery here. Why did Spedan not just get on with enjoying his life of luxury? What makes a wealthy young man take to heart the fate of the people who work for him? Why doesn't he just carry on helping himself to the great flow of cash that they create for him? An income of £2m a year is enough for any family to be happy on, or to be miserable on if that is their bent – at any rate, it is enough. Nobody would have criticised him for accepting it. The attempt to change it would risk so much: his family might end up paupers; he himself would probably be treated as an outcast by the people among whom he had grown up; perhaps worst of all, the workers might be incapable of making it succeed.

Beatrice Potter, later famous as Beatrice Webb, had studied the early workers' cooperatives. In a book published in 1891 she lamented their failure. Her firm conclusion was that they would always fail, quoting a comment by Professor Stanley Jevons (a prominent nineteenth-century economist): 'No such concerns can possibly succeed unless ... shareholders working as operatives are prepared to submit to a manager who is their servant.' Potter, listing examples of failures, did not see this problem as even potentially solvable – no good manager would ever be allowed by worker-owners to rule them day to day, and none would be attracted to such a company – so she despaired of ever seeing a viable 'association of producers'.[16] So popular were her ideas that her book had been reprinted three times and still enjoyed considerable standing when Spedan was lying in hospital, wrestling sleeplessly with the problem of unfairness towards his father's employees and its unfortunate effects on the business. He was eventually to be instrumental in demonstrating that Potter could not have been more mistaken.

Within a year of the accident he had fleshed out in his own mind the main elements of what would become the constitution of the John Lewis Partnership. He returned to work after two years' recuperation, filled with the zeal of a man who has discovered a transformative insight and determined to convince his father. Spedan's advice was to keep the employees informed about the enterprise in which they were all engaged. His father should also be listening to them, he said, and sharing the profits with them.

Everyone who knew Spedan recognised the power and focus of his personality. However, his father was the equal of him and even more stubborn. Spedan's every attempt was blocked. By 1915 the relationship had reached breaking point, and in 1916 in a deal with his father Spedan exchanged his quarter-share of the John Lewis business for a controlling interest in a single large shop, Peter Jones in Sloane Square. This store was in trouble, losing serious amounts of money. Spedan was at last free to experiment. Over the next four years he reduced working hours, kept the employees systematically informed, granted a third week's holiday and distributed annual bonuses in the form of preference shares. The decline of the business was halted; it became profitable and started to grow.

But it was only in 1928 with the death of his father at the age of ninety-two that Spedan was free to implement his ideas more widely. He did not wait long. The following year he passed his shares into a trust for the employees, taking in exchange a thirty-year interest-free bond for £1m, equivalent to nearly £50m today. Until 1950 he retained control, shepherding the company into its new way of working, and above all establishing its constitution. But he took no more salary, fee or dividend – it seems from the archive that he did not even take the payments he was due on the bond. There was a single payment in 1934 and no record of any others.

His father proved to be not the only one who disagreed with his plans: all the advice he received was against putting the company into the hands of the employees. In 1950, when he was about to pass final control of the company into the trust that owns it still, he sent a letter to the *Gazette*, the company magazine. 'If I make this gift to the Partners present and future,' he wrote, 'I shall be doing so in the teeth of strong advice from an experienced lawyer and from some other friends.'

He could also have mentioned their bankers, the whole business community and all theoretically inclined economists. But the resolve, formed through sleepless nights in hospital over forty years before, stayed with him, bolstered by the facts that would not leave him in peace: £4,000 a year each for 300 workers; £2m for three family members.

There is no saying exactly why he did what he did, but fairness was undoubtedly an important consideration. In 1954 he wrote in his book *Fairer Shares*: 'Our world of millionaires and slums is more and more volcanic. The present differences are far too great.' The differences are greater today: in 2008 the most comprehensive measure of income inequality, the Gini coefficient, indicated the worst level of inequality in the UK since recording started in 1961.

Spedan Lewis did something that most people who transfer the ownership of companies to their employees neglect to do: he thought deeply about constitutional matters – corporate governance, as we know it today. The people at the top of a corporation have a great deal of power. And power corrupts. To counter this tendency, Spedan incorporated a number of mechanisms in the constitution. One of them is a free press. In the political world he observed that a free press played a key role in keeping powerful people honest. Accordingly, he built one into the John Lewis constitution, and to this day all letters, including the anonymous ones, are published every week. That was a stroke of genius.

The current chairman of the John Lewis Partnership, Charlie Mayfield, summarises the point today: 'What Spedan Lewis talked about was the sovereign authority of public opinion. It's as simple as saying: "What partners think, matters."'

In conventional companies, directors from outside the company – non-executive and part-time – are supposed to ensure good governance. With nearly all their information coming from the CEO, they know far less than the employees, and they have on their agendas different considerations. In the John Lewis Partnership, however, the employee-partners have the weekly *Gazette* in which to make public their views, and this court of public opinion constantly reinforces good governance. Difficult issues are raised in the letters, and they are answered by the directors – thereby continually educating all concerned. Against a background of everyone being involved as a co-owner, the overall purpose behind the letters is generally constructive.

By contrast, in a conventionally structured company the regular publication of anonymous letters from employees would be likely to call forth expressions of antagonism. Employees in these companies are being used to serve the financial ends of the shareholders: although most people bring goodwill with them to work, the fact of servitude will always tend to breed cynicism and hostility.

Brian Henry, an employee-owner in Litecontrol in Massachusetts, for example, put it like this, talking of his experience with a previous employer: 'You come in, do your job and go home, and somebody else makes the money. You have a salary and that's it, that's what you get paid. If you do better, well, you might get a raise.'

Across the world in Loch Fyne Oysters, a sustainable-seafood company that has been owned by its employees since 2003, David MacDonald, a fish-filleter, says exactly the same of the time before the company became employee-owned: 'Before the buyout it was just coming in and doing my job and going home and not really knowing what was going on. I didn't have a clue really. All I knew was that it was my job to fillet fish and go home.'

This traditional model of employment is not inspiring for those on the receiving end; it does not intrinsically even attempt to gain the interest and commitment of the employees. They are treated as servants, passive recipients of instructions. Not surprisingly, this results in a need for them to be watched, supervised and disciplined, to the frustration of the managers, who often come to look down on the employees as a result.

Why don't the employees care? Because the employment relationship treats them not as partners but as instruments.

In the John Lewis Partnership, however, every employee is a partner, sharing information, influence and profit. The free press operates effectively because the experience of partnership breeds a genuine will to solve problems together. Moreover it keeps the managers subject to daily scrutiny by the employees, which is in many ways a more powerful incentive to good behaviour than occasional pressure from even the most upright and imposing of non-executive directors.

The constitution of the John Lewis Partnership includes other mechanisms, probably even more important than the free press, equally designed to hold the powerful senior managers to account. Every quarter, executive directors report to the council and are subjected to interrogation by the sixty-seven elected members. The questions and answers are printed verbatim in the *Gazette*, modelled after Hansard (which records the debates in Parliament). These meetings are self-evidently for real: very challenging questions can be asked. The current chairman has taken steps to intensify the accountability to the council. The council has always had the right and responsibility to get rid of the chairman if things are not going well. In anybody's book, that is accountability.

There is also a separate group of people, called the Registry, with one person in each department store charged with checking up on the managers to make sure that they are acting in line with the letter and spirit of the constitution. This seems designed to cause conflict, but it actually helps everything work better. It has distinguished antecedents – the Censorate in the Chinese imperial system first established at the end of the third century BC, and in Europe the 'separation of powers' discussed in eighteenth-century constitutional debates. Of all the founders, Spedan Lewis seems to have been the most aware that corporate structures involve the distribution of power and need appropriate structures.

ITALY: GIUSEPPE BUCCI

The earliest of these founders was Giuseppe Bucci, in Italy. In the early 1800s the Bucci family had started a ceramics-manufacturing company in Imola, a town best known today for its Formula One racing circuit, but distinguished also as having an unusually high proportion of people employed in worker co-ops. After Giuseppe's father died and his brother fell out with the highly skilled workers, Giuseppe himself became the managing director. In 1874, in poor health and inspired by the democratic principles of the nineteenth-century Italian republican Giuseppe Mazzini, he handed the company over to the employees. As the story has been passed down, the employees struggled with the problems of managing the business and after about a year they begged him to take the company back to run it again himself. He returned as general manager, but only to train the most gifted individuals to handle the management of the business. His mission completed, in 1877 he handed the company over to the employees for a second time. Today Cooperativa Ceramica d'Imola is a global leader in the design and manufacture of tiles. It is still structured in the way that Bucci set up: there is a board composed entirely of people elected from the employees, by the employees; the main task of the board members is to appoint the general manager and then to have him or her account to them every month. The elected board can sack the general manager at any point. This system has produced a very fine business, wholly owned by its employees for 135 of the 200 years of its existence.

GERMANY: ERNST ABBE

In Germany, Carl Zeiss started making scientific instruments in 1846 and soon became fascinated by optics. Twenty years later he teamed up with Ernst Abbe, a truly creative optical scientist. In 1888, just as the team led by Abbe was developing the ultimate lens – the anastigmatic camera lens that made the company world famous – Carl Zeiss died. In his memory Ernst Abbe set up the Carl Zeiss *Stiftung*, or 'foundation', the German equivalent of a trust, and in 1891 passed his own shares into that foundation. Zeiss's son Roderich, who had been a partner for ten years, took his lead from Abbe and likewise put his shares into the trust. In 1896 the foundation adopted its constitution, which among other things prohibits the sale of the shares and requires the interests of the employees to be a central consideration. As a result, the company is owned collectively on behalf of all its employees, and it cannot be sold. The foundation is also required to ensure that the business is profitable. The result has been a highly creative and committed approach by the employees: in the words of the chief executive in 2000, 'People love Carl Zeiss and the Stiftung.'

The company has continued to flourish in spite of many challenges: two world wars; the division of the company into two, one in East and one in West Germany; the rejoining of the companies following the reunification of Germany; enormous restructuring; and creative investment in difficult new technologies, such as large-scale lasers.

A major element in the drive that has led to that success is the commitment to engineering excellence. This is a drive that can be found in other, more recent employee-owned companies, often those founded by scientists. In the US, Science Applications International Corporation (SAIC) founded by Bob Beyster, a physicist, grew over three decades into an $8bn company owned entirely by its employees, with a commitment to scientific excellence. Arup, founded by a charismatic Dane, Ove Arup, is a globally successful consulting engineering company. It has been owned since 1970 by trusts for its 10,000 employees. Arup engineers have designed many iconic structures, including the 'bird's nest' Olympic stadium in Beijing and the bridge linking Sweden and Denmark. The company is overtly centred on its founder's vision of engineering excellence, which takes precedence over simple democracy in its constitution. A similar motivation drives Quintessa, an employee-owned environmental services company founded in 2000 by the nuclear physicist David Hodgkinson. During his time at Harwell, the UK government's nuclear research centre, he ran the multimillion-pound research programme in the storage of nuclear waste.

Engineers and scientists are of necessity humble before facts. They spend their lives dreaming up new solutions to structural and chemical problems, striving to ensure that every last detail is right. It is striking that engineers from a number of countries – Germany, the US, the UK and Denmark – have chosen the employee-owned model, building companies that have lasted for decades and stayed at the forefront of their industries. Against the triumphalism of the capital market enthusiasts, intent on self-aggrandisement often at the long-term cost of the companies with which they play their fee-generating games, the example of the engineers is worth noting. As well as achieving outstanding and long-lasting business success, they have brought happiness to the many thousands of people involved.

AMERICA: LOUIS KELSO

If you have a great idea about how to change things, what can you do to get people to listen? More important still, if you have a great idea *and no power*, what can you do to get people to listen? Louis Kelso, an American lawyer, started in that position and succeeded magnificently.

This difference in power marks a strong contrast between Kelso and the other founders.

Bucci had enormous power in the small world of his family's ceramics business. He could do what he wanted, and he did. As far as we know, his ambitions went no further than that business. Having seen the employee-owners achieve success despite their shaky start, he probably died content. His legacy has given hundreds of employee-owners more positive working lives, as well as bestowing the benefits of greater wealth on their families, generation after generation for over 130 years. It has also been an inspiration for the structuring of dozens more firms, many outstandingly successful.

Spedan Lewis eventually inherited similar power in the rather larger world of his father's department store business. Like Bucci, he could do what he wanted, and he did. But his ambitions went further than the business: he dreamed of triggering a widespread change in the ownership pattern of British industry – something that proved beyond his reach. Consequently, in spite of his enormously successful legacy – his efforts have brought happiness to tens of thousands of people, and their families, for eighty years – he died a frustrated and embittered man.

In Mondragón, Father Arizmendi had status, rather than direct power: he had the backing of the church hierarchy, which carried considerable influence in the Spanish outback in the 1940s and 1950s. A place in the lower levels in the church hierarchy was a mixed blessing: mindful of the conservatism of some powerful clerics he was careful not to give the authorities too much detail about what he was up to, and he was grateful that Mondragón was isolated from the main centres of power. His message was expressed in the things he did, the way he behaved, rather than from the pulpit. Gradually it became clear to the locals that he really was devoted to the interests of everyone in the mountains and valleys of the region, and that his ideas about employee ownership really worked. As a result, he attracted over time an enormous following for those ideas. Hundreds of thousands of workers and their families and communities have benefited, and his beloved cooperatives have provided an inspirational example to many more around the world.

Louis Kelso, on the other hand, had no power to speak of, other than the power of persuasion. He was simply a corporate lawyer in California. But in terms of the number of people affected, his legacy is greater than that of anyone else so far.

Kelso grew up during the early 1930s, at the low point of the Depression, which affected him deeply. He became convinced that, over time, ordinary employees would receive a smaller and smaller proportion of the income generated by the economy, while the owners of capital would receive more. He seems to have been right. In 2006 a newsletter produced by the respected National Center for Employee Ownership carried the following article:

Back in the 1950s, Louis Kelso, the creator of the modern ESOP, argued that the share of economic growth ordinary workers would capture from their labor would shrink over the next decades, while returns to capital would far outpace economic growth. Economists said Kelso was deluded. It turns out the economists were deluded. According to Labor Department data, the salaries of non-management employees have fallen to an inflation-adjusted 10% below their 1970s levels. In the last five years, the U.S. Bureau of Economic Analysis found that despite strong economic growth, the share of GDP going to wages and benefits dropped 2.5%. Meanwhile, the stock market has continued to rise at an inflation-adjusted 8% or so per year. An article in the *New York Times* on this subject (Oct. 15, 2006) says economists are still perplexed and insist this trend, so counter to classical economic theory, is bound to go back to the normal pattern of wage and benefit growth tracking GDP growth. Kelso, by contrast, argued that only by making workers into co-owners of capital would they ever be able to keep up or move ahead.[17]

If the economy was to stay healthy, Kelso thought, then working people would have to obtain additional income from elsewhere. Failing that, the economy could not function: if businesses were to be able to sell their products then the purchasing power of ordinary people had to be maintained. He proposed to achieve both objectives through spreading the ownership of capital; in his eyes this would turn the employees into capitalists, leading to the kind of committed behaviour that makes the capitalist economy thrive. His perspective eventually helped convince most politicians in both major American parties to support the idea. Again, the facts back him up: there is overwhelming support from well-designed and rigorous academic studies showing that companies become more productive in employee ownership.[18]

Kelso cut his teeth in 1956 on the all-employee buyout of Peninsula Newspapers in Palo Alto (the beautiful city south of San Francisco where Stanford University is situated). The retiring owner, in his eighties, had caught the Bucci–Abbe–Spedan bug, as many do, and wanted to sell the company not to another bigger company, nor to a handful of rich managers and investors, but to all its employees. By chance the owner's second-in-command had been a sailor in the navy with Kelso during the war; moreover, the company's legal adviser was a senior partner in the law firm where Kelso worked. Kelso was not involved in the discussions and try as they might, neither the lawyers nor the financial advisers could make the numbers work: they came up against the immovable mathematical fact that employees cannot afford to buy the companies that employ them.

Kelso happened to run into his ex-navy colleague, who was departing, rather depressed, after the lawyers' meeting. Listening to the story, Kelso told his friend that the senior partner's advice was wrong – something that junior lawyers rarely say to clients of their firm. He got permission to look at the file. That weekend, he found the solution.

The key point was that business assets pay for themselves; nobody buys a business except in the expectation that it will pay back within a reasonable time the money invested in buying it, and significantly more. Logically, then, there is no need to be rich to buy a company: you just have to find a way to borrow the purchase price. A successful company will pay for *itself* over time – it will pay back the loan, and then give you much more besides.

Kelso's partner had been assuming that the money would have to be raised up front by the employees themselves. But Kelso realised that the company's profit-sharing scheme could borrow the money, buy the company, and then pay off the loan in future from the annual allocations of profit. Since the main owner was eager to see the employee buyout proceed, the money could be borrowed from him, rather than from a bank.

They did the deal. This was the first time in America that an employee benefit structure had been used to borrow money to buy shares for the employees. The 1929 scheme in John Lewis is very similar (Spedan transferred the ownership to a trust for the employees in exchange for debt), but it is unlikely that Kelso was aware of it – he simply extended the principles of leveraged finance with which he was already familiar from corporate acquisitions. Good ideas tend to be discovered several times. A similar financial structure is used today by private equity investors, but for the enrichment of only a handful of individuals: Kelso, by contrast, developed it to spread wealth to all the employees.

Peninsula Newspapers stayed successfully employee-owned until well into the 1970s. In the meantime, Kelso worked on other employee buyouts and on his economic theories. In 1958, with the help of the philosopher Mortimer Adler, he published these ideas in *The Capitalist Manifesto,* his first book.

In 1975 he made a further key contribution. In a four-hour meeting over dinner in Washington, together with Norman Kurland (a Washington-based lawyer and a strong supporter of Kelso), he persuaded the chairman of the Senate Finance Committee, Senator Russell Long, to incorporate his leveraged buyout system into legislation. Russell Long was the son of the populist Louisiana senator Huey Long, who had been assassinated in 1935. (The murder was never solved. The fact that he had intended to run for President in the 1936 election, which could have threatened the re-election chances of President Roosevelt, may have been pure coincidence.) Russell Long, while conservative in his political approach, was strongly attracted to the idea of spreading capital ownership as a way of improving the lot of working people and the functioning of capitalism. The system was adopted under the name of the Employee Stock Ownership Plan, or ESOP.

Russell Long, like his father, had a good line in folksy communication: answering those who argued that workers should not have their eggs in one basket, he pointed out that most workers have neither eggs nor basket. If you have lots of eggs, then certainly put them in lots of baskets. But if you can get hold of only one egg, then it makes sense to put it in a basket and look after it as if your life depended on it.

The Kelso–Long legacy is extraordinary. It is directly as a result of that meeting that there are at the time of writing, as mentioned in chapter 1, ESOPs in some 11,400 companies in the US, holding shares with a total value of over $900bn, for the benefit of nearly 14 million employee-owners. The companies using these schemes vary from giving nominal amounts of shares with few rights all the way through to 100 per cent ownership with full voting and governance rights. Encouraged by a series of tax breaks, a high proportion of those companies have 30 per cent or more of their shares in the ESOP, and a growing minority have 100 per cent. Further schemes have been spawned to spread ownership widely, affecting similar numbers of people: for example, some 9 million employees have stock options and 11 million take part in officially endorsed stock purchase plans. (The numbers cannot simply be added together: some individuals will be members of two schemes, or of all three.)

Kelso did not have Spedan Lewis's insight into the constitutional control of powerful leaders, nor Arizmendi's fertility in spawning initiatives in many directions. Even among employee-owners, Kelso's ideas on economics, as expressed in several subsequent books, have remained marginal. But his idea for practical action, the Kelso–Long legacy of the ESOP, can justly be called the single most important step in employee ownership anywhere in the world. Publix, the enormously successful supermarket chain wholly owned by its 144,000 employees, is one of the companies using this system.

These five individuals were pioneers. They were admirable, strong characters, who acted on their intuition that companies and the economy will work better, and that people will be happier, if everyone has a stake. This is an instinct that is widely shared, and not just by business people: children get the idea easily and even people who have never worked in business see it immediately. It is a naturally appealing idea – not just because it is fair, but because it promises to work, to be more effective.

Ironically, capitalism itself is built on the idea that owners will work more energetically and creatively, and with greater commitment, than people who are employed by others. Instead of following through the logic of that insight, the owners of capital and their intellectual supporters have built company structures in which employees have none of the participation of ownership: they have no right to know what is going on, no right to be consulted, no right to influence the choice of leader or the policies set, and no right to participate in the wealth that they all create together. The vast majority of people are systematically deprived of any ownership stake. It is as if they are seen as coming from a different species, insensitive to the galvanising effect of ownership. Kelso put the point succinctly: capitalism is good at creating capital; it is lousy at creating capitalists.

Luckily, each generation produces more people who think like the five pioneers described above, and, generation after generation, others too have decided to pass their companies into the hands of the people who have helped build them, rather than selling them out to big corporations or financiers. In this way the logic of capitalism is carried further, into the lives of more and more people, and the wider it goes, the more beneficial it proves, for the economy and for the people involved.

These wise businessmen and businesswomen are far too numerous to list, but we will meet some more of them in the pages that follow.

3

Predictions

The ancient Greeks turned with awe to the Oracle at Delphi for predictions of the future, gleaning from the barely comprehensible utterances of the priestess some inkling of their fate to come. Today we listen with similar reverence to economists.

Ostensibly the priestess at Delphi was in touch with the gods, and politics played no part in her ravings. In much the same way, economists have striven for decades to raise their theories to the status of a science, whose tools are mathematical models and complex statistics. Like the Oracle, the sciences aspire to float above political considerations. Nonetheless the ancient Greek leaders turned to the Oracle to justify and add gravitas to their decisions, and in similar fashion present-day politicians, journalists and business leaders make use of economists' theories to shape and to back up their projects.

Mainstream economists are no better at predicting the behaviour of employee-owned companies than they are at forecasting the behaviour of bankers. Which means that they are very bad at it. They have consistently asserted that employee-owned companies will not work, just as they have uniformly claimed that markets – traders and bankers – will be able to price risk accurately. The risk involved in securitising sub-prime mortgages was so universally and badly mispriced that it nearly brought down the world economy. This chapter will highlight further examples of unreliable predictions – this time, about businesses co-owned by their employees.

As mentioned in chapter 1, a central academic paper in this tradition – one that is referred to frequently even today and was reprinted as recently as 2000 – is a 1979 dissertation by Michael Jensen, a major figure in the theory of the firm with an emphasis on capital market theory, and William Meckling.[19] I will quote several times from that paper in showing that the numerous actual employee-owned companies in the world demolish its predictions.

If there is a theme through and behind their pessimistic predictions, it is the oft-repeated statement of faith in the Market.

For example, Henry Hansmann, quoted again below, ignores questions of power and incentives, and repeats the faith: 'why do conversions from employee ownership to investor ownership occur so frequently? The most likely explanation is simply that employee ownership is not an efficient mode of organization for the firms involved.'[20]

Why? Because if it were efficient, the Market would see to it that it flourished.

Exactly the same assumption is seen again and again, simply stated as a given, not questioned or justified, and with no evidence produced. Another paper expresses the unsubstantiated view that: 'the ultimate conclusion on the labor-managed firm is clear. Whatever its contribution to industrial democracy, it is not an inherently efficient economic organization.'[21] And it is not simply economically inefficient – it is inefficient in terms of its governance. Yet another paper concludes that: 'Employee governance is rare in advanced market economies due to its relative inefficiency compared with shareholder governance.'[22]

Again, the Market would see it everywhere if it were efficient. Finally, from another of the classic papers frequently referenced even today, a prediction that enhanced employee commitment will be more than offset by reduced managerial commitment is followed by this flat statement: 'If this were not so, profit sharing with employees should have occurred more frequently in Western societies.'[23]

It is not that these economists have had to wrestle with any lack of data – they do not have that excuse. They have simply ignored the data that others have presented. Readers interested in the empirical studies will find the best source of references on the website of the National Center for Employee Ownership.[24] Above all, the research sustained over decades by Douglas Kruse, Joseph Blasi and Richard

Freeman repays study.[25] I will take just one example, a study of producer cooperatives written by John Bonin, Derek Jones and Louis Putterman.[26] Having shown – with an analysis mathematical enough to convince the most addicted economist – that the plywood cooperatives in the north-west of the US 'do not exhibit the perverse or inefficient behavior predicted', they note that 'Shirking by workers is never reported as a concern in studies of real world [producer cooperatives]; observers report that workers monitor each other successfully in cooperative organizations.' They go on to say that 'No strong empirical support for the underinvestment hypothesis is found either in France or the U.K.', and they end with the rather polite and moderate observation: 'Arguments put forth against worker ownership often rest on an ignorance of the results that we have surveyed.'

The theoretical, traditional, mainstream economists cannot be unaware of the empirical work. They simply ignore it. It does not fit with the fundamentalist market theory. The effect is as if the standard-bearers for the official view have sent the empirical professors to Coventry for daring to show that the dominant paradigm is mistaken.

In the case of growth, the prediction is that employee-owned companies will not be able to grow as fast as their conventionally owned competitors. There are three strands to this argument. The first is the idea that employee-owners (as distinct from wealthy company owners) are naturally cautious, with the consequence that they will reject projects proposed by entrepreneurial leaders. The second is that employee-owners will prefer to take cash out of the company rather than reinvest it to enable the company to grow. The third is that if a company is to grow it needs to be able to increase its capital by selling new shares to wealthy people outside the company; because employee-owners will never want to do that, they will not be able to take their businesses forward.

The lessons from experience – empirical data – show that these arguments are unfounded. Employee-owned companies tend to have high rates of reinvestment, and many have proved vigorously entrepreneurial. Besides, new shares issued on the Stock Exchange generally do *not* fund organic business growth, which is the only kind of growth that leads to prosperity.

The track record of Science Applications International Corporation (SAIC), headquartered in San Diego in California, rebuts this pessimistic prediction. It is a story of entrepreneurial growth, and growth, and yet more growth. In the thirty-seven years from its foundation by Bob Beyster, until 2006 when its shares were floated on the Stock Exchange as an $8bn company with 45,000 employee-owners, SAIC's sales grew at a compound rate of 33.5 per cent per annum. In the last seven years of that period sales increased from $4.7bn to $8bn. They didn't need to issue new shares to outsiders – they funded the growth from retained earnings. And not only did they follow entrepreneurial leaders but they bred them, with the engine of growth at every stage being employee ownership.

The most extraordinary prediction of all made by the traditional economists is that employee-owned businesses 'will respond to an increase in demand with a *reduction* of output and employment'.[27]

The SAIC numbers are sufficient comment on that.

Once again the founder shaped the way that the company and its ownership developed. Bob Beyster was in his own words an engineering brainbox (although, he confesses ruefully, not a great athlete). The middle-class Detroit family into which he was born was hit hard by the depression in the 1930s, which embedded in him a lively fear of bankruptcy and an awareness of how easily it can happen – along with the conviction that General Motors, his father's employer, was the best company in the world. He was encouraged in his childhood dream of becoming President of the USA. At the beginning of the Second World War he left high school and joined the navy, which eventually put him through college, where he discovered a talent for maths and physics. He continued in the University of Michigan and moved eventually to Los Alamos, New Mexico, the government nuclear research facility, where he stayed for several years. He then moved to San Diego in California, where he spent twelve years in the General Atomics corporation, working on the science of nuclear reactors. Secure in the exalted world of research, he looked down on people who left General Atomics to build their own businesses: 'Entrepreneurship was not for me – it was too degrading.' But the company started to focus on areas that did not interest him, and in 1969 at the age of forty-five he left to start the business that became Science Applications International Corporation. The aim was to work with a few friends and stay in San Diego.

From the beginning, SAIC was owned by the employees: his own stake, which started at 100 per cent, was down to 10 per cent by the end of the first year. Under the financial pressures familiar to those who start companies – not enough cash to pay his salary and a not entirely trustworthy accounting system – he was persuaded by an adviser to sell a stake in the company to venture capital investors. Beyster was clear that he did this simply because that was how it was done – it was the conventional route. Anyone who started a company and achieved an early profit was advised to sell shares. The company website summarises the result: 'Because of SAIC's success, the outside investors ultimately received $2 million for their $200,000 investment, although most had not contributed to the company's performance in any way.'[28]

It adds a comment from Beyster: 'If people get ownership make sure they earn it.'

That principle – make sure that employees earn their ownership – was combined with another one: make sure that the great majority of employees own stock. For decades, over 90 per cent of the employees owned stock.

To begin with there was no cash to pay decent salaries, but Beyster knew that if he didn't attract and keep the very best talent, he would not make a success of it. Shared ownership would be the key to holding them and inspiring them. Profit was never the main driver, simply the necessary condition that would allow them to attract outstanding people and grow the business.

One of the people attracted in was Peter Stocks, recruited in the UK in 1999. Joining SAIC was for him a form of liberation. 'SAIC had a business in Europe, but it was tiny. It was just one contract with BP Exploration up in Aberdeen, a small outsourcing contract, and it wasn't going very well. The deal with me was, "We've got this little contract: if you can grow it then you'll get a share of the company. And you'll have a lot of freedom to do what you think best to grow it."'

The promise of a share in the ownership was not just for him. The whole team would be rewarded, everyone included.

'Close to 100 per cent was owned by the staff and most of the staff owned stock – in the UK about 90 per cent had stock, through a mixture of buying and giving. We had new-entrant schemes where they made it attractive for you to buy in, "Buy one and get two options." We always thought it was a good idea if people coming in would commit to stock, even if it was in a small way. We gave employees interest-free loans, too. We tried all kinds of ways to get people interested in holding stock.'

Everyone was paid below market levels, but with a substantial performance-related supplement. This extra would be paid a third in cash, a third in stock and a third in options: it included cash, shares that you could sell immediately, shares that you had to wait for and options that allowed you to buy at today's price in five years' time. 'That had two interesting effects. You became much more interested in what the company was doing. But also you tended to take a long-term view, because people were affected very materially by the growth of the share price.' For someone in a senior position, the performance element might be as high as 50 per cent of salary. At the bottom, the proportion would be much smaller, but everyone would participate.

'There were secretaries in Los Angeles who were dollar millionaires. They'd worked for a long time, they'd always participated in the bonus schemes, and the stock price had doubled every five years. So their reward for staying and growing with the company was very significant. And that was fair, because they really had helped grow the company.'

Of course, when people own shares they want to be able to sell them at a time of their own choosing. For this there was an internal market that operated quarterly. If employees wanted to sell shares and nobody wanted to buy them, the company bought them. A regulated subsidiary company was established as a 'market-maker', handling all the trades. As a result, all the employees were confident of being able to cash in their shares when they chose. The fact that the share price rose pretty steadily through all those years provided an incentive to hang on for as long as possible. Only after the dotcom bubble burst in 2001 did the share price fall significantly, but it always stayed higher than the price in January 2000, and within eighteen months it rose above the dotcom peak again.

As in all the best-performing employee-owned companies, and indeed in companies of all kinds, good management was key. And, as always, it combined true empowerment with strong disciplines. On the empowerment side, everyone was given ownership training, which was delivered peer to peer – it was not top-down propaganda from managers. Along with that, everyone signed an ethical statement every year.

'My PA, who was the longest-serving employee-owner, used to run a lot of the ownership and ethics training. It was not done as someone coming in and lecturing you: "I'm the longest-serving employee-owner in this place and this is how you behave." It was a structured discussion, to get people to think about it, talk about it and sign up to it. For example, "Why do you think we should be frugal?" or "Would it be right if the senior guys flew first class?"'

One of the initiatives that Stocks took was to start a new business with new people in a new market – a combination that lies near the risky end of possible start-ups. The new division was in management consulting, for which Stocks recruited a number of experienced people. Given the freedom typical of SAIC, these new recruits decided they would fly first class. The grapevine worked instantly and Stocks himself brought them rapidly into line. Ownership breeds responsibility.

One of the fallacious claims about employee-owned companies is that they will lack effective supervision – the prevailing assumption being that top-down hierarchies do provide it. Supervision is by no means the main driver of performance when ownership is shared; nonetheless in practice the best supervisors are not senior people, but fellow owners at the same level or lower down the hierarchy. With ownership they feel responsible to each other, and have the power to intervene. Rather than being less effective, supervision is *more* effective than in conventional companies, because it is driven by the widespread sense of responsibility and actual empowerment that come with broad co-ownership.

The same tough-mindedness was evident all the way through. The freedom afforded to people who aimed to grow the business was enormous, but to be given that freedom you had to perform. The first test was called 'Red Teaming', somewhat similar to the TV programme originally invented in Japan and known as *Dragons' Den* in the UK and *Shark Tank* in the US. In Stocks's words: 'You could go to the board and say, "I've got a bright idea. I think I can make it work. I need £500,000 as a starter." I did that on two occasions.'

The company was run almost entirely by scientists, and the disciplines of science affected every aspect of it, including the Red Team of senior directors, who would examine each bright idea put forward. They were interested in establishing good evidence one way or the other.

'You stood up in a room full of very senior people and they would try and shred you. The notion was, "If it's a rotten idea, rather we shred you than the market shreds you." They would come up with huge holes in your proposal. If you came out of that with any dignity and any ambition still to go and do your project, then you probably would. It was a very brutal process, but it did give you a great deal of confidence when you'd got through it. I survived it a couple of times.'

This 'tough love' fostering of entrepreneurs was one of the two main drivers that built an $8bn company from scratch; the other was the share distribution system that made everybody a shareholder, while giving successful entrepreneurs the right to own significantly more shares. Employee ownership was not only compatible with sustained high growth – it energised it.

The response to stories like these often starts with the phrase, 'Ah, but . . .' followed by an attempt to explain it away, rather than accept the implications. In the case of SAIC the 'ah, buts' might include, 'Ah, but they depended on government contracts', or, 'Ah, but they were all highly intelligent scientists.'

On the government contract point, SAIC was of course not alone in competing for the Defense Department contracts: it beat off competition from some huge conventionally structured companies devoted entirely to that business. And its entrepreneurial growth was equally effective in the non-government parts of its business. There is simply no merit in that particular 'ah, but'.

As regards the intelligent scientists, that 'ah, but' at least has the merit of conceding that employee ownership is an ideal environment for intelligent scientists to build a company with sustained fast growth. To show that it is also an ideal environment for less formally educated people to do the same, let us look at another employee-owned company: the Davey Tree Corporation of Ohio.

This business was started in 1880 by John Davey, a self-educated English immigrant to the US. Over the next ninety-nine years of conventional ownership, turnover rose to $60m, at which point the company was sold to its employees. Over the next thirty years turnover increased tenfold, to $600m, and employment trebled, to 7,000. The operations of the company spread to every state in the US, and to five sites in Canada. The Davey Tree people hold the record for relocating the largest tree ever moved, at 141 feet high and weighing 542 tons; at the other end of the scale they take care of trees in domestic gardens. There is science involved, but the great proportion of the employees would not claim to be highly educated academically – just highly motivated, highly innovative and highly experienced. And they flourish in employee ownership.

Like SAIC, Davey Tree Corporation has tailored its ownership system to foster a dynamic, entrepreneurial approach, in which some 30 per cent of the ownership is held by all the employees in broad-based schemes, the rest owned directly by current and retired employees. With a strong emphasis on voluntary participation, the original ESOP has been rolled into a different type of pension scheme,[29] under which each individual makes the decision to participate, rather than being included automatically. Like SAIC, Davey Tree brought in a number of schemes that used share purchase rights to reward performance. In 2009 no individual held more than 4 per cent of the shares; 28 per cent were held by retired employees, the rest by current employees.

The organisation structure is necessarily decentralised, and a central objective of the ownership system is to help ensure that the people in each local unit feel able and encouraged to do everything possible to take their business forward. As always, the key is good management, but the employee ownership system plays a vital role in motivating and sustaining the superb record of growth.

These stories of growth in these two significant employee-owned companies are sufficient to establish that the prediction on growth is wrong. Employee-owned companies can grow, and grow spectacularly. And these are just two among many, many companies that have grown well in employee ownership.

The second argument against the ability to grow is the idea that employees will bleed the company dry rather than retain profits to invest. Once again this is a theoretical argument, and once again the empirical evidence simply does not give it any support whatsoever.

The Jensen and Meckling paper is clear on this point. It says that employees will want to make an investment 'only if the cash flow per worker rises'. This means that they will not invest in any long-term project. Further, Jensen and Meckling predict that each employee will not want to invest in any project that runs past the date when he or she retires. This means that the last thing they will want is to hand their company on to the next generation stronger than it was at the beginning. They will literally want to bleed it dry. To this end, they will leave it positively decrepit, spending the least possible amounts on maintenance, let alone on capital projects. 'To the extent that today's workers can pay themselves higher salaries by reducing, postponing, or eliminating maintenance where the major negative effects on cash flows will occur in the future beyond their own horizons, they will be more likely to do so.'[30]

The full extent of the Jensen and Meckling nightmare, which has gained such wide currency and is still quoted today whenever the academic literature is discussed, is seen when they go on to talk about governance issues. This, to my mind, unaccountably respected paper predicts the following dangers not just with employee ownership, but also if the employees are given some voice in a democratic structure such as the German co-determination system. 'Upon gaining control of the firm the workers will begin "eating it up" by transforming the assets of the firm into consumption or personal assets.' This will have effects not just on the individual firm but on the economy as a whole.

'The result of this process will be a significant reduction in the country's capital stock, increased unemployment, reduced labor income, and an overall reduction in output and welfare . . . The final result will be fairly complete, if not total, state ownership of the productive assets in the economy.'[31]

That hasn't happened yet in Imola, where since the 1920s there has been a large group of companies owned and very definitely controlled by their employees. Nor are there any signs of co-determination in Germany leading to state control – in fact, very clearly the opposite. Since the reunification of Germany, the old East German economy has been largely privatised.

And this prediction did not apply in the case of two large companies, SAIC and Davey Tree. In John Lewis, whose 70,000 partners elect half of the board, there is a palpably fair profit distribution every year, with each person in the company receiving the same percentage of pay. Over the last couple of decades the range has been between 9 per cent and 24 per cent, on top of pay rates which are competitive with the general market – except for senior managers and directors, whose pay is below market rates. But, in addition, over the five years to 2009 turnover grew from £5bn to £7bn, and in that time the company retained nearly £1.5bn in cash for investment. In 2007 the board – in which nearly half the directors are elected by the employees – announced plans to double the turnover in ten years, creating 35,000 new jobs, adding twenty-four new department stores to its existing twenty-six, and completing a similar level of expansion in its 180 supermarkets – by early 2010 there were already 225. This investment in growth continues a tradition running from 1929, when the employee ownership was first established. Over eighty years of employee ownership there has been no sign of a tendency to extract too much cash. It is baffling that economists still give any credence to the prediction, which at the very least is seriously undermined by what has happened in practice in the case of John Lewis and many other companies.

The best test of the idea that employee-owners will take out too much cash lies with small companies under wholly democratic control – if the problem is going to appear it is most likely to appear in those circumstances. UBH, a business based in the north-west of England, is one such company. As a subsidiary of a large corporation it was bankrupted in 1999 by the corruption and incompetence of some managers, some of whom went to jail as a result. Ninety-one newly redundant employees put up £5,000 each to buy the assets of their company, which manufactures tanks to carry liquids in container transportation systems. It is noteworthy that far from extracting cash and spending it, these blue-collar engineers invested the cash they were given as redundancy money. Having appointed an MD with experience in the industry, they licensed the basic technology to a Chinese company, which earned them millions in royalties over the next few years. With substantial cash in the bank, they could easily have paid it out in bonuses and dividends and had a ball. What did they actually do? They invested the cash in developing their business, turning themselves into world-leading manufacturers of cryogenic tanks – a type of tank that operates at ultra-cold temperatures to carry gases in liquid form. It is worth repeating for the benefit of any mainstream economist who has read thus far: these blue-collar workers *invested* their cash in rescuing their business; made a small fortune from licensing know-how; extracted *none* of it; and *invested* it to improve their skills and their business. In other words, their behaviour was the exact opposite of what the economists predict.

I sympathise with the economists. It is always hard to accept facts when to do so would require a radical change in world view. Like the bishops outraged at the insights of Galileo and Darwin, they are committed to a paradigm that no longer works. But their belief in the scientific method will perhaps help them accept the need to change their model.

For the benefit of 'ah, but' merchants, let me say that the UBH case is by no means unique. For example, when in 1986 Margaret Thatcher defeated the miners' union and closed all the deep-coal mines in the UK, the employees of Tower Colliery, a deep mine in one of the Welsh valleys, invested their redundancy pay to buy their mine. They achieved this feat under the leadership of the local union official but with no support from the national union leaders or from the government. They continued to operate it very successfully until the coal ran out twenty-two years later, by which time they were ready to sustain their company, having developed other businesses. The buyout lifted the whole local economy – the economic multiplier of an employee buyout for the local community is orders of magnitude greater than any other form of business ownership. It also inspired a transformation in the spirit of the community. The final closure of the pit was accompanied by a party for the whole village, a party that combined a proud and dignified ceremony with joyful celebration.

Elsewhere, there are similar instances of employees refusing to behave as they are typecast by the prejudices of the mainstream economists – investing their cash to acquire and sustain their businesses.

In Spain, since 1986 there has been a type of employee-controlled company called a Sociedad Anónima Laboral, or SAL, which has had widespread use in taking over businesses that are on the point of collapse. In almost all cases, the employees have had to invest their own money as part of the deals. A significant proportion of all 12,000 SALs in existence by 2006 were of this type. In a 2006 study of nine such SALs in the engineering industry, Anthony Jensen reported that on the shop floor he found a high level of enthusiasm.[32] As one worker stated: 'In the old days I reported to the boss. Now I am both employee and boss. There is no conflict in that, but I lose more hair and have to think more.'

Between them, these nine companies were employing a total of 938 people when they got into trouble. In the reconstruction process that number fell to a low of 380, but by 2005 it had recovered to 675. If the ownership had stayed in the conventional system most if not all of these jobs would have disappeared. Instead, through committed investment by the employees, the future holds the prospect of work and active involvement in high-performance work systems, with the resulting wealth spread widely in the community.

All of these cases, involving different-sized businesses with different governance models in different countries, give the lie to the prediction that employee-owners will bleed their companies dry rather than using their cash to invest in them.

The third strand making the case that employee-owned companies will not be able to grow is the view that they will not have access to capital.

Like the other arguments, this one is theoretical. The thinking is essentially as follows: in order to grow, companies need capital; companies get capital by selling shares to outsiders; employee-owned companies don't sell shares to outsiders; therefore employee-owned companies will not be able to grow.

It looks logical, but the logic is flawed.

It is certainly true that companies need capital to get going initially. This capital is usually provided by the founder selling shares to himself or herself, and perhaps to friends and family; if a substantial amount of capital is needed, then shares can be sold more widely. Once established, most companies never again sell new shares to outsiders. In the US and the UK about half of private sector GDP is produced by private as opposed to listed companies; in most other developed economies the proportion is higher. Most private companies do not sell shares to outsiders.

In 2009 I put the 'access to capital' point to John Logue, a professor at Kent State University in Ohio. John Logue was a great man (the past tense is necessary, because to the huge sadness of very many friends, colleagues, business people and employee-owners, he died in late 2009). With his large frame and languid Texan drawl, John always gained attention, from professors, managers and blue-collar workers alike. People listened to him, not just because of his style, but because what he said was always well informed and carefully thought through; because he was a man who cared about people; and because he had a sense of humour. John looked at me steadily and said without a flicker of a smile: 'You just indicted the 4.1 million American closely held family-owned companies, which in recent years have accounted for 100 per cent of the job growth in the US.'

And he was right. The great majority of those companies, once they have got going, never again issue new shares in exchange for new capital, and many of them develop into substantial businesses. They fund their growth firstly by investing cash which they retain from their profits, and secondly by borrowing money. When they borrow money, they repay it from retained profits in future years. None of this needs the sale of shares. Business investment is funded from retained profits.

The fact that the anti-employee ownership prediction is driven by ideology rather than by facts is shown even more clearly when we look at companies whose shares *are* quoted on the stock markets. People who advise companies to float their shares on a stock market include 'access to capital' as one of the supposed benefits. They tend not to state clearly their own 'access to capital' – the fees that they will charge for helping in that flotation. Often 10 per cent of the new money raised goes in fees, and sometimes much more.

Do the companies that float their shares make use of their 'access to capital' to invest in their businesses? No. Just as in private companies, new business investment in the vast majority of quoted companies is funded from retained profits and borrowings. Instead new shares are generally issued not to build businesses, but to expand through acquisitions. And acquisitions have been shown to be as likely to destroy value as increase it. They do not increase GNP, the real economy – they simply pass companies around from one set of managers to another. But acquisitions, like flotations, earn huge fees for the advisers. Acquisitions also provide supposed justification for enormous rises in the pay of chief executives. The companies they agglomerate through acquisition are thus likely to be less productive than companies owned by their employees. Such companies therefore give a poorer deal and worse service to their customers. Their senior managers are likely to be distracted from actually running their real business. But simply because the companies are bigger there are large payouts to the handful of people at the top, and their advisers. So the effect of the stock market, together with the acquisitions it facilitates, is to concentrate wealth and to build less productive companies.[33] Employee ownership does the opposite: it builds effective businesses and it spreads wealth more fairly.

In this context it is worth highlighting again the case of Mondragón in Spain, the globally outstanding model of how to fund the start-up and growth of new employee-owned businesses. As we saw in the last chapter, in the 1960s, after they had built from scratch four businesses in four years, they were in the eyes of the bankers getting too big, too fast. For the benefit of any mainstream economists, let me repeat: these *employee-owned* companies were *growing* too far, too fast, in the opinion of the conventional bankers, who – wait for it – were much more *risk-averse* than the *entrepreneurial* employee-owners. These are facts. Which part of this do the economists not understand?

It looked for a moment as if the economists' prediction was going to prove true – the employee-owners could not raise new capital, so they could not fund growth. The reason was not that they could not afford to borrow, but because the bankers looked askance at them, on the grounds that the businesses were owned not by one or two rich individuals but by all their employees. The problem was a reluctance to support something owned by workers; just as there is a hesitation to accept the empirical facts about employee-owned companies today.

As explained in chapter 2, the response of the employee-owners, inspired and pushed along by the local priest, was to start a bank themselves. The bank went on to invent the most successful entrepreneurial support programme ever seen anywhere. Over the following decades experienced people in the bank mentored and funded the start of well over 100 businesses, virtually without a failure, all of them employee-owned, independent and with entirely democratic constitutions. As the supervisory rules for banks were tightened, the bankers passed the entrepreneurial support programme to another body, which continues to work closely with the bank and with the network of established businesses.

The bank itself is not owned solely by its employees: they own just under half. The rest is owned by the businesses that founded the bank and those that it later helped set up. It is therefore a hybrid between employee and mutual ownership.

In the 1990s Mondragón faced another enormous access-to-capital challenge. The local cooperative supermarket, Eroski, was a small player in national terms, with its outlets limited to the local geographical area. But with the advent of the open market across Europe, two of the large French retail chains began to acquire Spanish stores and also to build new ones in Spain. It was clear that unless Eroski moved quickly, and on a large scale, they would become marginal in their home market and might eventually be driven out of business.

Was the response of the employee-owners and managers anything like the predictions of the economists? Did they take too much time to make decisions? Did they retreat in the face of risk? Were they too busy extracting bonuses and indulging themselves? Were they unable to raise the capital required to expand fast?

No.

In short order they created a multibillion-euro venture fund. They did this with money from the bank, from the other employee-owned businesses in their voluntary bottom-up network, from the charity for the blind (the most cash-rich charity in Spain) and from the Italian cooperatives (which include a very large financial sector). One key to the success of the fund was the fact that the partners involved were chosen because they were supportive of the concept of companies being co-owned by all their employees. This is a condition which is almost wholly lacking in the financial markets elsewhere. Eroski then went on the acquisition trail, lifting the business by 2001 into the position of second-largest retailer in Spain, after the giant French chain Carrefour.

This expansion was characterised by speed of response, large strategically driven decisions and massive funding raised in many different ways, including the use of the public markets – but without selling any equity. If they had sold equity the end result would have been ownership by outsiders, not by the working people involved.

In the process of doing all this, Eroski was operating with multiple ownership systems. The original base was a workers' cooperative with some consumer members. Most of the expansion came from acquisitions of conventional companies, but they also expanded through building new supermarkets and hypermarkets. When a conventionally structured company moves into employee ownership, years can pass before the employees begin to feel and behave like full partners in the business, so accustomed are they to the conventional passive role of 'employee'. The managers of Eroski were faced with the very large problem of integrating the employees in the various acquisitions – employees who far outnumbered the original members, and were scattered right across Spain. To help this process they invented a transitional ownership process, quite complex technically, but essentially designed to allow the combination of outside funding and ownership by all employees. Should any economists fail to notice, this constitutes the unthinkable: a form of large-scale international structural and financial innovation by a network of employee-owned companies. By 2010 they had worked out how to build on that transitional form to create a single employee-owned structure for the whole Eroski retail group.

That experience of the creation, building and expansion of the Mondragón group shows up the economists' predictions for what they are: empty ideology.

No doubt the 'ah, but' fraternity will be in overdrive, generating reasons why this is uniquely limited to this one occasion in this one place. But however long a list they produce of specifics unique to that place and that time, they will be missing the point. In any situation there are always specific conditions that will never be replicated identically elsewhere. The key is to identify the transferable principles. The underlying principle here is this: the way to fund the growth of employee-owned companies, and to foster their decisive and entrepreneurial potential, is to form financing institutions that are supportive of them. At the moment employee-owned companies face financiers infected at best with scepticism and sometimes with ideological hostility. These attitudes are reinforced by theories designed to back the current stock market and banking system – theories which are not confirmed by the empirical facts. Financial innovation is required, aimed not at generating huge bonuses for a few speculators, but at helping human beings build genuinely productive businesses co-owned by those involved.

The advisers may end up being paid less in fees than if they continue to pursue flotations and acquisitions. The chief executives may have to get used to lower 'earnings', if that is the right word for their plunder. But the customers will love the service they get from the employee-owners who look after them, and above all the people who work in the businesses they own together will lead happier, more productive lives: these businesses will do more for the economy and for the people as people than can be dreamt of under the prevailing system of ownership.

4

Creative and Inventive?

You see creativity in people and you just go with it.
　　Kate Hall, Arup

It is hard to see why employee-owned companies come in for such disparagement, when they perform so well. There is another cluster of predictions – again based on theory, again not looking at the facts – giving reasons for the doom that must inevitably attend the foolish attempts to build employee-owned companies. This time the focus is on the idea that such companies will be slow, cumbersome, unimaginative and lacking in innovation.

Innovation is absolutely central to staying alive in business. Competitors are constantly improving their products and reducing their costs. Keep up or you lose out.

Innovation abounds in the natural world. The impala on the plains of Africa, dodging for their lives, race away from charging cheetahs. Just enough are killed to keep the cheetahs alive. Then a cheetah is born with an innovation – perhaps a gene enabling slightly quicker responses – and over the succeeding generations the cheetah and its descendants catch more: the death rate among impala rises. The impala that survive to reproduce are the ones that are a bit better than average. When an impala is born with a gene which enables it to be quicker still, or more elusive, the balance is gradually restored; the cheetahs may even decline in numbers as more and more of the impala have the new gene, allowing them to escape. Over time, with each successive innovation, the balance swings between the two. If the successful innovations are mainly in one species, the other may become extinct. If cheetahs that lived 500,000 years ago were spirited into the present, they probably wouldn't be able to catch a single one of today's impala; nor would the impala of long ago succeed in evading any one of today's cheetahs. Innovation has done its work.

Likewise in business. The successes – the ones that survive and prosper – innovate constantly. The ones that don't innovate ultimately get eaten or starve. The main difference is that business innovation takes place in months or years rather than over generations. Innovation has to be driven, constant, each step implemented as quickly and as flawlessly as possible. Ford would not attempt to sell today a Model T, except as a curiosity.

The last chapter pointed out the sheer snobbery evident in the idea that, instead of investing, workers will squeeze money out of their companies. A similar level of disrespect lies behind the idea that any employee-owned company will inevitably tend to be slow on its feet.

The prediction rests on three arguments. The first is that the managers will have to spend time – Heaven forbid – *talking* to the employee-owners and even *listening* to them. This will be such a time-consuming and confusing distraction that they will not be able to make decisions quickly enough.

The second is that once employees own the company, they will become complacent. They will not want to make any changes, preferring just to hang on to what they have. Economists know that companies must innovate or die – ordinary workers, so they claim, will be unable to embrace that fact.

The third is that employees may disagree about the way forward. This was expressed in an influential academic work by Henry Hansmann, an economist:[34]

employees are far more likely than investors to differ among themselves concerning the firm's policies. To begin with, employees may disagree about their relative wages . . . [As a result,] successful instances of employee ownership will remain largely confined to firms with highly homogeneous classes of employee-owners.

Once again, these arguments have no substance. They are utterly disproved by the facts – they are even diametrically opposed to them.

Of course, it is possible to construct a nightmare scenario where, for example, the experts have to stand by while even the decisions on technology or marketing are resolved by majority voting. While that system may have been tried by small workers' cooperatives it is not characteristic of employee-owned companies, nor even of workers' co-ops generally.

In creating the worry about slowness, a great fuss is made at the theoretical level about the problem of 'collective decision-making'. But this problem has been largely solved, and there is absolutely no reason why the employees cannot make use of the solution that has been found. And they do. That solution is the prevailing business organisation: the company or corporation. The invention of the joint stock company largely solved the problem of collective decision-making – a group of investors needing to make decisions about their enterprise. The solution is to delegate to one among them, the president or managing director or chief executive, the responsibility for making the day-to-day decisions, and periodically for the others to hold that person accountable for the actions taken and the results achieved.

Thus the Italian cooperatives, which are, for example, globally successful in exporting robots, do not subject each technical or commercial decision to a vote. They use the company solution: they delegate to the general manager the responsibility for ensuring that these decisions are properly taken by the right people, and then periodically, just as in a conventional company, the top manager must explain to the owners the actions taken and the results achieved. Equally, in the Mondragón network in Spain there are well over 100 businesses; each one uses the same solution as any corporation – an elected board of people (in this case – unusually – with a significant number coming from the shop floor) whose main job is to appoint the general manager and hold him or her to account every month. The problem of collective decision-making is solved.

As to talking and listening, the MD of a company owned by outside shareholders is well advised to spend the time necessary to keep the shareholders informed. Chairmen and CEOs of quoted companies sometimes lament the amount of time that it takes to talk to institutional investors and to report to Wall Street or the City of London. The MD of an employee-owned company is also wise if he or she keeps the owners of the company informed.

But there are differences. A major difference is that in an employee-owned company, when the leader talks to the owners, he or she is also talking to the employees – and vice versa. They are one and the same. This means that the owners are much better informed already. They know what has gone on through the year; what has been done well and what badly, and they have a pretty good idea of where responsibility lies for both the successes and the failures. There is little point in using up valuable time on spin.

As well as being better informed, the owners can contribute to solving the problems, to making improvements in what is done and how. And because they own the business, they care about it. They want to make a difference, in the knowledge that it is theirs and they will share in any profits.

In this context, the time spent on communication and consultation is highly beneficial. First of all, the people who are involved in putting any decision into practice will have a good understanding of why it has been taken, and as a result they may well generate ideas that can improve it.

An example of this kind of innovation came from Woollard and Henry, a small engineering manufacturer of specialist rolls for the paper industry. The business, based in Aberdeen in Scotland, was sold to its employees in 2002. A short time after the buyout some of the shop floor engineers proposed to the MD that they should make a very simple alteration to one of the machines: cut through two steel pillars supporting the machine, and weld two additional pieces of steel into the gaps. They themselves carried out the work, at a cost of next to nothing. As a result the company was able to manufacture larger rolls, expanding its market significantly. The innovators involved said that years before the buyout they had suggested this improvement more than once to the owner, but he did not listen to mere shop floor workers.

A year or two later the same company developed a completely different product for a new industry, manufacturing safety cages for transporting people by crane from ships on to oil rigs. The team that developed the product came largely from the shop floor.

In America, Floturn, based in Fairfield, Ohio, and 80 per cent owned by an ESOP since 1988, has achieved a dominant position in its industry, the manufacture of drums for laser printers. This triumph is the result of constant innovation. Needing to double the rate of production – then forty per hour – to achieve break-even, at first the chief executive sought in vain a solution through automation of the manufacturing process. Failing with that approach, he appealed to the employees, now owners of the company, to improve their productivity. When the *Wall Street Journal* reported the story in 2000[35] they had reached over 200 per hour, were using less expensive materials and had improved the design. Most of the improvement had come from the inventiveness of the shop floor workers, who, according to the chairman, Robert Glutting, had simply been given some free rein and clear direction and had not been criticised when they made mistakes. Floturn could have used this low-cost position to make extraordinary profits, but instead whenever net profit margins rose above 10 per cent of sales, they shared the benefits of innovation by cutting prices to the customer. Not surprisingly, they continue to dominate the market. When everyone shares in the ownership, and is allowed to help make improvements, innovation makes everyone rich. In a report published in 2007, the 290 people benefiting from the Floturn ESOP had an average stake of $170,000.[36]

Economists seem to have a fantasy picture of how managers should take decisions: they should do it quickly, firing ahead with absolutely minimal explanation or consultation. Supervisors will then ensure that the employees carry out those decisions. In the real world, however, such rapid-fire, unexplained decision-making, without any input from the people who have to do the work, is likely to run into problems. The processes of communication and consultation have the effect of shaping better decisions and of leading above all to quicker and more effective implementation. People who are aware of what is being done and why, and who have had the chance to contribute their ideas, will understand the project and feel that it is theirs. They will be keen to make it succeed.

This may provide an explanation for a somewhat unexpected conclusion in a study of the major UK retailers by two economists from the London School of Economics, published in 1993.[37] It did not surprise them to find that over a twenty-year period the only significant employee-owned retailer, the John Lewis Partnership, had the highest marginal productivity of labour. In normal human language that means that, with every new person employed, John Lewis saw a greater increase in sales than any other retailer. It is easy to understand that the co-owner of a business will be more committed, think harder and work more energetically than an employee in a 'normal' company. That was the unsurprising result. The surprising finding was that John Lewis also had the highest marginal productivity of *capital* – for every £100 invested, it achieved a greater increase in sales than any other retailer. This result offends against basic economic theory. According to the theory, the highest marginal productivity of capital *must* be achieved through the capital market – the Stock Exchange and the discipline that it brings. But it wasn't. It was achieved by the employee-owned company. The key to understanding this result lies in the fact that in John Lewis the employee-partners are involved not just in the day-to-day business but also in the design of all capital projects. More time is spent on communication and consultation in the early stages of each project; as a result, the design is improved and when the time comes to put it into practice the people are fully on board. It is human beings who make capital projects succeed or fail; the employee-owned company treats human beings as human beings – partners – rather than 'resources', and their response confounds capital market theory. They achieve greater productivity of capital than the conventional companies driven by the capital markets. This inclusive process liberates the creativity of the people involved. In other words, it fosters innovation – exactly the opposite of the prediction.

This is something that the more progressively managed conventional corporations have been discovering for some time. In particular, many successful manufacturers have introduced involvement programmes aimed at constant improvement. A good example dates from the 1970s at Toyota in Japan: the managers gave every employee on the assembly line the authority to stop the line, and indeed insisted that it *must* be stopped every time a problem was encountered. In contrast, the American car manufacturers had honed to perfection the art of keeping the assembly lines going. It cost a small fortune every minute that the line was at a standstill. As a result, stopping the line was anathema: problems would be sorted out at the end of the line.

But the Americans were overtaken by Toyota, because in Japan every time the line stopped a team of improvement specialists raced to the scene and worked with the line operatives to understand and solve the problem at its root. As a result the problems did not recur. Over time the costs of rework were reduced to close to zero in Toyota.

This kind of innovation through participation flourishes in particularly fertile territory when the people involved actually own the company. A good example of the near limitless possibilities of this approach can be seen in another Ohio company, in the ever-changing and expanding group of businesses centred on the holding company EBO, which stands for Excellence by Ownership. The group's move into employee ownership started in 2000 and reached 100 per cent in 2008. The growing ownership galvanised one of the company's management systems, called 'Excellence by Objectives', originally designed to turn the widely used 'Management by Objectives' on its head, through changing it from a top-down to a bottom-up process. Included in everyone's objectives for every quarter is that of producing ideas for improving how things are done. These ideas are then discussed and, if possible, implemented. The sheer fun of generating and working up improvements together is intensified and raised to new levels because they all share the ownership of the company. Or rather, of the companies. Since the move towards co-ownership started, EBO has developed many new products in its traditional field of engineering, and also in three new fields – medical, solar energy and hybrid drives – each launched in a separate new company. Building on that experience it has now developed yet another new business: providing support for entrepreneurs going through the process of business incubation.

Many people have the talents to be natural innovators. When they are 'just' employees – uninformed, uninvolved and not respected – this potential for innovation is repressed and lies dormant. When they own the company together, they are informed and involved and respected, and the talent can flourish. Not only do employee-owned companies innovate, but they have a particular strength in innovation, stepping far beyond the level that conventionally owned companies can attain.

The second argument is that employee-owned companies will tend to become complacent, choosing to hang on to things as they are, rather than welcoming change and making improvements.

This is of course possible, but it is not unique to companies owned by their employees: conservatism is a general human tendency. The view that people tend to be conservative lies behind the idea that conventional companies should be constantly prodded by the capital market, that is to say, by outside shareholders. However, the capital market is neither necessary nor even very effective at providing the stimulus to innovate. By far the most effective prodding towards innovation comes from the product markets, as long as they are reasonably competitive. But stronger still is the drive of people who see that things can be done better. The internal motivation of inventors is legendary: many become so focused on their ideas that they find it hard to bother with the distractions of normal life. But to build a business out of an idea takes more than just the application of an inventor: it takes joint commitment and problem-solving by whole groups of people. Shared 'psychological' ownership is often the result. And psychological ownership becomes enormously stronger when it is matched by real ownership.

Over several decades the electronics industry in America was a beacon of innovation. It varied according to quite local factors. In Silicon Valley in California, for example, it remained successful and developed continuously, but in the Boston area, which started with a similar cluster of innovative companies, the process gradually seized up. A seminal study[38] argued that the fluidity of the networks of people in Silicon Valley and the lack of proprietorial authority, together with the inability of owners and managers to contain the flow of information and of people, all contributed to that creativity. The Boston area was characterised by a more authoritative top-down culture, with networking being harder to achieve. This seems to have been the root of the relative sclerosis that overtook the cluster of companies in the Boston area.

It is notable that a major driver of the Silicon Valley businesses was a form of employee ownership. The companies could not afford to attract good people by paying cash, and because of this they had to use share options to entice people to join and to stay. As a result, not just the managers but over time virtually all the people involved had the potential to build a stake if they made the company successful. This proved to be the greatest motivating factor in the most sustained eruption of creative business innovation yet seen in the world. The only other factor that came close was the excitement of doing the work itself. [39]

Most business innovation does not happen in great leaps. Even Nokia's unparalleled move from forest products into mobile phones resulted from a series of logical steps, first into cable manufacturing (originally telephone cables were insulated by paper), then switches (telephone cabling needed switches, which in time led to electronics), and from there into mobiles. Most innovation happens in small-scale improvements in the products themselves and in the processes that produce them. It has become clear over recent decades that such innovation can be achieved better if everyone is thinking along those lines than if the creative effort is limited to just a few scientists and other specialists. The involvement of everyone is achieved more thoroughly and to greater effect if they all share in the ownership of the company than if they are working for a few rich guys at the top. Once people understand the business, and understand what is required to keep it successful, then as owners they will contribute with enthusiasm to making the necessary changes.

A case in point is provided by Arup, the globally successful firm owned by its 10,000 consultant engineers and other employees. They design engineering structures of great complexity and on a considerable scale. More than most, they depend on making innovations, in this case in engineering design. Their approach is facilitated by their employee ownership, which has been in place since 1970.

A vital strength is the way they solve problems by helping each other, regardless of their locations across the globe. At the time of writing they are heavily involved in the infrastucture development in East London, in preparation for the Olympic Games to be held there in 2012. This is a complex process with multiple commissioning agencies, and it covers many fields, from road- and bridge-building through stadium design to the creation of electronic security systems. Unlike Arup, their major competitor is divided rather rigidly into separate specialist businesses. A branch of this competitor's bridge-building business is based in London. As a result, Arup faces intense competition on every bridge project in the capital. But the culture inside Arup fosters the sharing of skills – there are only the most porous of lines between different business specialties and across geographic boundaries. Arup's leader for the whole Olympics project is a woman in her thirties, Kate Hall. She manages a team of 400 people, but that team is in many ways a virtual team. For example, three of them are based in Hong Kong and four in Australia. The ones in the UK are scattered across every office in the country.

At a meeting in the Arup office with one of the Olympics clients, a complex problem was raised. No one present had the expertise to address it. A relatively junior member of the team suggested showing the client how Arup solves problems in these cases. There and then, Hall summarised the problem in a quick forum posting on their skills networks, which circulate any query to all engineers with the relevant experience in the global Arup network. This was easy to do, not least because the computer network is set up to facilitate it. Before the end of the meeting, replies came in from around the world, from engineers who had solved similar problems. Because of this information- and skill-sharing approach, which is founded deeply in the shared ownership of the company, Hall can lead a team on a London project for which there are no experts at all in London. Several bridge specialists are working in Birmingham, for example, on projects for the Olympics in London.

Hall has practised her profession all over the world, often on projects where Arup has been required to collaborate with competitors designing different aspects of the same schemes. She has gradually become aware of the contrast between Arup and the conventionally owned competitors. The ease with which the Arup people cross boundaries, whether geographic or business, gives them a creative edge.

It is worth listening to her talking about creativity in generating new ideas and building new businesses. The ownership structure, and the sharing culture that has been built over decades on the basis of that ownership, fosters both the creativity and the entrepreneurial innovation.

'We don't have to respond to shareholder pressure. We're allowed a lot more freedom to do what we want. We've got groups who just do stuff called "foresight and innovation". They come up with great ideas, they lead conferences and have all kinds of contacts with researchers outside Arup. And that group doesn't have to be accountable. How can you have part of a firm doing stuff like that, that isn't instantly revenue-earning? Their value will be downstream: other people may get work as a result of what they do. It will not be directly attributable back to them.'

The same spirit is carried over into the formation of new business units.

'In Arup there's a lot of freedom. For example, we never did airports, we did structural design. Then some people proved to be great at it and those people decided to develop an airports business. And that's gone from strength to strength. That's people in the right place, and just going with it. For example, you see creativity in people who say, "I've always wanted to develop underwater engineering" and they get on and do that. Or you look at the guys in the Midlands office that work on car crashes, and they're individuals that have had the freedom to develop. One of my friends in that team was allowed to develop a business to write the code that simulates crashing cars. He was very good at it so he developed this whole program, which is now marketed to Jaguar and Aston Martin and others. He developed that simply from his love of writing code. I think people here take it for granted that you can just do that kind of thing. If you contrast that with other firms, they need a lot more rigmarole, they need a lot more approval, they need a lot more business planning. So our ownership allows us that flexibility. It also probably means some things go well and some things don't, but at least you can have a go at it. People are not constrained by red tape. They're allowed to go with what they're thinking and what their natural skill is, rather than managerial red tape.'

It is hardly a surprise that Arup has been growing rapidly. As a major employee-owned company it manages not only to keep up with the market but to lead it, largely through creative innovation.

Once again the mainstream predictions prove to be out of touch with what is actually happening across the globe. Instead of fitting the depressing forecasts presented by theoretical economists, employee-owned companies are constantly finding exciting ways to innovate, both in improving their existing businesses and in starting new businesses. Co-ownership and sustained fast-paced innovation belong naturally together.

5

Decisions, Decisions

The ideology that shapes perceptions among economists and businessmen alike has it that a key role of managers is to make difficult decisions – something that will characteristically not be possible in companies owned by their employees.

The reasoning is threefold. Firstly, *any* decisions will be hard to make and slow, because everyone will want a say. In the confusion, decision-making will be delayed. Secondly, no self-respecting manager will want to work in this environment, with the result that the quality of the managers will be low. And thirdly, employees will not allow these second-rate managers to make difficult decisions, especially those involving a reduction in jobs.

These predictions deal with quite intricate processes inside companies. To bring that detail into focus, it is worth telling some stories from the experience of converting Tullis Russell to employee ownership. It was through that process that I discovered the power and effectiveness of employee-owned companies.

The paper industry is a particularly tough one. Michael Porter, the Harvard Business School guru of industry analysis, cited it as an example of an industry where it is impossible to make a healthy return on capital over the long term.[40] There are many reasons: the investment is enormous and must be made in huge lumps – over a billion dollars for a new plant; new capacity comes on stream in large steps, disrupting prices; none of the competitors wants to allow the others to get an edge, with the result that they all build machines at the same time, creating overcapacity; the highly specialised machines are impossible to switch to other uses; the production process runs continuously 24/7 – to keep the machines running prices are slashed to win the last tonne of business; the business is cyclical, moving up and down rather violently with fluctuations in the economy; and the products are mainly commodities – there is not much difference between one copier paper and another, or one tissue paper and another.

As a member of the sixth generation I took over as chairman in 1985. My forebears had made good strategic decisions, investing in new equipment, specialising in technically difficult papers and building a reputation for high-quality products. They had also set out to be good employers, albeit in a paternalistic way.

However, there were problems. Competitive pressures were building, our costs were high and our speed of response was slow. Part of the difficulty was that right up to director level people were not kept informed about the business, and as a result were not in a position to contribute all they could. At the beginning of the quarterly board meetings the financial accounts were handed out to the directors – and taken back at the end.

It became clear that we would prosper only if we got everything right, from the big strategic decisions right through to the most detailed daily operations. That would be achieved only if those involved cared about the business, and about what they were doing. Passive obedience would never be enough.

The level of loyalty to the company was high, especially among the longer-serving employees. This was in part because of the history and personality of my uncle, who preceded me as chairman. Born into a very wealthy family, he had come to know and love the ordinary people who worked in his mill, not least because all through the Second World War he had fought alongside them in the local infantry regiment, the Black Watch. To me he was a hero, decorated after the battle of El Alamein, Britain's first victory, and officially reported wounded six times, the last when he lost a leg fighting in Normandy after D-Day.

Although the longer-serving people were committed and did their best, the management approach, deeply embedded, was very much top-down, leaving scarcely any room for initiative. And, as mentioned before, for me there was an insoluble problem: how would I get the *youngsters* to be committed to the company and to give of their very best? I could hardly inspire them with the story of how lucky they were to be working to make my family rich. So how could I expect them to work actively and creatively to improve things? The conviction of economists – that good performance is achieved by good supervision – was patently inadequate. We needed to do more than supervise intensely a barely willing workforce. We needed to give them a reason to commit themselves. The solution, reached after long years of experiment, and initially in the teeth of scepticism among the directors and sustained resistance from our advisers, was the all-employee buyout, completed in 1994.

There was also a desperate need to move the approach with which we managed the company from top-down authority to openness and involvement. The first distribution of shares to all employees together with the first briefings, the first consultations and the first programme to involve employees in improving things all started in 1985, shortly after I became chairman. To make the transformation effective we had to change the managing director, appointing in his place the operations director, who understood better how to inspire people. It took another three whole years to convince a core group that all this was for real, that it wasn't simply a species of diabolical trickery by the new regime. After this, a sense of freedom and commitment gradually spread through the company.

But there were tough decisions to make. With a workforce of 1,500 people, the company was overmanned. Our nearest competitor was achieving about 70 per cent more sales per head than we were. The inexorable conclusion was that we had to reduce the numbers employed. And so, at the same time as taking all the positive steps, we made about 200 people redundant, a shock that was particularly terrible given the paternalistic tradition. People had felt safe under the umbrella that my uncle could be relied upon to hold above them. The moment he handed over to me, his nephew, 200 people were thrown out of work. No wonder it took time for people to commit themselves.

One of the surprises on the way was that once it became clear that we were going to complete a full employee buyout, we began to attract better managers. Again this is exactly the opposite of what the 'experts' predict. In 1991, for example, Fred Bowden joined as operations director. He came from Wiggins Teape, a quoted company that had been acquired by BAT, a tobacco company (making large fees for merchant bankers), then been floated off on to the Stock Exchange (making large fees for merchant bankers), before merging with a large French corporation (making large fees for merchant bankers). Bowden's view on the speed of decision-making was not theoretical, but direct from the front line.

'When Wiggins Teape were taken over by BAT, decision-making slowed dramatically. Suddenly injected into the pot were lots of other people who wanted to take an interest in the decisions being made, some of them at a fairly low level. So suddenly there were more committees to go through to get things approved, and more people to talk to, to get things done. Those changes in ownership I don't think were beneficial to the business in any way whatsoever.'

His own approach to management had been disrupted in the process, with schemes to train and involve people simply abandoned. He was by nature a business builder, not a financial manipulator.

'I fundamentally believe that the best people to actually take business ideas forward and to get things done are the people themselves, in whatever job they're doing. They know what the issues are, they know the right things to do, and where we've singularly failed in quoted companies – and indeed in some private companies – is to really engage them and to take them on board.'

Engagement was often the aim of well-managed companies, but there was a flaw. 'In quoted companies you can, in the best businesses, get involvement and participation to a very high level, but there's still a magic ingredient that's missing, and that's the sharing of wealth.'

Bowden could see that Tullis Russell would be different. With the commitment to independence in employee ownership, there was every reason to expect to be able to implement his ideas. The company would probably never be sold, and certainly not over the heads of the employees. He was giving up the possibility of progressing up the ranks of a large international company, but he was gaining a leadership role in an environment that gave every hope of being able to put his basic values into practice, to build a really successful business. With the support and involvement of the employees – very likely to be given because they owned the company and would want it to do well – he expected to be able to do things more quickly.

Bowden recognised that he would have to submit himself to re-election by the employees every three years – and relished the prospect of engaging with that constituency, giving as good as he got in the generally good-natured exchanges. He would have to spend time communicating with them and listening to them and involving them. What is more, we gave the right to veto strategic decisions to the company's top elected body, composed of fourteen elected representatives who met with the board four times a year. Conventional predictions would always forecast that this would make it hard to manage effectively. But Bowden understood that all this might well work a lot better than the system in the quoted company he had come from. To begin with, however, a whole series of tough decisions lay ahead of him, first as operations director, then as MD, and finally as chairman.

One of the first steps Bowden took as operations director was to change the rotas to bring Tullis Russell into line with the rest of the industry – to have the machines running 24/7 instead of stopping every weekend. This meant increasing the number of crews or shifts from three to five. In theory, the number of jobs in the mill would rise by 66 per cent, something that in a normal company the union might be expected to propose at the beginning of the negotiations. The national paper industry body for the UK advised that this was a very difficult process to embark on. Because of the necessity to renegotiate so many aspects of the union contract it took mills on average two years to agree and implement the change.

Bowden put together a joint management-union team – all of them, of course, employee-owners. He then took them on a tour of papermills in several European countries to see different shift patterns in action, after which he asked the team to propose at least two acceptable shift patterns to be voted on by everyone in the mill. One of the constraints he set was that they should minimise the increase in the total number of jobs – to be achieved by getting each person to take broader responsibilities. For example, on each shift there were separate teams for controlling the machines and for testing the paper qualities: might the machine teams take control of their own quality testing? This was one of the many things they had seen working on the Continent.

Instead of taking two years, the change was negotiated and implemented in six months. And not a single additional job was created, thus achieving a significant step up in productivity. Virtually every operative faced a challenging expansion in his or her responsibilities, and during the first few weeks after the new system started there was a real wobble in performance, with higher levels of 'broke' paper manufactured. But as the people involved rose to the challenge of their wider responsibilities, performance returned to normal quality levels and eventually reached beyond them.

The speed and success of the decision-making and implementation were achieved in part because of good leadership by Bowden as operations director. But there is no doubt in his mind that without the years of developing employee ownership and participative management the process would have been much more fraught and would have taken far longer. Everyone could see from the start that any improvement would benefit them all, not just a distant owner but all the employee-owners. They would all share in the additional wealth.

A decision made by a vote of all the employees is one of the horrors that economists and conventional business leaders recoil from. Yet in this instance it had the effect of *reducing* the time taken to achieve a major strategic change. The employee-owned company took 75 per cent less time than its average conventionally structured competitor.

According to the conventional model, the leader of this company is in a dreadful situation, one that will undermine the whole decision-making process. He is subject to re-election regularly by the employees; he has to spend a considerable amount of time communicating with them, consulting them and involving them in decisions. But even if he manages to persuade them to let him make most decisions in reasonable time, there is still an appalling problem: the employees can veto all major decisions. As a result the prediction is that he – or his counterpart in any similar employee-owned company – will simply be unable to make difficult decisions, such as a decision to declare people redundant. The idea of closing a plant, for example, or moving operations overseas must, according to this view, be unthinkable.

A chapter from the recent history of Tullis Russell is apposite here. After ten years of employee ownership the company was faced with the need to move an operation to the Far East. This was the result of the increasing globalisation of the ceramics industry. The background was that one of the most successful parts of Tullis Russell's business was the production and marketing of the highly specialist paper used to carry decal transfers for decorating ceramics, such as plates and cups. The problem faced by producers of ceramics is that it is impossible to print directly on to anything but a flat surface. Since plates and cups are not flat, the solution is to print the glaze decorations on to paper, then wet the paper and slide the printed picture or pattern on to the plate or cup before firing it in a kiln. The paper is technically difficult to produce, and requires a number of coatings on the printing surface. In the 1980s Tullis Russell was the world leader in the industry, exporting the great majority of production. One of the reasons for this pre-eminence was the success of the British ceramics industry pioneered by Josiah Wedgwood in the eighteenth century. There was a cluster of world-famous 'potteries' round Stoke-on-Trent in England, and the Tullis Russell coating plant was right beside them. Being close to the customers gave the company an important edge in terms of technical innovation and keeping in touch with the industry grapevine.

China, with a much longer history behind it as a great producer of ceramics, expanded sales aggressively throughout the 1990s. One by one the pottery companies closed their Stoke-on-Trent plants, replacing their capacity with factories built or acquired in China. With the potteries in China its largest customer group by far, Korea developed a strong competitive position in decal papers. When one of the Korean decal paper producers went bankrupt in 2002, the Tullis Russell team of decal business managers convinced the board that they should acquire the Korean company. It was clear to everyone that the Stoke-on-Trent plant would be affected, probably drastically. The veto lay with the elected body, two of whose members came from the Stoke plant.

There was a long discussion. But the situation did not come as a surprise to the employees. Year after year, Bowden had kept the elected representatives and the employees as a whole fully briefed about all the significant developments for the business, about the objectives and plans, and about the initiatives taken by Tullis Russell. The employees in Stoke could see what was happening around them – they had witnessed the gradual closure of almost all their major customers. And they were involved in the plans to develop new products: they were already experimenting with coating different types of paper for different industries. With this full understanding of the strategic position of the business, they joined their colleagues in voting 100 per cent in favour of the acquisition. They understood that there was no gainsaying the change in the global structure of the business.

Eventually the board decided that the Stoke plant had to close. The experiments had succeeded, but with investment and improving productivity in the other Tullis Russell coating plant some miles away in Bollington there was no need for Stoke to remain open.

The board decision had to be ratified by the elected body. Once again, it had been kept fully informed about all the significant developments. Once again it voted 100 per cent in favour. This time, it had to agree to keep the decision confidential until the people in the plant had been briefed.

The board set a timescale of fourteen months for the closure, giving time for a measured pace in transferring production entirely to Korea. Bowden finished the board discussion by saying that the following week he would brief the people involved. This startled the two outside non-executive directors, both of whom had enjoyed distinguished careers in quoted companies. They both advised against making it public, saying that there was a huge risk of hostility from the people involved. They might start producing poor-quality paper. There would be a risk of large claims against the company from customers who might spoil whole kilnfuls of valuable ceramics as a result of using bad paper. Much better to prepare in secret until the last minute.

Bowden, fully supported by the executives, had to call on all his personal authority to insist that openness and honesty were not optional: they were vital to the employee-owned culture.

'I said to the directors, "You just have to trust me on this. These guys will not let us down. They will be appreciative of us giving them proper notice. We will put money in to help retrain them for other jobs, and be sensible about when we can release them from the plant. They've got a future to think about as well. It's not just about us."'

By 'us' there he meant the managers. 'It's not just about us.' There is a humanity about this approach that highlights a key requirement for managers of businesses owned by their employees. In human terms they have to be better than conventional managers. That does not in any way mean being soft. It means considering the human effects of decisions; and dealing with them. It means treating others as one would want to be treated – always with the common purpose of building a successful business. Managers in conventionally owned businesses, who are used to working with authority rather than leadership, find that hard to understand. They think it is about them and the outside owners, and, given the legal structures involved, it invariably is. But if they want to build a business that is truly productive, both economically and in terms of common humanity, then it isn't. It is about all the human beings involved. When people are treated as human beings and involved as partners they will achieve hugely more for the business and for themselves.

Bowden went to Stoke and did the briefing himself.

'I came away from Stoke-on-Trent very humbled, because people were so understanding and supportive of what we were doing. Because we had shared this information with them, because they knew we had done everything we could to save their plant, they knew we would do everything we could to help get them into other jobs. I've probably never had a harder challenge in my life than that, but I came away from it thinking these people were fantastic people. That's what *made* it hard.'

Managers sometimes think that keeping everyone informed is not part of 'real' management, the essence of which is taking tough decisions. But keeping people informed allows them to understand and therefore support decisions, even the most difficult.

Information in the conventional ownership structure 'belongs' to the shareholders. Even if a manager wanted to achieve this level of good management, he or she would be prevented from doing so by the legal structures. Bowden explains:

'The people in Stoke clearly understood the business situation, because we'd been sharing the information with them. But could you or would you do that in a public company, with the legalities of sharing that information, and the possible impact on share price? Would they allow you to do it? I don't know if it would be possible. Not in the way we handled it anyway.'

The conventional ownership structure, far from promoting good management, actually hinders it.

The effect of all this inside Tullis Russell was to increase the trust between managers and the others throughout the whole company. Increased trust led to increased commitment, which added to the constantly improving productivity. Far from shaking or contradicting the employee-owned culture, the difficult decision fitted perfectly with the best aspects of that culture. The managers had been walking their talk for a long time: when they were seen to do so even in tough conditions, the end result was a boost, not a disaster.

Tullis Russell's direct competitor, Inveresk, also based in Fife, had identical total sales but much higher productivity – some 70 per cent greater sales per head in 1990. From the late 1980s onwards the two companies adopted very different ownership strategies. Taking their advice from investment bankers, which included the idea that they might become very rich personally, in 1990 the managers of Inveresk achieved a highly leveraged management buyout from their American parent. The handful of top managers came out holding much of the equity, but by the terms of the investment agreement the private equity backer had control. The MD fought hard to get acceptance that the top 100 people or so – not just the top handful – could buy shares at the favourable buyout price, but their backers insisted that the offer be limited to managers. This did nothing for the commitment of absolutely key employees, the 'machinemen' who led the production teams, one on each of the enormous paper machines.

Driven by the frankly stated requirement of their backers to make as much money as possible as quickly as possible, they then went for a flotation on the stock market. The intention of the managers was to keep control of their own destiny. Stefan Kay, CEO at the time, looks back ruefully on that hope. 'We felt we had taken our destiny into our own hands, and we didn't want to lose it. That was a misapprehension. That was wrong.'

The process leading up to the flotation in 1993 absorbed the time and attention of the top group of managers for months. After the flotation they were placed under enormous pressure to make acquisitions – the investment analysts said that paper was too boring an industry to rely on organic growth, and that expansion by acquisition was therefore vital. Tullis Russell had also been looking for companies to buy, but it had rejected on several grounds the only UK mill for sale at the time. Inveresk, towards the end of a year in which it had publicly committed itself to make an acquisition, found itself backed into a corner by that commitment to the City. It paid well over £20m for a mill whose parent, it later transpired, would have parted with it for a fraction of that sum. The judgements made in the course of due diligence failed to take proper account of certain risks, and the risks turned out badly within months of the acquisition.

Through the 1990s, as the two companies went through their ownership transformations, the sales per head – a key measure of productivity – in Tullis Russell climbed ever higher, while those in Inveresk remained static. Both companies were facing relatively steady total sales, but Tullis Russell, by involving everyone positively in the business, carried on improving productivity. Because overall sales were not rising, this improvement in productivity necessitated redundancies on several occasions. In other words, the employee-owned company was better at making 'difficult' decisions than the quoted company. They did this successfully because all the employees in Tullis Russell were, as fellow owners, more or less on the same side. In 2000, for the first time, Tullis Russell moved ahead of Inveresk in sales per head, and then carried on climbing. Three years later Inveresk began to collapse. Four of its five mills were forced to close. In the process it put its main brand up for sale and Tullis Russell bought it.

In 2009, with the Inveresk sites in the hands of property developers, Tullis Russell announced a joint venture with a utility company to install a new £150m biomass power station, able to use recycled wood as its main fuel. That project alone was forecast to contribute 6 per cent of Scotland's environmental improvement targeted to be achieved by 2020. It would also help make Tullis Russell one of the greenest paper manufacturers in the world.

The employee-owners had taken the difficult decisions, not just once but several times. They were able to do that because the managers kept everyone informed and involved, treating them with respect and humanity. In the process they all made their company constantly more productive and more competitive. As a result they were in a position to make not just the difficult but the positive decisions too.

Tullis Russell is not unique. The economists' predictions are absurd. The company that took the traditional management-enriching and investment-bank-enriching and outside-shareholder-enriching route failed utterly to improve productivity. It was driven to make a misguided strategic decision in order to try to impress the stock market, and it ultimately failed.

The nearly identical employee-owned company attracted better managers. Decision-making was always up to speed, and sometimes much faster than in the case of conventionally owned competitors. And on the basis of communication and involvement it was able to make more difficult decisions more effectively and more consistently than the quoted company that failed.

Employee ownership works.

6

The Discreet Charm of the Employee-Owner

According to the current ideology, which seeks to justify the capture of enormous rewards by shareholders, CEOs and their advisers, a company owned by its employees will become complacent. The managers of conventionally structured companies are goaded constantly by the need to report to knowledgeable investment managers and analysts. This is posited as an article of faith by, again, Jensen and Meckling: 'The existence of a well-organized market in which corporate claims are continuously assessed is perhaps the single most important control mechanism affecting managerial behavior in modern industrial economies.'[41]

Not being subject to that stimulus, the managers of employee-owned companies will inevitably become slack. They will become bogged down in navel-gazing; they will spend their lives on internally focused discussions; and consequently the customers will come low in their list of priorities.

Previous chapters have examined the notions that employee-owners will fail to grow or innovate, will be unable to take difficult decisions and will extract too much cash from their companies. The prediction examined here follows inexorably from this picture of how employee-owned companies will work: it is that employee-owners will fail to give their customers sufficient priority.

As with the others, this prediction is comprehensively wrong.

Just how wrong it is is well illustrated by an employee-owned company called ChildBase, a group of thirty-six nurseries in the south and east of England. The nurseries are independently rated by the national Care Commission on the quality of care and on the quality of educational stimulation that they provide for the children. Across the whole country, 2 per cent of nurseries attain the rating of 'outstanding'. ChildBase does ten times better: among its nurseries the proportion is over 20 per cent and rising. The company is also consistently the most profitable in its industry. The key to its success is the way the people who work there treat their clients: the children and their parents.

Intuitively, the parents of the small children understand that far from neglecting customers, employee-owners will strive to serve them well. Alison Beard, one of the nursery managers, is a strong character with a powerful presence and a ready laugh. She has noticed that, not unexpectedly, many parents do serious research before handing over their beloved children into the care of people who run a nursery. One effect is that the nurseries which gain 'outstanding' ratings quickly fill up. She summarises something she hears often from parents: 'We noticed it's employee-owned, and that's great. It means the staff will really look after the kids well, because they're doing it for themselves.'

This basic intuition is one of the fundamental insights behind capitalism itself. There is no earthly or unearthly reason why it should apply only to capitalists, and not to other people. People are people, and when they own something they tend to look after it better than if they don't own it. In the case of a business, when they own it they care about it more and want to make it work better. And that means also that they want to make sure that the customers are happy with the way they are treated, and as a result will come back.

In the retail industry a very high proportion of employees meet customers face to face. Two of the most successful large retailers in the world, as judged by their customers, have been owned by their employees for decades. The first is Publix, based in Florida and employing some 140,000 people – the largest employee-owned company in America. The second is the John Lewis Partnership, headquartered in London and employing about 70,000 – the largest employee-owned company in the UK.

Founded in 1930 by George Jenkins, Publix has introduced since 1945 several stock ownership schemes to include all employees. The various employee schemes together own all the stock, which outsiders are not allowed to buy. The company is one of only thirteen to have featured in every year's *Fortune* list of the best places to work in America. It has grown consistently over the decades, adding $5.4bn in sales from 2004 to reach its 2008 total of $24bn, with over $1bn in profit. Above all, it is ranked by its customers as giving superlative service.

A comment made by the National Center for Employee Ownership in 2005 still applies in 2010: 'It consistently shows up on lists of the most admired companies and best places to work, and, year after year, has the highest customer satisfaction scores of any supermarket (and sometimes of any kind of business, period).'

The company website http://www.publix.com/about/Awards.do lists thirty-seven awards won. One that no mainstream economist would ever have predicted is its 2008 recognition by wRatings as the most *competitive* retailer in America. And it is worth noting that it has been the top supermarket chain as ranked by the American Customer Service Index in every year since 1995.

But its commitment to customer service does not indicate that other areas are neglected. The awards include recognition as one of the *Fortune* 500 companies with multiple women directors; as achieving green environmental and recycling credentials; and as a family-friendly employer. This is typical of well-run employee-owned companies. The subtitle of this book points to the fact that people at work are human beings: wherever people work, as humans they have multiple objectives, many of them with a high ethical content. They want to make their business successful, but they want to do it in a way that satisfies their deepest human instincts and leaves them feeling proud. Looking after customers is part of that.

By contrast, if the employees feel neglected and treated with a lack of respect, they will hardly be ready to lavish attention on customers. This will be examined further in Part Two, which looks at what it means to have a job.

PART TWO
HAVING A JOB

Mankind are more disposed to suffer, while evils are sufferable, than to right themselves by abolishing the forms to which they are accustomed.

United States Declaration of Independence, 4 July 1776

When a man tells you that he got rich through hard work, ask him: 'Whose?'

Don Marquis

Arbeit Macht Frei
(Freedom through work)
Slogan of Dachau Concentration Camp, 1933–1945

Prologue: The Deal

So, the employees do the work, and you get the money? That's the deal?

Yes. That's ownership. We own the company – the employees just work in it.

And that's a fair deal?

Yes. We own it – so we get the money.

What about the employees?

They do what they're told.

Isn't it their work that makes the money, creates the wealth?

Well, yes, in a way. But they've just done their jobs, done what they're paid to do.

But if they create the wealth, why is it you that gets the profit?

Because we take a risk. They don't take any risk. We do.

Risk?

We bought the shares. We paid a lot for them. When we sell them again we might not get back what we paid for them. So our money is at risk.

So why did you buy them?

Because there's a good chance that they will make us a *lot* of money. Once the employees have been paid, if it's well managed, there'll be a lot left over, and that's all ours. That's shareholder value.

What if there's not much left?

You have to make sure that there is – keep the managers on their toes, keep them improving things. Making better products, making cheaper products, getting more people to buy them. Keeping costs down. That's the market at work, the drive that keeps our great economy going. The creative innovation of the market.

And how is that achieved?

Well, you employ good managers, pay them the market rate, and tell them to get on with it. Better, cheaper products, and lower costs.

How do you keep costs low?

By automation and IT systems, by reducing the number of jobs, by moving the operations to cheaper places, like China. A host of ways.

So the risk that you take . . .

Is that they won't come up with the good ideas for products, or get the costs down fast enough, won't get rid of enough people in time. But if they do it right, we make a fortune. That's ownership.

'Get rid of enough people' . . . *so the managers reduce your risk by passing it on to the workers?*

Yes, if you like. And the quicker they do it the better.

Surely that means the employees are sharing the risk? So shouldn't they share the rewards?

No. They get paid for what they do. It's only fair that we get the rest.

How is it fair? You risk some cash and get all the profits; they risk their working lives and get no share in the wealth they create.

Nonsense. That's just the way it is. It's a marvellous system. Ownership can make you seriously rich. What's the problem? Everyone's doing it. Just get on with it and enjoy it. It's a good deal.

7

Working for Shareholder Value, Under Capital Market Discipline

What is it like to work on the shop floor in the retail industry? Companies that are *not* owned by their employees supposedly have all the advantages attributed by economists to the conventional ownership structure, with their shares listed on the Stock Exchange and their managers subject to 'capital market discipline'. According to the standard model, there are enormous benefits to be gained from this system. These benefits include a ready access to capital and, above all, the active scrutiny of management behaviour, which is instantly either rewarded by investors buying their shares, which pushes the share price up, or punished by investors selling them, which pushes the price down. The share price is thus a more or less perfect index of informed opinion about each company's performance. If the price falls to a very low level, the company can be bought by another corporation, which will install better managers. Under capital market discipline the rule is: perform for the owners or you're out.

This chapter is not about statistics or theories. I simply recount the stories of some individuals, as told to me. Here my interest is less in refining a conceptual understanding and looking at numbers, than in seeing how it works out in the lives of real people. It is worth listening to ordinary workers talking about their working lives. One person I interviewed started as an enthusiastic salesman and has reached a stage of disappointment and disillusion; another is a woman whose positive approach undoubtedly underlies her clear success as a manager. But although she herself does not complain, she is not treated well. Much of her success comes because she persists *in spite of* what the senior managers, with their eyes on their masters in the stock market, are driven to do.

A number of books have set out to capture what it feels like to work for low pay in large corporations: this ethnographic approach gives important insights. For example, the story of Kenny Dobbins in Eric Schlosser's *Fast Food Nation* illustrates the real meaning of how a large corporation keeps health insurance costs low – a financial achievement much lauded by Wall Street analysts. Kenny worked for sixteen years for a meat-processing company in Colorado, during which time he was injured several times. According to Schlosser, every year an average of one in four employees suffered a work-related injury or illness requiring more than just first aid. Kenny in his sixteen years had experienced on separate occasions damage to his back (requiring surgery), chlorine poisoning (a month in hospital), severe trauma to his back and forehead (two weeks in hospital), a broken leg, a broken ankle, and finally a heart attack. Along the way, through loyalty to the corporation, he had helped break the union; he had also won an award for a courageous rescue of a fellow worker who would other-wise have been killed. After the heart attack he was fired, without notice or explanation, not even being informed of it, finding out only because his medical insurance cheques were returned. At the age of forty-six he seemed to be decades older. But the company kept its medical costs low, which was good for shareholder value. Kenny's verdict was: 'They used me to the point where I had no body parts left to give, then just tossed me into the trash can.'

Barbara Ehrenreich, in her book *Nickel and Dimed: Undercover in Low-Wage USA*, reports her experiences working as a waitress, a cham-bermaid, a cleaner and a Wal-Mart 'associate'. The cleaners worked in small teams in large and beautiful mansions, whose sometimes mean-minded owners would set traps for them, placing piles of dirt in hard-to-reach corners to check that they cleaned thoroughly. Ehren-reich asked her fellow cleaners what they felt about the opulence that surrounded them as they worked. Colleen, a single mother of two, said: 'I don't mind, really, because I guess I'm a simple person, and I don't want what they have. I mean, it's nothing to me. But what I would like is to be able to take a day off now and then . . . if I had to . . . and still be able to buy groceries.' And 24-year-old Lori, deep in credit card debt and suffering from a serious back problem, expressed the age-old American dream: 'All I can think of is like, wow, I'd like to have this stuff some day. It motivates me and I don't feel the slightest resentment because, you know, it's my goal to get to where they are.'

Joe Bageant, in *Deer Hunting with Jesus*, picked up this theme – how the American dream has fooled the poor. He was brought up in less than prosperous circumstances himself in Winchester, Virginia, and escaped to become a journalist. He goes back to meet his old friends and acquaintances in the bar, the Royal Lunch. The perceptions of the people he meets are shaped by a mix of economic theory and traditional values:

the almighty market is rational and rewards efficiency, thrift and hard work; and free competition 'rationally' selects the more worthy competitor. Thus the wealthy are deserving of their elite status. According to the conservative canon, if you haven't succeeded, it can only be because of your inferiority. Nearly everybody at Royal Lunch feels socially inferior. But in any case, they feel they can at least be self-reliant. They can accept personal responsibility.

Another book, *Gig* (modelled on Studs Terkel's classic *Working* and compiled by John and Marisa Bowe and Sabin Streeter), consists simply of monologues distilled from interviews with 126 people on the theme of work. A UPS driver, for example, resents the use of corporate power:

Every day there's a meeting in the morning to tell you what you did wrong the day before. Every day. They get you all together in a group, all the drivers and everybody, and then they yank you in the office and yell at you personally for about five minutes. It's like roll call, like, you know, a police station show. Except they just yell at you.

But he still considers his relationship with his supervisors to be 'pretty workable'.

It's functional. But you can never trust them because they're company people. The managers are worse. UPS treats their own people – the managers and supervisors – worse than they even treat their drivers. It's like the theology is 'shit rolls downhill'. So you can *never* trust anyone, and every driver has this attitude. You know, it's 'us against them'. Totally.

In the same book the chief executive of a very large insurance company tells of his working life. The world as he relates it does not contain any employees, but is filled with stock market analysts, major share-holders, the general public, sponsorship of the World Series, other decision-makers in the business, lawsuits, the corporate jet, his two sons, the difficult decision to require a vice-chairman to leave the company, high financial rewards, team-building and the need to work weekends and eighteen hour days.

In Britain, Polly Toynbee followed in Barbara Ehrenreich's footsteps and reached very similar conclusions in *Hard Work*. The rise in wage inequality had been dramatic through the 1980s and continued, more muted, in the 1990s: those at the bottom were struggling to partici-pate at all in Britain's rising GDP per head. Moreover, employment rights had been undermined, especially through the use of contract labour organized by agencies. Seeking work with an agency, she was presented with a 'take it or leave it' contract to sign. She read the small print.

The terms exposed in these tiny words explain why the NHS [National Health Service] is using casual workers employed by agencies at pay and conditions it would never itself dare to offer in public. The Casual Work Agreement is an 'agreement to provide occasional services', in other words a zero-hours contract. One clause automatically opted me out of the 48-hour maximum working week protection. 'The temporary worker hereby agrees that the working week limit shall not apply.' No sign no job.

Like Bageant, Toynbee points to the widespread existence of false consciousness supportive of right-wing political programmes, although in Britain the illusions have not been so successfully transferred to the poor as they have been in America to the rednecks. Within the Euro-pean Union the only country refusing to accept legislation setting a maximum working week of forty-eight hours is Britain. As a result British employees were permitted to opt out individually. During the political debate the argument had been couched in terms of high-fliers in top jobs, who would have to be free to put in all the hours they chose. But in practice it fell on the poor: 'Four million workers have "voluntarily" opted out of the 48-hour law.'

Like the people working under totalitarian political systems, these people – the chief executive as well as all the others – are trapped in the system that governs their working lives. They cannot step out of it. The driver has to submit to his treatment by his supervisors or lose his job, and if he leaves he will almost certainly have to take one that is not very different in the way that he is supervised. The chief executive either has to respond to the Wall Street analysts and the major shareholders or lose his position; and again, to find another job at anything like the same pay he will have to accept very similar conditions elsewhere, conditions that require him to exercise his considerable power in such a way that the owners are happy with the results. The temporary agency workers cling on at the bottom, falling back on charity from time to time, with not a hope of rising much beyond that, no matter how hard they work – the pain alleviated for some by the dream, which will almost certainly remain no more than a dream, of one day having wealth.

In 2010 from across the world came the distressing news that the Chinese factory where Apple iPads were manufactured at the time of the product launch had seen a spate of suicides by the low-paid and highly regimented workers. It was no surprise that they too are forbidden to speak together. They were, after all, working for their Taiwanese owners, who had the right to demand a complete focus on producing shareholder value.

This system can be changed. It is determined essentially by the legal contracts of ownership and of employment. In the end those contracts need to be altered. In the meantime, employees can alter them for themselves by acquiring the companies where they work, so that, as in John Lewis, the roles of owner and employee are combined.

In Oxford Street in London I interviewed a number of individuals who work in the large retail companies that have the supposed benefit of their shares being traded on the Stock Exchange. These companies are direct competitors of the John Lewis Partnership, which, on account of its being employee-owned, lacks the benefits of capital market discipline.

The method used to select the interviewees in London was to walk around the department stores, approaching people who looked as if they might have worked there for some time and asking them whether they would talk to me about their working lives. This was unusual, even startling behaviour. Some people were shy, others afraid that they might break a rule by talking to me, and yet others said any interview would have to go through management. I am therefore particularly grateful to those who agreed. The only way in which these individuals are not random is that they are unusually brave and independent-minded.*

Oxford Street is one of the great bazaars in the world, a concentrated, unending, barely-controlled explosion of buying and selling, on a scale equalled in only a handful of city centres around the world. There you can find the flagship stores of the great British retail chains – some of them, like Marks and Spencer, known around the world. In Oxford Street the Market comes alive. Competition drives change after change – change of fashion; innovation in design; constant transformation of window-displays; the complete refurbishment of stores long before they have become worn out; and new things everywhere, every day. Compared with a hundred years previously, Britain has fewer industries ahead of the game internationally, but British retailers are very much in the global league. And it is the Market that drives them.

Actually, the perpetual change is driven by *two* markets: first, the product market, visible all along the street, in the shop windows and on every floor of the multi-storey buildings to which the crowds flock daily; and second the capital market, centred on the changing and unchanging buildings of the City of London a few miles away – all of them unseen by the shoppers in Oxford Street. The labour market is not a significant influence on all this. There are always plenty of people ready to take jobs on Oxford Street.

The chairmen of corporations probably spend rather less time thinking about the buyers of their products than about the buyers of their shares, and perhaps even less thinking about the people who work in the lower levels of their companies. They swear annually in their reports to the City that their employees are their greatest asset,

* For chapter 11 I conducted three further interviews, in John Lewis, in order to establish whether there were any fundamental differences in how employee-owners experience their working lives.

but the behaviour of many shows that what really drives them is their reputation in the capital market. They know who has the power to unseat them – the people who manage the billions of pounds and euros and dollars in the mutual funds, pension funds, private equity funds, venture capital funds and hedge funds. These are the people that grab the attention of the chairmen.

The customers in the stores have *some* power – they can stop buying. The employees have a little power – they can refuse to work. But the important power lies with the institutional shareholders, because they *own* the business – they can unseat the directors, or sell the company to someone who will. Shares seem to speak of value and price, but the underlying language of the stock market is the language of power. Power also lies behind the language spoken inside the companies, running through the management hierarchies from top to bottom, with little chance for those at the bottom to reply.

Close to the bottom of any conventionally-owned retailer's hierarchy there are many people who would be an asset in any business. Many of them *love* selling and always have. 'Selling is in my blood,' said one, who at the age of thirteen had started working for a market trader after school. By the age of seventeen he had acquired two stalls of his own.

Some are very knowledgeable, having been through formal or informal apprenticeships – sometimes at considerable personal cost – and have gained the expertise that comes with long experience.

When I met her, Ingrid Elliott worked in the flagship store of Debenhams,* one of the major retail chains. She was proud of what she did. As she moved energetically round her department there was an impish spark in her face – she looked ready to break into a smile or even into an outright grin. But her body language was purposeful – she was clearly prepared to mix it if she had to.

Like the others, Ingrid was a considerable asset to the business that employed her. She had worked faithfully for Debenhams for 25 years. When she arrived as a youngster from Belgium, following her boyfriend back to England, she was happy to get a job – any job. Then the job became a career. Training helped her step onto the first rung

---

* For accuracy, I am using the past tense, because I am reporting what I saw and learned. This does not imply that she does not work there still.

of the management ladder. Nowadays training was delivered by computer programmes, but back then training was done by real live people, and she was grateful to them for the encouragement as well as the knowledge they gave her. Her role now was to manage the four areas where food was served in the Oxford Street store. When she explained what she liked about her work, the language was the ordinary language of a human being, free from jargon or overtones of power.

What I enjoy is working with people. As Food Services Manager you tend to work with the same people for a long time. On the shop floor the managers are moved around, and they never get a chance to build their team. Also, on the shop floor they don't see their people from one hour to the next, because it's such a vast area. With us it's all compact: you can see who's doing what, and where they are. So it's more personal.

Her team of fifty people rose to 100 on the busy days. Asked how she helped them develop a sense of being a team, she still did not resort to jargon:

'Working alongside them. And being fair to them. It's very much give and take, old-fashioned style.' She laughed, a little ruefully, and repeated the last phrase.

By contrast there was the modern style of management, practised by younger people, who did not see things in shades of grey. For example, everyone had to be totally flexible – for them that was an inflexible rule. As a result, at short notice the managers could tell the employees what hours they had to work, and they had to work those hours. No arguing. But actually people's lives do not let them be totally flexible – except at great personal cost – and Ingrid took account of that. So she tweaked the rules.

If someone had a history of being late, she would first have a chat with him or her – 'gently,' she added with a laugh. 'A lot of sound people have good reason for being late: sometimes they've got another job they have to travel from, or college, or children – all sorts of things. We see if we can maybe adjust the hours we ask them to work, see if we can accommodate them better. That's harder for the manager, but it's much more friendly and you get a lot more out of your staff.'

One indicator of the success of this approach was the fact that absences in her area were running at an average 4 per cent, which was less than half the rate for the store as a whole.

But when necessary, Ingrid could also be tough. If people just couldn't get out of bed, she got rid of them. There, at last, was the language of power. She had moderated it almost completely – she looked after her people, she talked to them, she worked with them, she cared about them, she bent the rules for them – but when there was no alternative she exercised raw power.

This is the power that runs right down from the chairman. Chairmen of companies like these perhaps feel that power most rapturously at the annual general meeting, after their city investors have re-elected them to their posts with another pay rise and a huge dollop of share options. To gain re-election they have had to promise constant improvement. Consequently, they and their fellow directors have to make sure that their companies' performance improves. The important judges of what 'improvement' means are not the customers, and certainly not the employees, but the shareholders. The measure of improvement is the amount of value that can be wrung out of the business in the form of share-price increases and dividends. This, of course, is 'shareholder value', a phrase with semi-religious overtones, evoking reverential acquiescence and bringing debate to an end. How could anyone not believe in shareholder value?*

The directors of Debenhams have a lively understanding of what can happen if shareholder value grows too slowly or unpredictably. So do the managers, and the employees. In 2003, after a period of poor performance, the whole company was sold, and its shares taken off the Stock Exchange. Power was transferred to a group of private equity investors, backing a new chief executive to lead the company. As reported at length in the press at the time, they bought the company for about £1.7bn – a 37 per cent premium to the value on the Stock

---

* The concept can be traced back to a 1981 speech by Jack Welch, shortly after he took over as chief executive of General Electric. It came to dominate the corporate world. But the economic crisis seemed to have a significant effect on his views. In March 2009 he was reported in the *Financial Times* as saying: 'shareholder value is the dumbest idea in the world. Shareholder value is a result, not a strategy . . . Your main constituencies are your employees, your customers and your products.' This turnround is nearly as significant as that of Alan Greenspan, who, visibly chastened, admitted to Congress on 23 October 2008 that his credo of decades, that the best outcomes were achieved by letting markets regulate themselves, was flawed.

Exchange. The way they structured the finances, however, allowed them to achieve that acquisition while investing a total of only £606m of their own money, just over a third of the price. The remaining £1.1bn was added to the company's debt, more than quadrupling it. Among other things, this greatly reduced the tax that Debenhams was paying, because interest is allowed against tax.

It's ingenious. You buy the company, but the company pays most of the bill for you, with the taxpayer picking up a fair bit of the tab too. When this method is used by private equity buyers to make a few people very rich, this leaves a bad taste, but as Spedan Lewis and Louis Kelso showed, the employees as a whole can use the same technique to acquire the companies where they work. The difference is that having got hold of the company, the employees naturally want to strengthen it over the long term; the financiers' main goal is usually to extract the maximum cash from it in the short term – a few years at most. In the case of Debenhams they quickly set about squeezing cash out of the company.

By selling and mortgaging many of the buildings owned by Debenhams the new team repaid substantial amounts of debt and lowered the cost of much of the rest. They then set about generating more cash from the operations – and also from the suppliers. Before the acquisition Debenhams was paying its suppliers an average of 27 days after the goods were invoiced; before long the suppliers were being paid only after about two months. That was equivalent to forcing them to give Debenhams an interest-free loan of over £100m. This carries not a single benefit to society. It reduces the speed at which capital is circulated, which reduces GDP. It places a financial burden on suppliers, often smaller weaker companies, which can in some cases cause them to fail. So a company managed to extract cash will often reduce its own borrowings by using its power over suppliers, nakedly in the company's own financial interest but at the expense of the suppliers and of society as a whole. The invisible hand becomes visible, and is used for the benefit of the owners of a company, but *against* everybody else's interests.

At the same time, according to financial analysts at the time, while Debenhams continued to open new stores they invested on average 39 per cent less on them; and, even more drastically, they reduced their capital expenditure on refurbishing stores by 77 per cent. This reduction in capital expenditure is the kind of thing that does not affect results immediately, although it tends to weaken the business in the long term. Still, why worry about the long term when you can clear so much money out of it in the short term? If I can buy a company and get it to give me more cash than I put in to buy it, then I have effectively got hold of it for free. Consequently it does not matter much to me if it has been weakened. I can still sell it on for a considerable further sum, and the consequences will be someone else's problem.

All this is the very opposite of building a business – it is extracting cash from a business that other people have built. The aim is to get back the total original investment, and much more, as quickly as possible, before the cash extraction possibly weakens the business, with the result that the business begins to fail its customers, and the customers turn away.

What else did the new owners of Debenhams do in search of cash? As Ingrid remembered she looked down and talked in short staccato sentences. 'It was hard. There were quite a few big cut-backs. They weren't very popular. There were a fair few redundancies. People were frightened. It was a rough ride. It's always personal – you hurt people for a long time.'

City analysts argue that this is exactly the sort of 'difficult decision' that the leaders of companies have to make, so that the flow of cash to investors can be maintained and grown. Chief executives who develop a reputation for a ruthless streak will carry a great deal of credibility on the Stock Exchange. As a result, some of them will be able to negotiate enormous rises in their personal incomes.

The redundancies carried out by Tullis Russell when they moved their decal coating operation to be near their customers in the Far East were aimed at strengthening the business in the long term. The Debenhams redundancies coincided with substantial cash extraction for the private equity investors in the short term. To repeat, the aim of private equity acquirers is often to get out quickly with a large haul of cash, not to invest in building the business for the long term.

In the food service areas in the Oxford Street store, Ingrid had been training a deputy manager, who was proving highly competent. In 2003 this deputy was ready to take on full managerial responsibilities. Instead, she was made redundant, and she was in effect replaced by somebody with a different title on lower pay. 'I did resent that. The new person wasn't ready for the job. It was so wrong – totally the wrong move for us. I wasn't in a position to stand up for my deputy. All I could do was help her find another job, outside the company. Totally the wrong job for her, as it turned out.'

In this particular instance the managers were making redundant a long-service employee, someone committed to and enthusiastic about Debenhams. 'She only ever wanted to work for Debenhams,' said Ingrid.

The new owners also got rid of the employee share scheme. Debenhams had been giving out small amounts of shares free to all employees who were eligible – and most of them were. In the 2003 acquisition the shares were all bought in, and no more given out by the time of writing – at least at Ingrid's level and below. There seemed no longer to be any attempt to share even token wealth widely with the people that helped create it. Instead the owners were keeping it for themselves. During the three years in private ownership the investors who had bought the company with an investment of £606m were reported as having paid out to themselves over £1bn.

Three years after the acquisition by private equity, Debenhams' shares were floated back on the Stock Exchange, at a price of 195p per share. The investors were reported as cashing in another £200m and still keeping 35 per cent of the company. They left the company laden with close to £1bn of debt, and some of the tactics used to generate cash were said by analysts to have backfired on the brand name. For example, Debenhams was holding sales for sixteen weeks each year, in contrast with eight weeks at Marks and Spencer and only six at John Lewis.

The overhang of debt meant that in the event of a market downturn, they would struggle. The downturn came, and in November 2008 the share price fell to 20p per share. Still, that's how the capital market works – the Capital Market, I mean. Enormous sums paid out in short order to financiers; a business undermined; people damaged; and a fortune lost by the pension funds. The share price of 20p proved to be the low point, and the price at the time of writing (early 2010) has recovered to about a third of the price it was at the time of the flotation.

With her two boys to look after, Ingrid was now working part time: her career was on pause. But she was just as committed to the company.

'I'm doing almost a full time job in three days. It's a bit unusual to have a part time manager, but they're getting just as much out of me as they were when I was full time.'

Her company mobile phone was switched on at all times, even at home, although a supervisor, who managed the department in her absence, protected her from being called too often.

Ingrid often laughed, and she did not speak against the company at all. At each stage she explained away the painful and difficult things she described – they had to do it, it was the right thing to do, it made the company more efficient, it couldn't be helped. Asked if her feelings changed with the removal of shares, the sacking of her deputy and the 'hard' experiences, she reflected for a moment, and then: 'No. I suppose I must be Debenised. I'm very tough. [She laughed, and then became serious.] My role was to make sure that my team were as little affected as possible. You can't be seen to be struggling yourself, otherwise you can't help the other people. So you've got to say, "Yes, it's a bit tough at the moment, but we'll get through it. Let's do this . . ." And you carry on as much as possible a normal life.'

So she kept things going *in spite of* the effects of the 'discipline', which in theory works to strengthen the company. Without her efforts, and the efforts of similar people, the shareholder value would have been destroyed. Capital market discipline depends on the good will of people who work hard and creatively and caringly to preserve the capacity of the business, even as the wielders of that discipline extract billions at their expense. This voluntary willingness to go beyond what is said in the employment contract is absolutely vital for every single business – that is why the 'work to rule' is so effective a tactic when people are disgruntled: without the extra commitment that is normal, the business struggles.

Pressed on how things might be done better, on what she would change if she were in charge, she thought for a long time, then told the story of how new IT systems were introduced. She was simply handed a pile of system manuals. 'You don't have time to read them. You don't get trained on anything. And the systems don't always work. They've been trialled in some piddly store somewhere, and because Oxford Street is so much bigger and so much more complex than anywhere else, they sometimes don't work.'

She looked as if she might never smile again as she gave the example of the clocking-in system. It was supposed to enable the managers to spend less time in the office and more with the customers. She would have loved to do that. But the new system would never pay the staff correctly – she had to redo it all manually, which took longer than before it was introduced.

Like other interviewees, she could raise these things with her managers, but it was not easy to be heard. 'We can stamp our feet, but they won't necessarily listen to the individual. So you've got to have quite a few people getting off their butts and saying, "This doesn't work for us." And people won't always do that – they are busy with day to day stuff.'

The result was that the people became resigned to having to do the extra work. Once again Ingrid gave a rueful laugh.

Another thing she would do if she were in charge would be to bring back the share scheme or profit sharing. Like others she cited John Lewis as one company that still shared its profits with everyone. She thought that would really get people going.

But she did not let these things get her down. 'Debenhams is a successful business. Over the years it's always been run pretty well. You've got to have pride in what you do. You feel you're part of something that's successful and good.'

And that is how people in their millions live. There is heroism in these lives. Having no alternative, and filled with goodwill, they make the best of it. And if that means ignoring or reinterpreting what the people in power are doing, then so be it. There is no option.

It called to mind the song of the crucified at the end of the Monty Python film, *Life of Brian*. Always look on the bright side of life.

Unfortunately, the stories told by the other interviewees were not happy ones. My publishers showed to their lawyers a draft of this chapter that reported accurately and in detail what my interlocutors had said. The lawyers' summary advice was simple: 'You will be sued.' Britain's libel laws are perhaps the most repressive of debate in the whole of the developed world, and consequently it is too risky to tell the honest truth, naming the companies and the people. The following is therefore an amalgam of what I heard, but with the companies and the individuals unidentifiable. If you, the reader, do not yourself work in a large store, then to find out if it rings true perhaps you can show it to someone who does. I am grateful to the people who talked with me, and sorry that I am able to thank by name only Ingrid, who made no serious criticism of her employer.

For these remaining interviewees, frustration lay just below the skin. Some felt they were not allowed to use their skills. It pained them that so many opportunities to sell were missed – the perception was often that sales could be so much higher. Some were dispirited at the fact that fellow workers were allocated to sell complex products when they knew little about them. The biggest criticism was often that the managers could make so much more of the business. 'This place could be a *goldmine*' was typical of the comments. They really wanted to see the business successful, but tended to feel that because of the managers' approach it was not. The hierarchy of power seemed to get in the way of creating a good business – rather than teamwork, the managers often seemed to be preoccupied with their positions in the hierarchy. The interviewees frequently felt that their views were of no interest to the managers.

A repeated complaint was that the people recruited to sell were not given the training they needed, with the result that their attempts to sell were less than successful. It was not fair on the customer, who might not be knowledgeable or accustomed to buying the particular product; nor on the staff member, who had not been given sufficient training to make him or her confident and skilful. A typical extract from one interview ran like this:

'Once I heard someone say to a customer, "Have a look at this – it is more expensive." You don't say, "This is more expensive"! You say, "This is a better technology", or "better quality", "This is a different manufacturer" – things like that. But you don't use the word "expensive". Straightaway you ring alarm bells for the customer.'

When youngsters start their jobs, they all want to succeed – they want to make progress and do something they can feel proud of. But enthusiastic, good-willed youngsters often do not last long in an environment where position in the hierarchy is a dominant force around them. One person said that the politics got on the youngsters' nerves, and they soon left. Another reported that there were many people off work with depression and stress, brought on by the management approach. In one case: 'For example, they have reduced the number of staff. Someone initially is employed on the floor, selling. Because of the reductions in staff she finds herself selling, putting stock out, working behind the till, working in the back room, working in other areas. She's like a spinning top, and doesn't know when she's going to stop. It gets you down in the end.'

According to some, the lack of teamwork and leadership made it worse. Managers were rarely around to supervise or help solve problems. 'Since there are no managers on the floor,' one commented with a grin, 'they shouldn't take any credit when the company makes money.' Most recognised that the managers could play a key role, but felt that to do so they would have to be present much more than they were. One listed four important consequences if a manager spent time on the floor: 'One, the manager's working with the staff. Two, the staff can respect the manager because she's actually pulling her finger out. Three, she can see the problems and solve them. And four, she will see what merchandise is moving – which stock to promote.'

A frequent criticism was that the people on the floor were not listened to. Some wanted to contribute ideas and see the good ones put into practice. But the trend seemed to be for decision-making to become more centralised, with less flexibility.

In theory, pressure from the capital market should force companies to improve their performance, including the way they manage people. For example, in 2004, with performance declining, the threat of capital market discipline appeared over the horizon for Marks and Spencer (M&S), in the form of a bid from a billionaire. The board, reportedly in turmoil, ousted the chairman and the chief executive before appointing Stuart Rose as the new chief executive. The resistance he organised to the threatened takeover saw off Philip Green, the would-be acquirer, and was seen in the City as successful. Among the 'successes' was the fact that the company paid out nearly £2.3 billion – £2,300,000,000 – in cash to its shareholders. One of the many steps that M&S took to help improve profits and fund this huge payout was to squeeze their suppliers; another was to get rid of 650 jobs.

It is not clear exactly how the suppliers were squeezed. The document sent to shareholders in 2004 said: 'We have renegotiated terms with our suppliers.' This was predicted to save £140 million per annum. Whatever M&S did, the phrase 'renegotiating terms' often implies both cutting prices and taking more time to pay. As discussed above, this brings about no benefit to the economy or to society.

In the City this 'discipline', as applied to M&S, and the response to it, were seen as excellent things. The board of M&S had been punished for allowing the company to perform less than optimally – that is, wringing out for the shareholders less cash than had proved possible once capital market pressure was applied. In many cases the discipline is applied through the actual sale of the company – a sort of corporate corporal punishment, as happened to Debenhams. In the case of M&S the threat alone was sufficient to force them to change their ways.

As to the removal of 650 jobs, M&S had always had a reputation as a good employer. To the City disciplinarians, that sounded like complacency. Less money should be spent on employees, and the money saved should be given to the owners.

One thing that redundancies fail to do is encourage the remaining employees to work more enthusiastically for the company. The fact that the business itself depends to a great extent on the quality and energy of its employees often seems in these circumstances almost to be beside the point. In the world of the management hierarchy, mesmerised by the concept of 'shareholder value', supervised and disciplined from outside by the shareholders, with power running one way, down from the top, the effect on the employees does not seem to be a significant consideration, according to those low down in the organisation. To people who care about selling, that is anathema.

When not under the sway of greed and fear (the motivations that are reputed to keep owners doing their best), the human race as seen by mainstream economists is driven by supervision. It is supervision that keeps people performing at a high level. On the stock market, this means that the chairman and chief executive will become complacent and allow performance to decline, unless they are supervised by the shareholders and disciplined if they fail. Inside the company, people will try to get away with doing the minimum, unless they are supervised and, when necessary, disciplined. The staff, however, report a different effect. 'You are walking round the floor afraid to scratch yourself in case somebody is watching you. It is very uncomfortable. So the people on the floor – there's no life in them. There's no enthusiasm.'

In some cases the philosophy of 'management by supervision' reaches such extremes that staff find themselves ready to laugh out loud – or to weep. One person reported: 'Some days there will only be one manager and that manager will spend half a day in the CCTV room. The CCTV room is meant to be there to prevent terrorism and theft, and for the safety of customers and staff. It is not there for staff to spy on other staff.' The feeling engendered is that the staff are being watched, and there is little confidence that the managers will take a supportive approach. 'They're looking to isolate someone, to identify people who are weak, to get them out of the door. Which is completely wrong. Instead of working with those people on their strengths, to improve them, they are looking at their weaknesses. Everybody's got a weakness: there isn't a human being without a weakness. They shouldn't just focus on the problem – they should look for the solution. And the solution isn't to punish, it's to help that person improve.'

There was a feeling of neglect taking effect in many ways. One talked of a decline in simple housekeeping standards. 'There is complete disregard for the store. If you look at it you'll see the place is falling apart. The floor is scratched and dirty. Don't just take my word for it: you go in there tomorrow and look at the dust on the counters. It is dirty every single day. It's the people managing that section who are ultimately responsible. But they show complete disregard. You wonder where the managers are and what they do all day.'

In the stores too, it often seemed to the staff that they were not valued. There were reports that managers had over time closed a social club, taken away a pool table, and shut a staff cafeteria. One employee summarised it thus: 'Anything that is there to cool your mind, they take away.'

It would be normal for employees to raise these and similar issues with their managers, especially where there are ways to sell more goods. However, people said that they and their colleagues had raised things many times, but in vain. In the words of one individual, who had worked in the same company for many, many years – the words were said with sadness and a touch of anger – 'You don't feel valued. It seems they're not interested in what we think, in the ideas we put forward.'

Another said that there could be discussions, but the next day they would be forgotten. The effects were cumulative: 'People just give up. There's no motivation. Who do you approach? When you hardly ever see a manager on the floor, who do you approach? And when you do see one they say they haven't got time – "I'm busy, I'll catch you later" – just to avoid you.' After trying repeatedly but without success to be heard, some ended up just doing the minimum required to keep the job. 'I wash my hands of it. I leave it to them. That's the kind of attitude they get.'

One said that in the old days the company had been better run, with more focus on customers. There was also greater incentive for the staff – a bonus scheme and other benefits. 'But all that is gone. Now it's all about reducing costs. Even receipts – you can get a better receipt in a corner shop. In a multimillion pound business, a receipt should stand out. You want your company to stand out from others in every little way.'

The City believes that by changing the CEO they can change the company's performance; similarly one interviewee looked to the top management to lead a change. But the prescription for a solution was different from the City's. 'What is needed is for the people right at the top to make a change. They're making mega mega money, and the workers making the money for them are like ants – the top people can't see them. But I think they should concentrate on those people, because those people are at the forefront of the business. They're the ones who open the doors and they're the ones who are on stage. Once you lift the blinds you're on stage, once you open the door you're on stage, and it's up to you to act.'

Characteristically, people got on well with fellow workers. 'They are very nice people. And we are all in agreement. Sometimes we just laugh about the whole thing, because it's a joke. It's like a circus.'

One particularly brave person very much wanted to be named. Unfortunately, legal caution makes that unwise. 'I'm just telling the truth, that's all. Probably they aren't going to like it, but it is the truth. You have to stand up. Otherwise things don't change.'

At bottom, they wanted to see the company succeed, and wanted to be allowed to make a full contribution to that success. Most people want to be able to feel proud of what they do. But in a big corporation with a large hierarchy driven by capital market discipline, they tend to live lives of frustration. For some the frustration is extreme.

8

Power and Accountability – Corporate Governance – and CEO Pay

According to *Business Week*, the average CEO of a major corporation made 42 times the average hourly worker's pay in 1980. By 1990 that had doubled to 85 times. In 2000, the average CEO salary reached an unbelievable 531 times that of the average hourly worker.[42]

In the catalogue of bad faith that characterises statements on 'corporate governance', few can equal the sheer brazenness of the supposed justifications for the unending rise in the pay of chief executives.

Many numbers are quoted, sometimes varying widely, but everyone is agreed that year after year CEO rewards have been rocketing up. According to the American unions, the AFL-CIO, 'A chief executive officer of a Standard & Poor's 500 company was paid, on average, $10.9 million in total compensation in 2008.'[43] This compares with median pay of $5.39m for the same group as listed by *Forbes*.[44] Either way, it is a big number.

Several prominent entrepreneurs figured in the *Forbes* list for 2008. Towards the very bottom were Steve Jobs, the founder of Apple, with no pay at all (he held shares worth about $660m), and Warren Buffett of Berkshire Hathaway with his steady $100,000 a year, a minor contribution to his wealth, given that his shares were worth over $38bn. Larry Ellison, the founder of Oracle, played things rather differently, and ended up top of the list. His five-year total pay came to nearly $1bn, of which around half was paid in 2008. The value of his shares, at $20bn, was just a little over half of that of Warren Buffett's, and one wonders if he feels poor by comparison. Perhaps it is to scratch that itch that he needs an income of $2m for every working day.

Most of the people on the list were not entrepreneurs but professional managers. The people in every 100th place, for example, were all professional managers, holding shares in their companies valued at only (in this group it is 'only') between $1m and $7.5m. However, these sums were dwarfed by what they could earn: in 2008 they were paid $2.4m, $4.1m, $6.9m and $12.9m respectively, and their total earnings over the last five years ranged between $35m and $74m per person, on average between $7m and $15m a year – at least ten times the value of their shares and in most cases much more. One of the arguments in favour of giving CEOs large numbers of shares is that this will line up their interests with those of the shareholders. But even if you are given $1 million of shares every year, your ability to earn far more from your employment means that what counts is preserving your position at the top of the company, rather than looking after the interests of the shareholders.

The situation is broadly similar in the UK, albeit at lower figures. Even France and Germany seem to be headed down this route.

Ellison, Jobs and Buffett, as genuinely entrepreneurial leaders, are usually accepted as being in a different category from the professional chief executives. How to reward somebody who starts a company that goes on to thrive is an important subject. High rewards for people who achieve it is something most people find acceptable; similarly high rewards for the professional managers who follow along behind is another matter.

Perhaps the most common justification of CEO remuneration is the refrain that it is caused by 'market forces'. The claim is made seriously. A well-fed chief executive, fresh from the remuneration committee with a raise measured in thousands of dollars a week, as well as vast swathes of share options, can simply sigh, 'Market forces!' with a contented chuckle as he settles back comfortably into the leather seat of his limousine.

The ancestry of this argument goes back again to Adam Smith's invisible hand. Market forces are supposed to guide the players in any market, such as the chief executives (the sellers) and the directors who appoint them (the buyers), to ask and to pay prices – in this case, salaries – that properly reflect the balance between supply and demand.

When that happens, everyone benefits: there are exactly the right amount of goods – in this case, chief executives – to do the jobs available, at the minimum necessary cost.

If it feels a bit strange to talk about people as products in a market, perhaps we should look at a less complex product – the latest electronic gizmo, for example. If there are fewer gizmos available in shops than the number that people want to use, then the price will rise. That being the case, either the existing suppliers will increase their production, or new suppliers will be encouraged by the high prices to start production. As these extra supplies become available, so the prices will fall again. The invisible hand has guided the players in the market to improve the situation for all concerned: everyone who wants a gizmo will have one, and at a reasonable price.

The argument is that this same invisible hand is at work in deciding the pay of chief executives.

The first clue that this may be bunkum is shown by the fact that at the top end the demand for chief executives has remained pretty constant. The *Fortune* 500 companies need between them 500 chief executives, just as they did in 1980, when the average chief executive's pay was a mere forty-two times the average pay of the employees. But year after year the rate of CEO pay has risen, to a ratio of hundreds of times the pay of the typical employee in 2007.[45]

How to explain the rising prices? Has the supply gone down? Are there fewer potential chief executives available? Has our failing educational system reduced the average level of competence? Or have alternative highly paid careers – football, perhaps – tempted those who might have been chief executives off on to other paths? In this scenario all those additional millions in pay might be necessary to prevent a further exodus from the corporate world. This is theoretically possible. But there is no evidence that it is the case. There are vastly more MBAs entering the workforce every year than there used to be. That seems to suggest that the supply is rising rather than falling.

All of this is a conundrum. We see fixed demand and rising supply: therefore, the market model predicts falling prices (that is, falling salaries for chief executives). Yet salaries are rising steeply, year after year, with hardly a break.

Fixed demand, rising supply, but rising prices – it's enough to shake an economist's faith in the market model, assuming that it could be shaken. Actually, it is impossible to shake an economist's faith in the market model. The theoretical market model is true, beyond question. So it *must* be market forces at work. It *is* market forces at work. But mysteriously so.

There are many theories as to why this market moves in mysterious ways. A recent evaluation was carried out by Carola Frydman of the Sloan School of Management at MIT.[46] She found that the 'explanations' offered to justify today's rises failed to explain the movement of CEO salaries over the long term. For example, one argument is that CEO jobs have become more complex. But she showed that during the thirty years following the Second World War CEO jobs expanded hugely in scope and complexity without triggering any such change. Another argument is that, today, ownership is dispersed, weakening shareholder control over CEO pay; but actually it was more dispersed through the period of steady CEO rewards. Her conclusion was that the market is indeed moving in mysterious ways: 'most of the common explanations for the recent changes in compensation cannot individually account for its evolution over the long run.'

If we look more closely at markets, however, we find that there is a catch. If the market mechanism is to work, then one of the actors in the market must *want* to achieve a low price, and secondly that person must be in a position to exercise some influence, by refusing to buy if the price is too high. In the case of technical gizmos, there have to be people out there with cash in their pockets *looking for* the best price. If everyone buying a gizmo is so excited at the prospect of using it that he or she does not care about what it costs, then the price may not fall, no matter how many are available. Or if the act of purchase, for example, is an opportunity to display flamboyant generosity to a friend or to be seen as the coolest person on the block, then no time will be spent comparing prices. If you don't shop around, market forces may be of no benefit to you at all. Because you are not creating any drive towards lower prices, the market mechanism will not work.

In reality there is no great mystery to the chief executive conundrum. And it has nothing to do with market forces. It has to do with power.

The people who want the prices to fall – who want the chief executives to have lower salaries – don't have any power. So there is no *effective* market. The shareholders would ideally like to lower the costs of the top managers, as indeed the costs of all the employees. But the shareholders have long ago succumbed to the lure of liquidity. They are rather like over-excited gizmo buyers, in that they have no intention of getting involved in achieving the best price. If things go in directions that they don't like, they don't get stuck in to try to influence things, to turn them round. Instead, they sell their shares. It is a position of complete irresponsibility, a total lack of commitment. Thus they have no influence, and as a result no one is trying seriously to get top salaries down.

The employees, of course, have no say in this, or in anything else about how the company is managed. If they did have any influence, might they set out actively to keep top salaries down? It is perhaps indicative that the salaries of the 100-plus chief executives in the employee-owned Mondragón group are significantly below 'market' rates, and the pay of the leader in employee-owned John Lewis, the UK's most successful retailer, is also orders of magnitude below that of his peers in other companies.

Economists have described the problem quite well. The chief executive is appointed to act in the interests of the shareholders – to act as their 'agent'. As their agent, he or she is supposed to be looking after their property, their company. In essence the problem is how to get your agent to do what *you* want, rather than what *he or she* wants. And the answer is: if you do not keep your eye on him or her, and take every opportunity to exercise your influence, then you can't. Your 'agent' will do what he or she wants.

It is obvious that chief executives have a great deal of power *inside* the companies they run. It is less obvious, because less palatable to the powers that think they be, that chief executives have a great deal of power to influence the shareholders. Theoretically, the shareholders own the companies, and therefore it is the shareholders who employ the chief executives. But who provides the information to the shareholders? The chief executives. In a markedly different arena Tony Blair, we now know, exaggerated the danger posed by Saddam Hussein, and so persuaded much of the British public to back Britain's co-invasion of Iraq. (Except for the huge and vocal proportion who did not count. The further huge proportion who, while suspecting that the open story was threadbare, nevertheless trusted Blair, thinking that he must know something he could not make public, eventually realised they'd been fooled.) Managers in quoted companies shape and spin their actions to create a good impression on the stock exchange. In theory the best they can do is to build strong businesses. In practice there is much to be gained by gaming the system.

Who forecasts the future? The chief executive. Who writes the annual report to shareholders? The chief executive. Who determines senior salary pay levels? The chief executive. Who decides what additional perks are needed to convince senior people such as the chief executive to get out of bed? The chief executive.

Hang on, I hear you say. What about the corporate governance structures? The non-executive directors who dominate all boards in the US, and are supposed to be pretty dominant in the boardrooms of the UK too – they are governing and controlling all this, are they not? The remuneration committees? The audit committees? The social responsibility committees? Even the corporate governance committees? They are all dominated by non-executives. Surely *they* are there to see that these things are properly done?

But who, pray, are these non-executive directors, who supervise the boards and sit on the audit committees and remuneration committees and social responsibility committees and corporate governance committees? Why, by and large they are none other than the chief executives of other corporations. To be sure, there is a sprinkling of non-executives from other sources too. They are highly paid for little work, they are flattered to be involved, and their pet projects are treated with great solicitude by the chief executives.

When it comes to setting the chief executive's pay, why would the members of the remuneration committee demur? They themselves are raking it in for very little work. Why would they want to saw at the branch they are sitting on? To bite the hand that gives them loads of cash and high status? To deflate a fellow chief executive, whose confidence is key to the success of the company? Many of those sitting round the table, chief executives elsewhere, will themselves soon have their own pay subject to scrutiny by non-executives. Where is the incentive to control the rise in pay? If I agree to a good raise here, then I will be more likely to get a good one myself. The wolves don't even have to worry too much about putting on realistic sheep's clothing – nobody is watching them. At any rate, nobody with any power.

Let us glance for a moment at a hypothetical report on the pay of chief executives, typical of those written for remuneration committees by management consultants recruited and paid by the chief executives. The report says that 50 per cent of chief executives are paid less than $5.9 million a year. But do we want our CEO to be in the bottom half? How would this look in the advertisement: 'Our new chief executive will be paid less than average'? Companies, like chief executives, have big egos to protect – they are *all* in the top half.

In theory the non-executive directors will have a humble awareness that they are supposed to be representing the interests of the shareholders. Might they perhaps consult those shareholders? Almost certainly not. The tendency will be to consider what they can get past the shareholders without triggering organised rebellion. That's not a very high hurdle.

PR people are paid small fortunes to make the reports to shareholders persuasive, so that there will be no objection to the inexorable rise of chief executive pay. And actually, as we have seen, shareholders always have an easy way out: they can sell their shares. That is much less trouble than organising a rebellion. In theory the sale of shares should trigger a fall in prices, eventually provoking a takeover. But in the case of CEO pay capital market discipline is an illusion. In the meantime the party goes on.

Market forces at work? Or a self-interested body of powerful people with the ability to set their own pay? The kids have taken over the sweetie shops, the cops have commandeered the betting shops. As the Nobel Prize-winning economist Joe Stiglitz pointed out, in real life, in every actual market, the reason why the invisible hand is invisible is that it isn't there.

A BRIEF WORD ON SECURITISATION

Corporate governance is supposed to enforce the accountability of those in positions of power. In theory the chief executives are accountable to the shareholders. We have seen that this accountability is not discernible in the setting of chief executive pay. The non-executive directors, appointed supposedly to supervise the chief executives on behalf of the shareholders, have rapidly been sucked into the system – probably lived there all their working lives – and do no such thing.

Why does this accountability not work? A contributory cause is in stock markets. The securitisation of corporate governance – the buying and selling of rights to hold the chief executive accountable – is as insidious as the securitisation of mortgages was in the early 2000s. It removes all sense of responsibility.

The holders of shares in an oil company are not interested in the oil business and have no commitment to it; it follows that they will not exert themselves to hold the chief executive accountable. They are interested in whether they can sell their shares for a profit, that is to say in whether *other people* are interested in the oil business. If others get interested, then the stock price will rise. If not, it will stay steady, or fall. The great British economist John Maynard Keynes was the first to express this point clearly.[47] In 1936 he pointed out that this is the opposite of what is required to build a healthy economy: for that, commitment is required, the commitment of large sums of money in investments that cannot be turned back into money, except over time, through the building of a successful business. If someone is in farming, as opposed to owning stock in farming companies, then like a spider in a bath he or she will discover that the only way out is down the plughole. A farmer has to be committed to solving all the problems that arise, in pursuit of which goal innovations are introduced round the farm, any necessary equipment is acquired, and large sums of capital are tied down for years at a time. There is no other way to keep a farm thriving. In the case of a holder of stock, on the other hand, it is 'as though a farmer, having tapped his barometer after breakfast, could decide to remove his capital from the farming business between 10 and 11 in the morning and reconsider whether he should return to it later in the week.'[48] There is no commitment, no effort to solve any problems. The existing, securitised ownership system – the stock market – undermines the building of business and the holding to account of the chief executive.

The idea that the pay of chief executives would be held in check by shareholders is intrinsically fallacious. Today, it is the financial institutions that are the main shareholders. As well as having the way out just described – selling the shares – the managers of the financial institutions are themselves very highly paid. They have a greater personal interest in seeing high pay for City and City-related jobs than they have in seeing the board costs of large corporations kept within reason. They identify with the wealthy and the educated – as do the legal and financial advisers who so often advise against employee buyouts – much more readily than they do with the pensioners whose interests they are supposed to serve. The mean performance of pension fund investment managers is consistently below that of their benchmark stock indices – because of the pay and fees charged by the fund managers. Security markets make up a gravy train that adds little to human wealth or happiness.

Where then should we look for people who are committed to building businesses, to improving them, to making them work? And who might possibly control the chiefs?

Of necessity, the people who are most committed to businesses are the people who work in them. When the employees, as owners, have the governance rights, then there is a rather better chance that the chief executives can be held to account, as in Mondragón and the John Lewis Partnership.

9

How the Employment Contract Came to Be

So far we have seen that the conventional, traditional capital market model fails to predict or explain what actually goes on in employee-owned companies. Moreover it makes several obviously false claims, not only about employee-owned companies but also about the best way to fund and organise productive businesses. However, we have to presume that the efforts made by economists and business thinkers are honest attempts to throw light on what is really going on. They are trying to expand knowledge. It's just that they've got it wrong. The result is that they can easily fall into the trap of justifying the status quo as if it were the best of all possible worlds. Science does not have the same danger – at least until it turns its attention, like economics, to human behaviour. There is no right and wrong in a volcanic eruption, a chemical reaction or the birth of a new star.

Ignoring the palpable flaws evident in the idea that markets function as predicted by the models, the economic ideology that has increasingly dominated the world since the late eighteenth century concluded that the market must be right. If it happens, it is ordained by the Market to happen, and therefore it must be right. Everything that happens, happens because it is efficient – otherwise the Market would not let it happen. If it does *not* happen, it is right that it doesn't happen – the Market has decreed it.

One of the biggest flaws of this approach is that it does not acknowledge adequately the issue of power. This creates the potential for economics to become purely ideological, justifying relationships of power and subservience. Things that have in reality happened through imposition by the powerful may be interpreted as rational, inevitable and proper. The accidental occurrences along the paths of history may be transformed by theory into necessary features of reality. Circumstances which could easily and perhaps should have been very different become viewed as the best of all possible worlds, simply because they exist. The effort is to explain why the Market has put them there, not to face the issue of power.

On the basis of the theories put forward by economists a considerable global structure of capital market operators and investors and advisers has been built, providing enormous benefit to relatively small numbers of people and perpetuating a legal system that does not acknowledge the humanity of the employees, or their right to share in the wealth that they create. In the quasi-scientific mode that deals in given facts, the economists discover the relationship between employer and employee – in its modern form, the employment contract – and set out to explain it. Today, the employment contract seems as if it is a natural feature of the landscape in which we live, as if it could not be otherwise. It is a fact of nature. Nobody thinks it needs to be transformed; indeed it seems to employers to be weighted so heavily in the interests of the employee that there is a widespread opinion that the law has gone too far. In the last few years the burden of maternity pay and holiday pay, for example, together with health and safety rules, seems to have feather-bedded those who work for the business, at the expense of those who own it.

Seen from the perspective of the employee, however, the result of the economic studies has produced a simple message for the great majority of the human population, who have to get a job to get by. The message is: work to create wealth for your employer, or live a life of poverty; sign an employment contract giving away your rights, or have an even more miserable existence. To summarise in one word: 'Tough!'

Look a little further back and it becomes clear that the employment contract had a difficult birth, in deprived surroundings, with abusive parents – and that it still bears the scars of that history. It would do it a world of good to unpack it, and thereby liberate it to take a different course in future.

PRECURSORS OF MODERN EMPLOYMENT [49]

By the year 1730 in England the countryside was peopled largely by an independent and relatively well-off yeomanry, subsisting as peasants on land over much of which they held rights in common. Without working extreme hours a yeoman could feed a wife and children reasonably well, growing grain or vegetables on his strip of land and allowing a cow and perhaps some sheep or pigs and chickens to graze and forage with those of his neighbours. It was the golden age of the English peasant.

Increasingly over the next hundred years, and particularly after 1760, the landlords appropriated the common land that had enabled so many people to live sturdily in the countryside – about one fifth of all the land in the country, supporting much more than one fifth of the population. The people were thrown off the land and lost their livelihoods. By 1830 the situation in the countryside was so severe that one day a traveller in Kent stumbled across four bodies lying by the side of the road. They were peasants who had starved to death. They were not the only ones.

During this whole period Parliament was entirely and corruptly dominated by the landed aristocracy – in 1793 it was claimed that over 300 MPs were 'elected' by or on the orders of just 157 landowners.[50] During this period the aristocrats and their tame MPs passed numerous Acts of Enclosure, appropriating mainly to themselves and to their relatives and friends the common land that had previously given the peasantry a living. Time after time petitions from the yeomanry, attempting to have their longstanding customary rights acknowledged, were ignored by Parliament. This naked use of power by the ruling aristocracy to enrich themselves at everyone else's expense was dressed in the rankest hypocrisy. In 1911 the process was documented by Hammond and Hammond in their book *The Village Labourer*, where among many others they gave this example:

on 10th November 1775 a petition was presented to the House of Commons for the enclosure of King's Sedgemoor, in the County of Somerset, the petitioners urging that this land was of very little value in its present state, and that it was capable of great improvement by enclosure and drainage.

The officially acknowledged motivation was thus entirely beneficial to society: the improvement of the land. The petition omitted to mention that this land included 80,000 acres of pasture used in common by thousands of yeoman-peasants.

This case was unusual in that the private letters of some of the people involved survive. The correspondence makes it clear that Lord Bolingbroke – whose brother was the main promoter of this bill – and others of his fellow petitioners had run up considerable gambling debts, and the enclosure would give them extra income to pay them off. The nominally independent chairman of the committee supervising the progress of the Act wrote to Lord Carlisle, another friend who was also owed money by Bolingbroke: 'Bully [Bolingbroke] has a scheme of enclosure, which, if it succeeds, I am told will free him from all his difficulties . . . I am ready to allow that he has been very faulty, but I cannot help wishing to see him once more on his legs . . .'

The real motivation was thus to provide income to a gambling aristocrat, so that he could recover from embarrassment and pay his debts to his fellow landowners. The ostensibly independent chairman of the theoretically fair-minded committee in Parliament was a friend of the person who would benefit the most. The fact that it would deprive thousands of yeoman-peasants of their main means of survival was of no account.

Indeed, mature reflection would show that depriving the peasants of their customary rights and means of living would produce a salutary reinforcement of the proper position of the aristocracy. The Hammonds quote from a report written for the Board of Agriculture in 1794:

'The use of common land by labourers operates upon the mind as a sort of independence.' When the commons are enclosed 'the labourers will work every day in the year, their children will be put out to labour early,' and 'that subordination of the lower ranks of society which in the present times is so much wanted, would thereby considerably be secured.'

The yeomanry who would be evicted by aristocratic appropriation of the commons saw the same facts from a rather different perspective. Documents of the time make painful reading. The peasants characteristically trusted in the parliamentary process, and spent their scarce pennies on hiring lawyers to draft petitions. When these appeals reached Parliament, they were routinely 'left on the table' – that is, flagrantly ignored, sometimes not even read, by the rapacious landowner-MPs.

A petition of 1797 against another enclosure included the following passage:

under pretence of improving lands in our parish, we will be deprived of an inestimable privilege, which we now enjoy, of turning a certain number of our cows, calves and sheep on and over the said lands, a privilege that enables us not only to maintain ourselves and our families in the depth of winter . . . but, in addition, to supply . . . young or lean stock at a reasonable price . . . for general consumption; and we further conceive that a more ruinous effect of this enclosure will be the almost total depopulation of our town, now filled with bold and hardy husbandmen, from among whom . . . the nation has hitherto derived its greatest strength and glory, in the supply of its fleets and armies; and driving us, from necessity and want of employment, in vast crowds, into manufacturing towns, where the very nature of our employment, over the loom and forge, soon may waste our strength.[51]

The petition was ignored by the MPs, the enclosures went ahead and starving labourers wandered the lanes, desperate for work. As we have seen, the word 'starving' is not an exaggeration.

THE RESPONSE OF THE PEASANTS, AND THE REACTION OF THE POWERFUL

In 1830 a series of what were described as riots broke out across much of south-eastern England. These 'riots' consisted of gatherings of poverty-stricken men, many having been turned off their common land. They went from farm to farm demanding an increase in wages, breaking up threshing machines, asking for money, and at the same time sometimes setting ricks of hay ablaze. The practice spread across all of the rich agricultural south-east of England. The 'rioters' used no violence against people, and where they won agreement from the farmers to increase wages, they dispersed without insult. Frequently they obtained a fair measure of sympathy, from small and large farmer alike – who saw them as potential allies in achieving reductions in the oppressive 'tithes' (fees paid to the church) and rents to the 'great' landlords.

In all the uprisings not a single person was wounded, let alone killed, by the starving peasants. A couple of officers had their hats squashed. One, who set about one of the peasants with a whip loaded with iron, was struck in self-defence and needed treatment. By contrast, at least one peasant was shot dead by a vigilante farmer-militiaman.

The landlords controlled Parliament and the army, as well as providing the judges. They were accustomed to deference from the lower orders and were not going to be lenient in the face of such insubordination. Revenge was cloaked in the trappings of official authority and the most complete hypocrisy. In Salisbury, opening the proceedings of the special commission sent to punish the 'rioters', the future Lord Wensleydale enunciated the reasoning of the judges. He pointed out that men could be executed for breaking machinery, as they could for riotous assembly. One of his fellow judges had help-fully elucidated the point that an assembly would become 'riotous' – justifying the execution of those involved – if a single one of his Majesty's subjects were prepared to say that he (or presumably she) had been made afraid. He went on: 'If that law ceases to be admin-istered with due firmness, . . . our wealth and power will soon be at an end . . .' [52] There we have the authentic voice of the landlords in Parliament, and of their friends and relatives in the judiciary: a fear of losing and a determination to protect and expand their privilege, their wealth and their power.

The special commissions went on to punish well over 850 people. About 400 were imprisoned. Nine were executed by hanging. A further 457 were exiled to the arbitrary brutality of penal settlements in the colonies. In the exultant words of Mr Justice Alderson addressing those to be exiled:

You will leave the country, all of you: you will see your friends and relations no more: for though you will be transported for seven years only, it is not likely that at the expiration of that term you will find yourselves in a situa-tion to return . . . The friends with whom you are connected will be parted from you for ever in this world.

As the Hammonds point out, this punishment was particularly severe for labourers, who had no education and led their lives within a network of close ties in villages made up of their extended family and lifelong neighbours.

The special correspondent for the *Times* newspaper was accustomed to strike a triumphant note at the suppression of the 'mob', and to interpret as a sign of low moral intelligence any trace of a spirited response from the labourers in the dock. But even he was moved by the distress of the wives and families of the condemned. Perhaps somewhere at the back of his mind he recognised that the men, having been deprived of their traditional living, had only, without violence, been trying to gain a reasonable wage.

The whole proceedings of this day in court were of the most afflicting and distressing nature. But the laceration of feeling did not end with the proceedings in court. The car for the removal of the prisoners was at the back entrance to the court-house, and was surrounded by a crowd of mothers, wives, sisters and children . . . The weeping and wailing . . . was truly heart-rending. We never saw so distressing a spectacle before.[53]

For the wives and children, already starving, the sentencing of their husbands or fathers condemned them, too, to even more desperate poverty, and perhaps the ghastly rigours of the poorhouse.

Once the landowning aristocracy and their friends had appropriated the common land, and even after they had moved a significant proportion of the king's subjects to the colonies, whether under sentence or not, this still left a very large number of poverty-stricken country people – men, women and children – desperate for work. The result was, in the words of the petitioners of 1797, to drive people 'from necessity and want of employment, in vast crowds, into manufacturing towns'. Where, of course, they sought ways to make a living.

ECONOMIC IDEOLOGY

At that time there were no employment laws. In Parliament the ideas of Adam Smith, selectively simplified, provided confidence that to benefit the whole of society it was essential to dismantle such of the old laws as were designed to protect the poor – the minimum wage, controls on the price of bread and the anti-monopoly provisions. Like the Big Bang in the financial world of the 1980s, which was a victory of bankers over regulators, this Big Bang was the complete victory of the owners of estates and businesses over those who would limit their power.

In that age of self-confidence of the rich and powerful, extraordinary claims were made without irony. In 1795 the English parliamentarian Edmund Burke, who had supported the American revolutionaries in their quest for independence and then recoiled horrified at the French revolutionaries' taking of the Bastille, explained in his paper 'Thoughts and Details on Scarcity':

In the case of the farmer and the labourer, their interests are absolutely the same, and it is absolutely impossible that their free contracts can be onerous to either party . . . It is plainly more the farmer's interest that his men should thrive, than that his horses should be well fed, sleek, plump and fit for use, or than that his waggon and ploughs should be strong, in good repair and fit for service . . . It is therefore the first and fundamental interest of the labourer that the farmer should have a full incoming profit . . . But if the farmer is excessively avaricious? So much the better – the more he desires to increase his gains, the more interested is he in the good condition of those upon whose labour his gains must principally depend.[54]

Exactly the same thinking was applied to and by the new employers in the rapidly growing manufacturing towns, which had little or no representation in Parliament.

The effect of these doctrines in practice was noted in 1836 for the Factory Enquiries Commission by Dr Charles Loudon. Appointed by Parliament as a man to be trusted by the authorities, he was far from being a radical. Having heard the detailed testimony of numerous doctors, he summarised the evidence about the children of the destitute labourers forced to work under the enlightened-because-self-interested regime of the factory owners:

In conclusion, I think it has been clearly proved that children have been worked a most unreasonable and cruel length of time daily, and that even adults have been expected to do a quantity of labour which scarcely any human being is able to endure. The consequence is that many have died prematurely, and others are afflicted for life with defective constitutions . . . [55]

It is worth looking at one incident in particular, typical of the many that occurred in the developing factories, but rather better documented. One evening in 1801, in a factory near Nottingham, Mary Richards, a girl of about ten years old, was coming to the end of her shift. For perhaps thirteen or fourteen hours she had been on her feet, watching over one of the cotton drawing machines. She was described as a pretty girl, but she was thin and weak, fed on potatoes and cheap gruel by the owner of the factory where she lived and worked. She was one of about eighty orphan 'apprentices' for whom he had paid a fee of thirty shillings per head to take them from orphanages in London. The orphanages were doubly delighted by the arrangement – the fee money was useful, and they were relieved of the obligation to meet any further costs for the children's upkeep. The apprentices were then entirely in the power of the factory owner.

As usual, that night Mary was wearing a pinafore and apron, filthy with grease. The unguarded drive shaft, geared up from the huge water wheel, was set about a foot above the floor. Her apron caught in the shaft. She was dashed to the floor and whirled round, her bones breaking with sharp cracks every time she was pulled through the space between the shaft and the floor, 'her blood thrown around like water from a mop'. Her screams were quickly silenced, but echoed by the only other person in the area, Robert Blincoe, aged only seven or eight and incapable of doing anything to help. Finally the shaft stopped turning, jammed by her broken body. 'When she was extricated, every bone was found broken – her head dreadfully crushed – her clothes and mangled flesh apparently inextricably mixed together, and she was carried off, as supposed, quite lifeless.'[56]

Amazingly, she survived, albeit desperately crippled. Neither the owner of the factory nor the rough charity of the local parish gave her any hope of compensation or support. In great pain, facing all this alone at the age of ten, she had no choice but to go back to work for the same man, in the same mill, on crutches.

The doctors called as witnesses in the parliamentary enquiry had heard time and again such stories as this, reported years later by the boy, Robert Blincoe, in a memoir written down for him by John Brown and published in 1828.*

Abandoned in a London orphanage at the age of four, Robert was passed three years later as an 'apprentice' – in essence a slave – to the owner of the cotton mill near Nottingham. There was no limit to the violence and cruelty used against the children by the owner and his two sons, as well as by the overseers they employed, who themselves were punished if their charges did not meet production targets. To make matters worse, in the words of one shocked observer, the girls were 'subject to the lust as well as the cruelty of their masters'. On one occasion, Blincoe recounts, the local surgeon discovered that the children reported as 'ill' were in fact simply starving. By law, the surgeon should have reported this to the magistrate. He did nothing. In the words of the memoir: 'The surgeon and magistrates were friends and guests of the master, and in the frequent habit of feasting with him.' On another occasion, over a short period of time so many children died in the mill that the master divided up the bodies to be buried in a number of different parishes, making the mortality rate less conspicuous.

Robert Peel, who had himself been a ruthless employer but had undergone a change of heart, proposed a law to reduce children's working hours to no more than eleven per day. But he met resistance from Lord Lauderdale, who represented the vociferous lobby of the factory owners, on the grounds that 'The employer was the person . . . most likely to avoid overworking them' because it was in his interests to do so. However, the employers' understanding of political economy was perhaps insufficiently developed. They seemed to think that their interests lay more in the opportunity to make huge profits – and in that era a successful enterprise made enormous profits – than in the condition of the children slaving in their factories. Or perhaps they had a better understanding than Lord Lauderdale of the iron law of supply and demand: when the children currently employed succumbed to exhaustion, ill health and accidents, there were plenty more available. In Blincoe's words: 'Parish children and destitute orphans could be had at a less price than sheep or pigs, to supply the place of those that died.'

The apprenticeship was a fiction – it was another name for slavery.

* The book is said to have provided the inspiration to Charles Dickens for his character Oliver Twist.

In 1830 Richard Oastler, a man of conservative bent, a Tory who was against trade unions and radical agitators but embraced factory reform, compared the position of these apprentices to that of the slaves in the Caribbean and in America:

Ye live in the boasted land of freedom, and feel and mourn that ye are slaves, and slaves without the only comfort which the negro has. He knows that it is his sordid, mercenary master's interest that he should live, be strong and healthy. Not so with you . . . You are not mercifully valued at so much per head; this would assure you at least (even with the worst and most cruel masters) of the mercy shown to their own labouring beasts. No, no! Your soft and delicate limbs are tired . . . at only so much per week, and when your joints can act no longer, your emaciated frames are cast aside, the boards on which you lately toiled and wasted life away are instantly supplied with other victims, who in this boasted land of liberty are hired – not sold – as slaves, and daily forced to hear that they are free.[57]

THE STRUCTURE OF THE CONTRACT

It was in this context that the relationship between the owner and the employee became fixed, with the key structure of the relationship remaining unchanged to this day. All the power, all the rights, in the hands of the owner; none in the hands of the employee. This was the basic relationship that was eventually enshrined in the employment contract.

It is no surprise that, as the starving peasants had done, the workers reacted to this treatment. Exhausted, illiterate, half starved as many of them were, they intermittently moved *en masse* to persuade their employers to increase – or at least not cut – wages or to reduce the hours of work. As they had done for at least a century, many employers resorted to Parliament for support in suppressing these outrageous demands. Sidney and Beatrice Webb list Acts passed by Parliament to counteract worker agitation in 1725 for the woollen industry, 1729 for shoemakers, 1749 for hatters, 1777 for silk weavers and 1795 for paper-making. Then in 1800, largely at the urging of William Wilberforce, famous for campaigning against the slave trade but apparently deaf to the cries of the children enslaved in the mills at home, the authorities decided to have done with 'combinations' of workmen for good – and for good economic theory. In great haste, giving no time for any representations or even apparently for any debate, a general bill against combinations was passed. The Webbs, serious scholars, believed that the impulse was the spread of trade unionism among the textile workers of Yorkshire and Lancashire. The bill was named the Workmen's Combination Bill.

In the annals of the efforts by wealthy and powerful legislators to enforce control over the weak and the poor under the guise of the 'rule of law', this bill has no equal. It made it a crime to go to a meeting; or to induce 'directly or indirectly' anyone else to go to a meeting; or to contribute to a meeting; or to collect money for a meeting. It became a crime to try to persuade a fellow workman to leave his work; a crime to refuse to work with any other person; a crime to combine with a fellow workman to raise wages or reduce hours worked. The right to a trial by jury was removed. Instead of a judge, the local magistrate could convict anyone charged and send the offender to jail. In many cases the magistrates would themselves be employers directly affected.[58]

In theory this law prevented the employers as well as the employees from acting in concert. In practice the employer-magistrates could combine with impunity to reduce wages. No employer was ever charged under the combination laws, but hundreds of workers were sentenced for such crimes as talking about wages.

As the Hammonds point out, the real effect of such an Act lay in the power it gave to the employer-magistrate to use it as a threat. Parliament had removed from the workers the ability to resist the demands of even the most aggressive employer. But given the prevailing economic ideology – the convenient belief, in defiance of all the visible facts, that the more avaricious an employer was, the more he would want to look after the interests of his workers – the MPs could rest content. With such laws, strictly enforced, their power and wealth would not come to an end in the foreseeable future.

It took twenty-five years for the Combination Acts to be repealed, and for working people to be allowed, at least in theory, to form trade unions. Even then, the repeal of the legislation was achieved in Parliament by subterfuge, and when the employers' friends in both Houses realised what had been done, they tried to restore the prohibition on combinations. This time the opposition on behalf of the workers was successful. The employers would never again manage to achieve quite such perfect power over their employees.

But the basic skeleton of the arrangements remained in place – moderated, yes, but still visibly the same. Even today, the company owners have all the rights: to be informed, to appoint and sack the managers, to vote on major decisions, to receive all the dividends and to sell those rights to anyone they choose. The employees have the obverse of those rights: no right to information, no right to have questions answered, no right to any vote on anything, no right to share in the wealth they help create, either in the form of dividends or as a capital sum, and no influence over who becomes the boss. When the owners sell their shares then the owners' rights in the employment contracts are sold too – the employees get a new boss, who has the right to instruct them and dispose of them as he or she will.

Adam Smith pointed out that it was cheaper over the long term for an employer to hire people as workers rather than buy them as slaves, because if the employer buys them, then even when they are ill he has to provide their upkeep. When he just hires them, then although he has to pay them enough to ensure that they survive, they have to look after themselves – which they will do more efficiently than any slave overseer. He concluded that 'the work done by freemen comes cheaper in the end than that performed by slaves'[59] – perhaps an argument that carried as much weight in the freeing of the slaves as did the concept of inalienable rights. In 2009 the widespread hostility among well-off Americans to President Obama's plan to give healthcare benefits to poor employees could arguably be seen in a similar light. If the employers through taxes were going to have to pay for the employees' healthcare anyway, then they might as well not have freed them from slavery in the first place. This point is expressed polemically, but the overtones are troubling.

The fundamental flaw in the system is that employers still have all the power, which they use to enrich themselves, while the workers have no rights at all to information, to influence or to a share of the wealth created. The more the worker gets, the less the employer gets. It is a system that no rational person would design – nobody with the slightest awareness of what makes people and organisations flourish. And it has grown up shaped by the accidental paths of history, from the time when the supremely confident early industrialists were given unfettered power by their allies, the landed gents in Parliament.

Gradually, certain limits were applied. Reformists persuaded Parliament to conduct investigations and to pass the Factory Acts, limiting the working day and improving conditions. Trade union activity developed throughout the nineteenth century, eventually achieving the election of the first twenty-nine Labour Party MPs in 1906 and the first Labour government in 1924.

In America the story was broadly similar. However, given the ability of employees to go west, even in the earliest times there was not the same degree of rampant exploitation – except of slaves. Tom Paine marvelled at the levels of wages available when he arrived from England some years before the War of Independence. On the other hand, the American employers were just as hostile to the idea of the employees getting together in trade unions, and the battle to establish negotiating rights sometimes took bloody forms. Nevertheless, over the ensuing century and more, gains were made for working people and limits were set on the powers of the employer. The end result was that in America the body of law covering trade unions created a highly inflexible system, which had the advantage from the union point of view that, once unionised, a workforce could count on their rights being recognised; on the other hand, it created a considerable incentive for employers to get round the rules, which from the 1980s onwards they increasingly did, notably by establishing plants in non-union areas and overseas.

Having powerful employers on the one side and powerful trade unions on the other, locked together in a perpetual embrace and at the same time in unending conflict, has huge costs, both in economic terms and, more insidiously, in social and human terms. Simply in operating the system there is enormous waste of energy. Every management initiative faces suspicion and distrust, and comes up against the rules. This tends to make life in the corporate world frustrating and unrewarding for a large proportion of those involved. For many it is even humiliating. But both sides accept the basic structure of the employment contract, even as they wrestle over the details of its terms. There is a design fault: the structure is simply incapable of reaching the heights of flexibility, innovation and productivity that are possible in a sharing model, a system of genuine partnership, in which every person at every level is an active participant – sharing information, influence, profit and capital gain.

The system of having all-powerful corporate managers without independent trade unions is even worse. China's recent history presents a clear example of what happens. The waste of human potential, the waste of lives, reaches extremes that should shock us into concerted action, or at the very least trigger outraged protest.[60] It doesn't. It is easy not to identify with the poor and the powerless, particularly if they live in another country and the information is hard to find. And if you are employed – and there is no alternative – then it is uncomfortable to face the reality of what employment means.

In 'modern' industries, where the employees are educated and skilful, and the main product depends utterly on their brainpower, the balance of power is moderated further – the employees have more influence. But as long as most employees are being manipulated for the benefit of the 'owners' of the corporation, the relationship gets no further than a form of mutual exploitation. Individuals will join a company because it is a good company to have on their CVs; having worked for this company, they will have greater opportunities to find interesting work elsewhere. Aware that the company will only maintain the relationship with them until they can be got rid of without damaging corporate performance, they will not be psychologically committed to the company. They will not stay beyond the point where they believe they are deriving direct personal benefit from the relationship. It is deeply natural to identify with the company where you work, but there is always a shadow when that company is clearly using you.

What does it take to build a business? Commitment above all. Committed leaders, committed employees, committed capital. The kind of commitment that comes with employee ownership, which as we have observed was recognised by the entrepreneurs of Silicon Valley, among others.

Throughout this whole period, however, and still today, the fundamental relationship remains unchanged: power to the owners, no rights to the employee-servants. All the rest is an attempt to moderate the worst effects of concentrated power. But until the basic system is changed, that power can always be reasserted.

10

Thinking It Through

David Ellerman is a tall rangy man with penetrating eyes. He would
be unusual in any company, a deep thinker in his mid-sixties who does
not hold back from telling it like it is, in a style that is avuncular but
very straight. Of all the people who have thought about employee
ownership, and devoted years to implementing it as best they can, he
is the person at the forefront of developing a conceptual mastery of
the subject. For most people involved in employee ownership it is
enough to follow intuitions, muddle through in practice, content in
the knowledge that the results improve productivity and spread happiness and wealth. For Ellerman that is not enough, and never has been.
He will not rest until he has teased out a theoretical understanding
of whatever he addresses – and he has addressed a wide range of
things, from the logic of mathematics to the role of aid in developing
economies.[61] For three years he was economic adviser and speech-
writer to Joe Stiglitz, Nobel Prize-winning chief economist at the
World Bank.

Having shown a considerable talent for mathematics, Ellerman
disappointed his engineer father by choosing the only department in
MIT where they did *not* study engineering: in 1965 he graduated with
a degree in philosophy. He then obtained a full scholarship to study
the philosophy of science at Boston University, where he decided to
use his thinking time in the quest to strengthen the philosophical
grounding of capitalism.

'I remember thinking that obviously the capitalist system was the
best thing around, as compared with communism. But I didn't think

the intellectual justifications were very good in terms of property rights. So, ironically, I started out trying to give a better justification for capitalism. And I failed. That was a great shock.'

The more deeply he examined the idea of the firm – corporations and companies tend to be called 'firms' in the more theoretical discussions – the less cogent were the accepted arguments. A major difficulty was that the product of the firm was not being attributed to the people who were responsible for creating it – the product was instead being appropriated by the 'owners' of the firm. At first it seemed to be a question of property rights – a property right to the product being attached to the property right to the firm – and Ellerman's first two papers framed it in that way. From one of those papers Noam Chomsky picked up and still uses a quote on the renting of people. But Ellerman moved on in his analysis to reach the understanding that actually the problem is not a question of property rights, but of contract, and in particular the employment contract.

In the employment contract the employee is rented. In theory and in legal terms the employee is treated as a thing, an instrument – like a rented car. But actually a person cannot be turned into an instrument – cannot be rented by someone else any more than he or she can be owned by someone else. A person cannot hand over to another the right to operate him or her: the person has to cooperate. In more theoretical terms, autonomy is inalienable. That is not a normative statement about how things ought to be, but a factual one about how things are. It has appeared in many guises, pre-eminently when Viktor Frankl realised as a prisoner in a Nazi labour camp that the guards could do what they wanted to him, but as long as he was alive they could not take away his mental or spiritual autonomy. The human spirit burns in every individual. 'Everything can be taken from a man but one thing: the last of the human freedoms – . . . to choose one's own way.'[62]

It follows that the employment contract is in fact a fraud, which has the effect of depriving the employee of the right to participate in the product of his or her work. Fundamentally people are responsible for what they do, and for what they create. If we are responsible for creating something – growing potatoes, baking a cake, building a hut, painting a portrait – then that responsibility stays with us, in the form of ownership. In a firm the employee is in reality a partner, cooperating in creating the product of the firm, and hence jointly responsible for that product. The wealth (or deficit) created is therefore attributable to the employees.

Ellerman shows the self-contradictory nature of the employment contract by taking the example of the attribution of responsibility in the commission of a crime. If the owner of a firm tells his employee Mr Jackal to go and kill someone, and he does so, then Mr Jackal cannot escape responsibility for the crime. The fact that his employer told him to do it is no excuse – Mr Jackal cooperated and therefore is responsible. The employer shares in the responsibility too, but Mr Jackal does not avoid it. If the product of the employment is a crime, then the employee is responsible for that product, that crime. In Ellerman's phrase, the servant at work has become a partner in crime. It is only when Mr Jackal creates something valuable that we switch to the fiction that he is not a partner, that as a hired hand he has no responsibility, and so no ownership of the product he creates. Ignoring the fact of cooperation, the 'owner' of the firm gets to keep all the wealth for himself. The fiction of non-autonomy becomes the institutionalised fraud of appropriation.

Even in the military, where absolute obedience is drilled into everyone throughout the whole hierarchy, and disobedience is punishable in extreme cases by death, soldiers who commit war crimes are guilty. Being under orders is no excuse. Human autonomy is inalienable: it can be put under enormous pressure, but it cannot be handed over to anyone else.

In terms of rights, the ownership of the firm is the mirror image of the employment contract. The employment contract removes from the employee any right to information, any right to be consulted, any right to influence policy, any right to have a say in who becomes a manager, any right to the profits, and any right to the capital value created through the work of the employee. The equity contract – the share – gives all those rights solely to the 'owner' of the share. The shareholders have the legal rights to receive all the information and influence, to appoint the managers, and to appropriate all the profit and capital value created. These rights are securitised, that is, they can then be passed on to others – given as gifts, bequeathed by inheritance or exchanged for money.

It is not all one-way. The business of the firm may result in a loss rather than a profit. The losses are also attributed to the 'owner' of the firm. Once the employee is recognised as a partner sharing in any wealth created, then he or she is also recognised as sharing in any losses when the activities are not successful. Each person involved is a full member of the company. That may sound scary to someone steeped in today's fiction that employees are protected from losses. (They aren't, of course. When there are losses their jobs are at risk.) But where it has been running for even a relatively short time, people realise the benefits: they build up a capital stake in the good times and lose some of it in the bad times, but with everyone driving for success together they characteristically achieve far greater success than under the old system. And if things fail completely, they are no worse off than they would have been with the prevailing system – out of a job, and without having built up capital. Only they would have been active participants in the fight to make it successful, and not simply passive pawns subject to the decisions of the stockholders.

Robert Oakeshott has pointed out that as long ago as 1944 a similar perspective to Ellerman's was expressed as a challenge to lawyers and politicians by a distinguished British judge, Lord Eustace Percy.

Here is the most important challenge to political invention ever offered to the jurist or the statesman. The human association which in fact produces and distributes wealth, the association of workmen, managers, technicians, and directors is not an association recognised by the law. The association which the law does recognise – the association of shareholders, creditors and directors – is incapable of producing and distributing and is not expected to perform these functions. We have to give law to the real association and withdraw meaningless privilege from the imaginary one.[63]

This right to appropriate the product of the firm – the 'meaningless privilege' – is what gives a share its value, as well as its volatility. Its value comes from the right to appropriate all the profits and capital gains created by the work of all the employees today, and of all future employees for ever into the infinite future. Its volatility comes from the same source: if conditions change for the better today (the employees create a successful new product, say) so that a greater stream of profit can be projected for the future, then, because the ownership is attributed not to the people responsible but to the shares, all that future profit is suddenly added to the calculation of what the share is worth. And if the change is negative (a widely used drug is shown to cause cancer, say), then the value of the share must take into account all that drop in future earnings, together with possible liabilities to pay medical costs. Even though the future profit stream is discounted, the change still makes a big difference to the value, because it affects the future to eternity.

But it is the employees, including the managers, who have created the products and taken them to market. They are responsible for having created that wealth – as also the liabilities incurred in creating them. Ownership is properly attributed to responsibility – the duty to pay the liabilities, and the right to the proceeds that will allow that payment, and the surplus that usually remains, are really theirs. In future the wealth will be created by the employees working in the company at that time, and that future wealth will properly belong to those future participants.

Sometimes the justification for removing that ownership, that wealth, is said to be that the shareholders provide capital: the appropriation of the product is in exchange for provision of capital. But in reality shareholders hardly ever provide capital: instead, they appropriate cash from the companies. The vast majority of companies fund all their investment out of retained earnings, or out of borrowings that are then repaid out of future retained earnings. Very occasionally, established companies issue new equity and invest in their business the cash they get in exchange for the new shares. The time when equity is essential to a company is when it starts up, and if it decides to invest in a project for which it cannot borrow enough cash. The funding of new companies and new investment is extremely important to the health of an economy, and any system which intends to flourish must find a source for that entrepreneurial investment. But even if investors provide funds for a business, that does not make true the fiction that they can rent people, or that people are not responsible for the wealth they create. The funding can be recompensed while still acknowledging the rights of the employee-partners.

Furthermore, even the start-up capital can be found without giving away for ever the rights of the people involved, for this generation and all who will follow. The story of the Mondragón Bank and its unsurpassed record of funding the start-up of new companies is told elsewhere in this book. The constitution of those companies has remained resolutely democratic, consistent with the fundamental idea that capital should serve people, rather than people being the servants of capital.[64] The need is for a new design of financial institution, one that is aimed at funding employee-owned companies. And a basic principle will be that it is fine to hire or rent or lease things, including capital, but that people, being autonomous, cooperate as partners in the enterprise. They are not to be treated as if they were things rented.

To most people it seems ridiculous to suggest that the computers manufactured in a computer company should be recognised as belonging to the employees, as opposed to the shareholders. Why, then, does this seem so ludicrous? One commonly given reason is that the employment contract is voluntary. In theory at least, nobody has to sign one. The fact that people do sign them means that they voluntarily give up these rights – to information, influence, profit and capital – and voluntarily agree to the myth that they are no longer autonomous, but subject to the wills of the company owners and their agents. As Ellerman points out, the same argument was used to justify slavery. To outlaw a voluntary contract would undermine the rule of law at its roots. If in principle a person could voluntarily sell himself or herself into slavery, then that voluntary contract had to be respected. It followed that slavery as an institution could not be abolished. The reaction against this argument was based on the concept of inalienable rights, which originated in the Scottish Enlightenment – particularly in the thinking of Francis Hutcheson and George Wallace – and came by way of Thomas Jefferson into the Declaration of Independence in America. People have an inalienable right to their own autonomy – they cannot hand it over to another person or corporation. This is as true for a day as for a lifetime. It follows that the product of work is attributable to the employees, and cannot simply be removed by an employment contract.

This argument comes hard up against a seemingly insoluble problem: nobody believes it. The reasoning just seems impractical. It may have been right when used against slavery, but slavery is mainly in the past, at least in the developed countries. And everyone knows that employees today have no right to the wealth that they create. Never have had, never will have. Further, if you give the employees the right to influence and even to choose the managers, then companies would self-destruct, managers would lose the right to manage, businesses would fail right, left and centre. Goddammit, they get paid, don't they? What more do they want? And if they don't like it they can leave.

In actual fact, if they leave, for most people the choice is unenviable: they can sign an employment contract with another employer, or they can live on the streets. Realistically, there is no choice. Accept the contract that removes from you your right to what you create or live as a beggar. Pretend that you can be rented as a thing; give up your natural right to your product; or live in more or less extreme poverty.

Because it is normal, this is not seen as a problem, which is a sure sign that we are swimming in a sea of ideology, as invisible to most people as water is to fish. It is extremely hard even to perceive, let alone to step outside, the frame of reference – the paradigm – that shapes *everyone*'s perceptions. It takes a bit of an oddball, like David Ellerman, to do it.

But he is right.

PART THREE

HUMANITY IN PARTNERSHIP

'The form of association, however, which if mankind continue to improve, must be expected in the end to predominate, is not that which can exist between a capitalist as chief, and workpeople without a voice in the management, but the association of the labourers themselves on terms of equality, collectively owning the capital with which they carry on their operations, and working under managers elected and removable by themselves.'

John Stuart Mill, *Principles of Political Economy*, 1848

'What we need is revolutionary change achieved in an evolutionary way.'

Lech Walesa, Warsaw, 2009

11

John Lewis: Partners at Work

A little further east along Oxford Street from Debenhams is John Lewis, the department store mentioned with admiration by more than one interviewee. Perhaps they were dazzled by the fact that John Lewis shares its profits with all the people who work there, and so did not properly understand all the problems that economists see with the facts that it is owned by its employees, its shares are not traded on the Stock Exchange, and it is not subject to capital market discipline. Economists lament the fact that the company cannot be taken over, even by billionaires, as was attempted in the case of Marks and Spencer, or by private equity investors, who made a considerable fortune from the takeover of Debenhams.

In John Lewis's Oxford Street department store, where some 2,400 people work, I interviewed three people:[65] Gill Wright had worked there for eighteen years and was in charge of food provision, the same role as Ingrid's in Debenhams; Shazia Chaudhry, a younger woman, had worked eight years in the sports and luggage department; and Mo Asif, a young man, had been there only two years, also in the food area.

Like all the others I interviewed, from any company, these three individuals wanted to see their company successful. They wanted to play a part in achieving that, to have a role they could be proud of, and to have the satisfaction of knowing that they made a difference.

MO ASIF

Mo was proud of the experience he had gained before joining John Lewis – a total of eleven years doing bar and café work in various companies – and it gave him some confidence. But of the three John Lewis partners – all the people who work there are recognised as 'partners' – it was Mo who expressed the greatest frustration.

Like most people interviewed from conventionally owned stores, he wanted things to go well and got frustrated when he could see that things could be done better. Six months before, he had been on the point of walking out, worried that senior managers, above his line manager, were getting things wrong. It felt as if their actions might run his department into the ground. But things had improved since then.

What Mo saw as poor management offended his sense of pride, his instinct for what the department could become. And, like the others, Mo had a lively sense of being in the front line.

'The people that run the department are *us*, the team that actually deals with the customers. We're the first to meet and greet the customers, we're the ones to sit them down, take their orders, take the food and the drink to them. So we know how they feel. It's up to us to make sure they are happy, and walk out the door with smiles on their faces. We make sure they come back – at the end of the day that is what is important to me.'

In pursuit of this, when things went badly he sometimes took matters into his own hands. If, for example, food was delayed, he would offer customers free drinks. He kept a note of the drinks given out, and at the end of the week would show it to his manager. Things had been pretty bad a few months before, when 'you'd have coffees and soft drinks flying out, free of charge.' But at the moment things were going pretty well, and the free drink count was down to three or four a week.

Like the other interviewees, Mo craves a directly supportive approach from the senior managers. And he has similar criticisms.

'They stay up in the offices, most of the time. We started a new menu just last week. The senior people need to be there on the day it goes live, to see how it's going, to see what is selling and what isn't, to get the customers' points of view. One of them came down after the lunch session and asked how it had gone. I was shocked. Surely he should have been down there to *see* how it went!'

However, Mo's major bugbear was not the managers. The tone he struck was very different from those employed in conventionally structured companies. He was full of praise for his immediate line manager, because she listened to him and held the reins loosely.

'I do get my ideas listened to by my line manager. She's French, she's worked in hotels, she's had a lot of experience. She knows what she's doing, she knows what she's talking about. I go to her first. There have been times when we've had our disagreements, but it hasn't gone any further – luckily, touch wood. I think that's because she understands where I'm coming from.'

He also held the MD of the store in high regard. The MD was often seen walking about the store, and had recently thanked him personally for (unknowingly) looking after a friend of his. This acknowledgement meant a lot to him.

Mo's biggest criticism was of the behaviour of some of his fellow employees. One interviewee elsewhere had said he wished the managers would work with staff members to build on their strengths rather than penalise their weaknesses; here, Mo was frustrated with the results of just such an approach. 'With a structure like John Lewis there are long procedures. You have members of staff who are not pulling their weight, and shouldn't be working here. They're lazy, they don't want to help anybody else.' Fellow employees could put in a complaint, but it might take a year to sort it out, even though something needed to be done immediately. Mo said that even the managers were frustrated, because they could only do so much. It was the structure.

Gill Wright, the overall manager of the food services, when pressed for things that she would like to see improved, also cited slow decision-making – the process of thinking everything through and collecting views sometimes took too long. But despite the frustration expressed by Mo and Gill, the results of this decision-making process are hard to argue with. The steady growth of the John Lewis Partnership has brought it close to the size of Marks and Spencer, which used to be an order of magnitude larger, and the 2007 growth plan included an increase in the number of department stores from twenty-six to fifty in ten years. At the same time as Marks and Spencer slipped to 11th in the customer ratings of retailers, and Debenhams to 67th, John Lewis and its food retailing arm, Waitrose, swapped places at the top. It seems that a business gains a great deal by taking the time to involve its people widely in decision-making.

When John Lewis increased the number of food outlets in the Oxford Street store by opening a new bistro and a new brasserie to add to the restaurant that had been there for years, Mo enjoyed shaping what they offered. He went down to the Waitrose food outlet in the basement and jotted down some of the biscuits on offer, worked out the costs and suggested to his manager that they add them. 'Yeah, that's fine,' she said. 'Let's do it.' And it worked.

On another occasion the store's sale period was about to start, and large crowds were expected. The order for replacement glasses had not arrived. Mo said he'd go down to the glassware department to buy some and asked his manager how much he should spend. Her answer brought pride to his voice as he reported it months later.

'"As long as you don't spend a stupid amount just get whatever we need," she said. Which was great – I did. And I know I can come back to her again if there's anything we need, and she'll say yes or no, and she'll give me a reason either way. And that's great.'

He did the same with nuts and crisps in the bar, and again got the immediate support of his manager. And as he told that story another aspect of ownership came through: 'They sell. So that is revenue for *us*: that extra bit for the company also adds to our bonus at the end of the year.'

The profit-sharing bonus is an integral part of the John Lewis constitution, which itself has been thought through more thoroughly than most. At the end of each financial year the board – in addition to the chairman it consists of five elected directors and five appointed directors – decides as the first priority how much of the profit is to be retained for reinvestment. All the rest is distributed among all the partners – everyone who has worked for a year or more – as a percentage of salary. The chairman gets the same ratio as the shop floor people. In recent years the percentage has stayed below 20 per cent, and it has been as low as 9 per cent. But the longer-serving remember it reaching 24 per cent – three months' salary in a lump sum. Base salaries are officially set at the local market rate, which means that the bonus really is an extra.

However, unlike the interviewee, who burst out with, 'Who do you ask?' and Ingrid, who stamped her feet and still could not get the attention of the managers, Mo has a clear channel to influence what is done and how. There is a 'Partners' Forum' in the store.

'There's a meeting every three months. You have a member or two members from each department, who take the views of the department to the meeting. It is the same throughout all the departments through all the company. It is good – lately it's been good, because the two people that we put forward to represent us from the Bistro and the Brasserie are experienced. They know what they're talking about.'

Every two years John Lewis carries out a survey of its partners' opinions. Through this, some years ago it became aware that the democratic bodies, such as the Partners' Forum, were not as highly respected as in the past. The new chairman set up an internal commission to find out why, and to propose how to improve things. The end result was a change in the way that elections took place, and Mo's confidence in the representatives from his department is the result.

In the past, people had had to stand for election. This meant putting forward their names, which deterred some people. And often people were reluctant to stand if there was an incumbent, or as soon as the first candidate came forward.

Now, a new rule was introduced: *every* partner in the department was automatically nominated. This was good for the paper industry: each ballot had a long list of names down the left-hand side. But it was also good for democracy. The people who were elected were then not those prepared to put themselves forward, but those who were most respected and trusted by their colleagues. Often these individuals would have been too shy to come forward, but once they had been elected they were given a great boost: they knew that their colleagues respected them. They also had a real sense of responsibility: they had a job to do, which their colleagues now expected them to do. As Mo said: 'The two people that we put forward to represent us . . . are experienced – they know what they're talking about.'

His views are shared throughout the whole organisation. The democratic councils at every level are seen as more effective, and the representatives too. There is more respect. Everything is running better. Sometimes freedom of choice – whether or not to stand in the election – is not the best way forward. Participation is one of the responsibilities of ownership.

Mo himself knows a great deal about the performance of his department.

'We get the cumulative figures for the week in the magazine. We're pretty much above the middle, so we're doing ok. Last week, like-for-like compared to the previous year, the overall average for all departments was up by 1.9 per cent and we were up by 3.2 per cent. So we're making money.'

There is, however, no sign of the dreaded complacency forecast by economists, nor of a desire to bleed the company dry. Mo wants to spend money so that they can provide good service.

'We're making money, so I don't see why we can't afford to hire staff, which we're short of. This is the time [summer] to start hiring because there are people out there, and we need the staff before the Christmas period kicks in, to make sure we're ready for it.'

Mo's summary, after only two years in John Lewis, is rather different from one interviewee's 'we laugh because it's a circus' and Ingrid's 'you've got to have pride in what you do': 'Working for them, for the company as a whole, is pretty good. I know what I'm doing, the guys around me know what they're doing, I've got a good team and that works for me.'

SHAZIA CHAUDHRY

As previously noted, John Lewis does not have 'employees' but 'partners'. It was noticeable that Mo did not refer to them as partners, however, except in one connection: the Partners' Forum. Shazia, who has worked there for eight years against Mo's two, and Gill who has worked there for eighteen, refer to their colleagues as 'partners' as a matter of course. Perhaps it takes time to work oneself into a culture where people are respected and treated as partners rather than servants.

Shazia is a lively and impassioned young woman, whose words tumble over each other as she communicates what it is like to work there, in the department that sells sports clothing, sports equipment and luggage. Her job is usually 'covering the bridge', which means that she has to know what is going on right across the department, and to make sure that every area has someone serving in it. 'You can't leave an area empty, with no staff, so if someone has a break I have to get cover for that area. So it's an important role and it's kind of a pressured role as well. If someone asks, "Where's so and so?" you need to know where that person is.'

The role is designed to make sure that customers have a good experience. 'When it gets busy, part of the role is to acknowledge customers. When people come in I need to find out if they need help, and make sure that every customer has been acknowledged.' This does not mean that she herself does the serving – she directs others to where they are needed.

There is a pretty intensive testing process for each department.

'We get "test shops" to see if we give good acknowledgement. We call it ABC – Acknowledge, Build the sale and Close. They want to see if we can answer all the questions that the customer may ask, and check that we're offering other products correctly. We get a test sheet every month saying how every department did. It's good, it tells us how we are doing. They look at everything – it's quite a few pages.'

That is not all: the department may be visited any time. 'We get a "weekly snapshot" every week as well. A manager from the steering group will come and see how the department is doing, and whether the customer service leader has control of the floor. This is done from the customer's point of view.' Shazia accepts that there is some stress in her role, and that not every person in the department would be happy doing it. But she enjoys the challenge.

'John Lewis is top at customer service, and that's our job, doing it right. It's not just because of the snapshot and it's not that we're going to get into trouble. It's because that's why we're different, that's what we're good at. And that's important to me as well. When I tell my family and friends where I work it's like, "Wow!" and they ask me what it's like.'

Unlike interviewees elsewhere the people on the shop floor see the top managers.

'When the chairman comes, and other high-up people, we are told they are coming. They are happy to talk to you. I've talked to many of them – the chairman, directors, buyers – even if it's just for one or two minutes. The head of selling came in yesterday – they're all walking the floor. They come shopping, too. One of the partners in the sports department has served the chairman, and it's not "Omigod what do I say?" It's just normal.'

The MD of the store, Noel Saunders, is clearly an inspiring leader. Mo sang his praises, and Shazia too waxes enthusiastic:

'Just last week he came to the department and asked just generally how we are doing and how the floor was doing and whether the stock was ok. He's approachable. If he was walking by I know I could stop him and he would listen. It's not, "I haven't got time for this"; he's somebody who's very busy and his job's really important but he's always got time for everybody and he listens. He would give his honest feedback to you. He inspires me, he really inspires me. He's just so enthusiastic: he wants it to work, he wants you to be happy, he wants things to go well for John Lewis and things to progress. He's just so passionate. So you think you could do that little bit extra.'

Shazia herself, although she has not yet moved into management as some of her colleagues think she should, is now doing a little bit extra: she has recently been selected by her colleagues to serve on the Partners' Council as the deputy representative from her department.

'Before a meeting we go round all the partners in our department and ask everybody what issues they have. Say they're not happy with the catering upstairs, or the Christmas hours, they would tell us and we would take it up to the actual meeting, with the steering group people. If others have the same issue then it would be discussed, and the steering group people have to answer us, or go and get answers later. If we're not happy about anything, that is the big opportunity: all the managers, including Noel, are there.'

But is this just a talking shop?

'No. We get things changed. And they give us good feedback: if they're not going to change something they will tell us why.'

She finds being on the council invigorating and challenging.

'You have to be very brave – it takes that. Only some people can do it, people not afraid to speak. And you have to be able to bring back what they say to you. The managers are not bad people, they're like us, but you still need to know what you're talking about. You give them the information and they give good constructive feedback.'

Her summary is unequivocal: 'Whoever I speak to, I'm always saying I love John Lewis. My friends say, "God! You've been there eight years now – aren't you going to move on?" But I'd tell anyone to work here.'

GILL WRIGHT

Gill, the third person interviewed from John Lewis, runs the food services. She's been a partner for eighteen years, seven fewer than Ingrid
has spent in Debenhams, but with broadly the same job. Here, catering
services includes a canteen for the partners. Spedan Lewis started the
canteen in the 1920s, when he became aware that some of his employees
were too poor to eat adequately. One of the complaints elsewhere
was that everything that 'cools the heart' had been taken away,
including the canteen; here in John Lewis, as a matter of policy, partners can get a healthy two-course meal for under £1.

Gill joined after working as catering manager for a reputable firm
of City lawyers, which shrank after its leader had been sent to prison.

'They had no concern whatsoever for anybody's needs at redundancy. I was called into the office, told I had ten minutes to leave, and
to tell my team that they were redundant. I said, "No – do your own
dirty work." Somebody stood over me while I emptied my desk and
that was it. Which would never happen in John Lewis. It doesn't matter
how short a time you've been here, you get the same thought put
into anything that's going to change your working life.'

On joining, she received about a week of induction, including time
spent explaining the constitution and the history of how the company
came to be employee-owned. She talks now, with the confidence of
long experience, about the values that underlie the undoubted success
of the business.

'I've never been asked to do anything that made me think, "Not
sure about that." Everything here has to be very legal, very above
board, very open, very honest. That of course is part of the John
Lewis "mission statement", if you like, that honesty and the happiness of partners are above everything. So I've never ever been asked
to do anything that I thought was in any way underhand.'

Nonetheless, like middle managers everywhere, she finds herself
with pressures from both directions.

'It's always been an odd job being a middle manager. You're sort
of taking instructions and defending them, and you're the person that
takes the brunt of it. But in every decision that's made here, everyone
is considered. So, for example, in the decision on hours of work at

Christmas, which used to be done by volunteers, they don't just consider what's good for the managers, they consider what's good for everybody. Obviously we can't suit 2,400 people – what suits one is never going to suit everyone else. But it's up to us as managers, as forum members, as section managers, as people who are in charge of groups of people. We have to be on the side of the decision-maker. But we must also make sure that the message is given in a way that helps everyone realise why those decisions have been made.'

One of the decisions that Gill has been involved in is an initiative to make sure that the standards of care of the building are maintained – something that an interviewee in another store complained about with disappointment.

'We decided that partners aren't taking care of the building as they used to, so we're going to remind everyone of their responsibilities to keep the place clean and look after each other and so on. That's probably me being a bit old-fashioned: I don't think chewing gum stuck under the table is good enough. We just felt that it's our responsibility, it's up to us.'

This initiative has a particular feel to it, which is in line with the spirit of employee ownership.

'It's not somebody coming along and saying, "Don't leave a mess! Don't do that!" – that's not the way to do it. We need to get people to buy into it and say, "This is the way that we'd like us to behave, and can you not see that that's just not acceptable?" and hope that they'll buy into it. I think they will.'

As always, the outcome is not left to naïve hope.

'It has to be policed internally – we have to police each other, really. We've come up with a phrase: "Are you aware . . . [she laughs] that you're not supposed to do this?' rather than just saying [she adopts a mean, snippy voice], "You're not supposed to do that!" That doesn't help really.'

People are treated as adults, with the responsibilities of adults.

'We're very much into coaching rather than telling, asking open questions, and getting people to think for themselves, to move themselves forward. Even the training is all self-motivated. The opportunity is there but it's up to each person to take out of it what they will and put into it what they want to, and move forward accordingly.'

One of the groups Gill listed as playing a role in decision-making is unique to John Lewis: the Registry. One of the questions that occupied Spedan Lewis when he designed the constitution was how to prevent managers from sliding into the essentially uncaring and faintly – or not so faintly – corrupt ways that so often overtake people in positions of power. He came up with two answers: a free press and a 'critical faculty' – the Registry.

As explained in chapter 2, the free press is guaranteed in the constitution by ensuring the weekly publication of letters to the *Gazette*. The key provision is that all letters are published, even the anonymous ones. The chairman and only the chairman has the right to stop publication of a letter, and only for reasons of personal abuse, legal confidentiality or commercial harm. That last term could be a broad umbrella, allowing the kind of attitude that the government takes in resisting Freedom of Information, but in fact the tradition is maintained. Even if a letter cannot be published in its original form, an edited version is usually published, with an explanation of what editing has been done and why.

The result is that the letters, which usually occupy several pages, are filled with delicious rumour and gossip, as well as information and gratitude and congratulations. People read them avidly. And having read them, they read the replies. The letters on each topic are printed with a reply from a director. The result is that, for example, if letters are received objecting to the latest rise in the chairman's salary, there is a letter from the HR director explaining the remuneration policy. If he simply wrote an article in the magazine on the remuneration policy, it is doubtful that many would read it. But when it comes in answer to a heated attack on the chairman's level of pay, everyone reads it. The result is that everyone's understanding is enhanced, making the anonymous letters a superb educational tool.

The chairman's salary for the year to January 2009 was £736k, and he received a 12.8 per cent bonus like all other partners, bringing his total income to £830k. This compares with £1.13m in Marks and Spencer, plus a large number of perfectly legal but – for any but the experts – very hard-to-fathom share allocations and share option schemes.

A further function of the letters pages is to act as an effective prod for the managers, to make sure that they do things properly. Before taking any major decision, each manager knows that it could be the subject of a letter in the *Gazette* in the coming week. So he or she has every reason to make sure that the people affected understand the decision, and have had a chance to influence it. The result is that the whole process of participation is reinforced.

Yet another benefit of the letters pages is that they build trust. Everyone knows that nothing nefarious can be hidden behind closed doors – someone will write a letter about it.

The system does also appear to be achieving the founder's aim of keeping in check the egos of the powerful. In 2007 Mark Price, the new MD of Waitrose, the food retailing arm of the group, proved to be the perfect public embodiment of a food retailer. His large frame, rosy cheeks and cheerful, outgoing personality were seized on with delight by the press, and he featured prominently in the company's public face. Soon afterwards a series of letters appeared in the *Gazette* making the point that the company was 'us', not just the MD. The personification of Waitrose was toned down. Few captains of great corporations have any such check on flattery. It is rather harder for a director of John Lewis or Waitrose to fall into hubris: he or she will be brought back into line by the letters pages.

The second stroke of genius, unique to the John Lewis Partnership, is the 'Registry'. This 'critical faculty' is an unthinkable nightmare for those who model good corporate structure on that of the military, for it gives the staff a direct line to the board, *outside the management hierarchy*. A market fundamentalist, or a traditional manager trained in the current orthodoxy, would have a heart attack if he heard about this. In each store, and in every group of supermarkets, there is at least one person whose job it is to keep in touch with those who work there, and to check up on the managers, ensuring that they are behaving in line with the John Lewis principles. They report up to board level, not through the managers, but entirely independently.

Any business student proposing such a structure would be failed, and any consultant sacked. It seems to be a recipe for undermining the managers, destroying their 'right to manage', certain to create conflict and disaster.

In practice, however, this unthinkable system, this insult to the idea of strong management, works well. Extremely well. Why it does not have the bad effects predicted is open to a number of interpretations, but somewhere in there must be the fact that the employees really are partners in the business that they own together, and consequently want to make successful. The basic fairness of the ownership system means that the managers do not regard as hostile the people put into the stores to report on their behaviour, giving the board independent feedback on whether the managers are carrying out the principles of the constitution. This is not a problem, because the managers really do want to carry out the principles in the first place. They want to know where things can be done better, because everyone wants things to be done better, all of the time, so that they all prosper together. The result is that in each store the local registrar becomes not a carping fault-finder but a bearer of helpful feedback, keeping the managers in touch with the feelings of people throughout the stores, and pointing out potential problems before they fester and erupt or demoralise the participants.

The end result is that the customers are treated well. Employees who feel a lack of respect from their superiors will never be able to show genuine care for customers. Resentment towards the boss will never encourage good customer service. In John Lewis the sense of partnership and common ownership, which is carried through into a genuinely caring approach towards every partner, then feeds into the ubiquitous shared aim: to do well in serving customers. That is why John Lewis and Waitrose are ranked top by retail customers, year after year. The opposite of complacent, the partners prosper by working in common to delight their customers. And they draw happiness from doing so.

12

Leadership

We're employed by the partners – not the other way round.
  Charlie Mayfield,
  Chairman, The John Lewis Partnership

Good leaders are vital if any business is to succeed. Bad leadership can wreck a business quickly. But what constitutes good or bad leadership is hard to pin down. Companies have thrived for years under tough, top-down, numbers-focused leaders; others have done equally well with more people-centred approaches.

Even in the army, the two styles are mixed: on the one hand there is a rigid hierarchy, reinforced all the time by required behaviour such as saluting the officers. But at the same time the officers have a duty to care for the soldiers under their command. Plutarch, writing of Alexander the Great, who was hunting down Darius, the Shah of Persia, was one of the first to identify this aspect of effective leadership. After covering enormous distances across desert Alexander and his soldiers were desperate for water. Some Macedonians came by who had water, and they offered some to Alexander in a helmet:

He asked them to whom they were carrying the water; they told him to their children, adding, that if his life were but saved, it was no matter for them, they should be able well enough to repair that loss, though they all perished. Then he took the helmet into his hands, and looking round about, when he saw all those who were near him stretching their heads out and looking earnestly after the drink, he returned it again with thanks without tasting a drop of it, "For," said he, "if I alone should drink, the rest will be out of heart." The soldiers no sooner took notice of his temperance and magnanimity upon this occasion, but they one and all cried out to him to lead them forward boldly, and began whipping on their horses. For whilst they had such a king they said they defied both weariness and thirst, and looked upon themselves to be little less than immortal.[66]

In contrast, in early 2010 the *New York Times* printed a description of a vignette from Afghanistan. An ordinary Afghan soldier traded his badge with an American marine, receiving in exchange a can of energy drink. An Afghan officer then instructed the soldier to hand over the can, opened it, drank some, passed it round his fellow officers, and the last to drink handed it back empty.[67] That kind of 'leadership' would tend to undermine the effectiveness of any organisation. An inhumane approach – as seen in the demand by large retailers for last-minute overtime even from women with children to look after – cannot possibly secure the voluntary commitment that makes companies thrive.

The context of leadership is important. A group of friends on a camping trip will usually have no formal structure of leadership. But leadership will be given by individuals, from time to time, when decisions are required. 'Let's camp here!' is a suggestion that may be heeded or not: if the suggestion is adopted, then leadership has been given. Leadership only earns that name when other people respond: if someone says, 'Let's camp here', and the others carry on tramping silently along the path, there has been no leadership, simply a failed attempt at it.

In other circumstances, where there is a clear decision-making hierarchy, it may not be possible for followers to ignore or disagree with the decision of a leader. Still, the quality of the leader's relationship with the followers can have a large influence on the success of any initiative: people may, with resentment, give minimal compliance, or they may leap forward in support.

With an employee-owned company as the context, hierarchy tends to be minimised – the effort is to make the most of the intrinsic commitment that can result from shared ownership. Commitment would be undermined by any attempt at a dictatorial approach. The leaders of employee-owned companies tend to communicate a lot and listen a lot.

In the case of normal business decisions – about products, markets, operations, finance and investments – there is often not a great deal of difference between the decision-making process in an externally owned company and that in an employee-owned one. The facts are gathered and proposals are made to the directors, who then decide. Day to day the executive directors and managers implement the resulting plans, making tactical decisions along the way.

A vital point is that employee ownership can never make up for poor business decisions. The directors make the strategic choices; if they are wrong, then employee ownership will not save the company from disaster. The top managers in an employee-owned company must be just as talented and competent in making business judgements as the directors in any conventional business.

However, the fact that the directors are accountable to the employees does change things. When you know that you can be sacked by the people you are leading, your attitude will be different from that of the Afghan officer. You will tend to be keen to make sure that your decisions are well understood, and that you have listened to the opinions of the people you are leading. You will also tend to pay attention to the reasonable desires and needs of the employee-owners.

In the context of the shared ownership of the company, where each person will participate in the benefits of success, good leadership will be far more likely to attract enthusiastic support than in a conventional company where leadership which elicits voluntary commitment is essentially deceptive.

The transformation of a company's ownership can in the early days stimulate unrealistic expectations in the new employee-owners. It is worth emphasising the *shared* nature of the ownership. Shared ownership has less of a feeling of out-and-out power about it than just the stark declaration: 'I'm the owner', which can carry awkward, aggressive overtones. Parametrix is an environmental services company in the north-west of the USA employing 600 people, mainly engineers and scientists. When the owner sold 68 per cent of the shares to their ESOP the receptionist said to him: 'You work for me now!' That may have been innocent jest and the owner may have laughed. But similar responses sometimes have an edge: people who have felt downtrodden can stumble into quite aggressive stances. Leaders have to deal with those reactions and the expectations of dramatic change.

It need not always involve aggression: simply unrealistic expectations. At the time of a buyout, employees in their new role as owners can suffer from some of the same illusions about employee ownership as traditional economists do – such as the idea that every decision will have to be discussed by everybody. It takes leadership to make clear the practical rules.

For example, Victor Aspengren, in Schafer, was faced with the widely held assumption that representatives of the employees as owners would be involved in most if not all decisions. A couple of times a week the company had traditionally paid for lunch for all the employees. A number of employees, conscious that they were now owners, suggested to their elected representatives that this was not a good use of their money, and Aspengren as CEO agreed to discuss it with the committee. The discussion went on for seventy-five minutes, concluding with a decision to ask one of the company's major suppliers to sponsor one of the lunches each week. Aspengren then said to the committee: 'This was a good discussion, but we just spent an hour and fifteen minutes discussing lunch. Do you think that a good business can afford to do that? That is why we have managers. We're going to have to trust these people to make good decisions. We can't spend an hour and fifteen minutes on every little decision.'

This interplay between participation and authority tends to settle closer to the participation end of the spectrum than it does in traditional companies. But the leaders do not give up the decision-making role or responsibility. Indeed, in addition to the traditional responsibility to make decisions, each manager faces a set of requirements about how to approach people. Kim Lowe, the manager of the John Lewis department store in Aberdeen, said:

'A manager's annual review is made up of two sections: one on behaviours and one on delivery of tangible results. Sixty per cent of the score is on behaviours, rather than just delivering on sales, profit and costs. So there's a huge emphasis on treating people with respect and helping them develop. When we tackle poor behaviour or poor results, we do it within a framework of care. Good leaders can get rid of people that aren't delivering, but in a way that doesn't damage their leadership. Often if you've got two or three people that aren't pulling their weight, it is much more powerful to do something about it. The rest of the workforce gossip about the ones who are slacking, and they want you to deal with it.'

In the case of Schafer, the ownership culture produced a different way of handling this. Aspengren said:

'It became truly peer to peer. People would go to a supervisor and say, "We've got a problem with this person. We're going to sit him down and talk to him, but we wanted you to know, as you're the supervisor." They were stepping up as owners – "We're owners, we can handle this." They didn't depend on the supervisor or HR department. Owners are adults, and if they know what ownership means and understand the business, do they really need that much supervision? They know what to do.'

In a shared ownership context leaders are expected to behave in line with the principles that they espouse. Peter Stocks in SAIC found it hard to establish and sustain the culture as the company grew rapidly. He had to recruit people whose experience had been gained in very different circumstances.

'A lot of bullies get to be senior managers, because bullying can sometimes get really good short-term results. People have learned all the way up the tree firstly that it's acceptable and secondly that it gets good results and rewards. So when they get to senior positions they just carry on like that.'

He himself had to set an example of how it might be done differently, although he was aware of the irony that to do so he had to give a strong lead.

'I went through a period when I became very unpopular. I kept throwing people out of meetings, people using their Blackberries, people who were behaving badly, fighting, not being collegiate, and so on. In terms of breaking down those behaviours, you've got to be very rigorous about what you will accept and what you won't accept. And in some ways it's odd, because you've got to become a dictator to do that.'

Of course, some conventionally structured companies have magnificent leadership practices. Charlie Mayfield of the John Lewis Partnership says:

'It's important to be outward-looking because you create the opportunity to measure your own performance against other benchmarks out there. If you assume that what everyone else does is inferior in some way or just not relevant, you miss out on the opportunity of inspiration that comes from going out and seeing that there are some great companies out there. They really motivate and inspire their employees, but they're not employee-owned. And actually as an employee-owned company, shouldn't we be just as good as that?'

The big difference for him is this: 'We're employed by the partners and not the other way round, and therefore we have to tread that path of prominent personal leadership with some care.'

Lower down in the same organisation, Jenny Ridley, in the Registry, sees the middle management leadership role as much more challenging than it is in a top-down, traditional hierarchy:

'It's *way* tougher being a manager in an employee-owned company. You've got all the usual key performance indicators to meet. Department managers will typically have sales targets and targets for almost every aspect of operations, in almost exactly the same way as managers in any other retailer. But on top of that, they've got the broader democratic leadership role. They've got to be a role model for the partners. They need to help and coach and encourage people to make the department forums a success. They've got to put a hell of a lot more time and effort and creativity into communicating with their teams than would ever happen in another retailer. It's not just communication, it's ensuring understanding. And they've got responsibilities for participation and engagement. All this comes on top of the day job of being sales managers.'

There is a sense of pride in leading people who are clearly all on the same side – the role can be deeply satisfying. It's a different leadership mindset, one that is seen clearly in the words of the president of Litecontrol in Massachusetts, who starts every address to her fellow employee-owners: 'I'm the President of the company. I work for the 200-some people that work here.'

Later I will make the case that it is a deeply natural mindset, one that people typically respond to with energy and enthusiasm.

LEADERSHIP SUCCESSION

One of the crucial tasks facing any organisation is the choice of the next leader. In the jargon this is known as succession planning. This is particularly problematic for companies that are a little apart from the mainstream, like employee-owned companies. They are looking for leaders who 'get it', who have drunk the ownership juice, who are happy to be coaches rather than bosses – and who seek in their jobs a wider satisfaction than top rates of pay.

Even for normal companies with a mainstream approach to management, the task is not easy. The problem is harder to solve for employee-owned companies because the default position of leaders coming from outside the company is often far from sympathetic to all this, and far from an understanding of how to get the best out of widespread ownership and participation. In the words of John Logue, the Texan professor at Kent State University in Ohio:

'Employee-owners are no better at interviewing managers than conventional corporations. They make the same kind of mistakes: they hire salesmen who are good at selling themselves but who turn out to be charlatans. It's very hard to differentiate a good from a bad manager until you've had them for a couple of years, and I think employee-owned companies are slower to get rid of bad managers than conventionally owned companies. Having said that, the successor generation in a family-owned company is rarely as energetic as the founder generation. Does this make employee-owned companies particularly weak? No – it puts them in a category with some other ownership forms.'

The National Freight Corporation in the UK achieved a very successful employee buyout from government ownership. Sir Peter Thompson led the buyout in 1982, in which some 12,000 of the 24,000 employees participated directly, a proportion which grew over time. They made a huge success of the company, which had been loss-making in government ownership. However, Thompson reflects ruefully on the question of succession.

'In 1991 NFC brought in a new CEO. He proved to be a man who did not understand the core values of the business. The other directors all got together and said, 'It's him or us', so he resigned. Then of course a new CEO was appointed, who saw these executive managers as a threat to his power base, so he got rid of them. Autocratic management came back, from the top. It was disappointing. A big mistake I made was to recommend to the board an insider to take over from me. I recommended the Finance Director, who I thought was absolutely immersed in the philosophy of what we were doing. In no time flat he'd got it all wrong.'

In Baxi Partnership Limited, which manufactured boilers for domestic heating systems, the same problem led eventually to a major disaster. When the long term MD retired in 1989 the company struggled with the appointment of a new leader. In quick succession three CEOs were appointed and departed. The fourth brought in a new operations director, who led a transformation in the performance of the company, achieving strong growth from 1993 to 1998. The CEO, who gained a great deal of credibility by this performance of the operations director, then led the acquisition of an Italian company, doubling the size of Baxi Partnership Limited and obtaining access to some key new technology. With his credibility now established, and with the polished support of an investment bank, some consultants and a new chairman with a good name in the City, he was in a position to convince the employee-owners and their trustees that a major acquisition was the way forward. Baxi Partnership had around £200 million of sales and £20 million profit: the acquisition cost £500 million – out of all proportion in scale.

It did not work. Fifteen months after the acquisition the whole group was on its back, and all the operations had to be sold. The employees got £6 million and the trust £20m, just one fifth of the value the previous year. The root cause of the problem was the lack of a planned and effective succession for the job of chief executive ten years earlier. In the increasingly desperate search for their new CEO, the company ended up with someone who really did not 'get it' about employee ownership. At root he was a traditional manager, who was much impressed by the City ideology and sacrificed the employee-ownership in his search for success. In the end the employee-owners lost their company and he lost his leadership position.

The world of corporate leadership can be as bedevilled by large egos as any human institution. The employees have to follow their leaders in all the day-to-day business of keeping their company successful. But that success can be sustained beyond the current generation only if the employee-owners can develop the structures and processes to choose good successors, and have the initiative to operate those processes successfully. Having chosen their next leaders, the employee-owners must on the one hand follow and support them, and on the other control them effectively. Only then can the employee-owners hope to sustain this productive and humane system into the future.

Finally, there is a salutary lesson in the story of SAIC, which grew to $8bn in revenues by 2006, the largest employee-owned research and engineering company in the US. Bob Beyster, the founder, remained the dominant leader in the company for over thirty years. Over the course of at least a decade he recruited potential successors (one from the outside, the rest from the inside) and then found that somehow they didn't measure up. Approaching his eighties, he found agreement on a successor, an insider widely seen as ready to take over the CEO role. Everything was set up for the handover, which would take place at the final dinner for the annual gathering of the scientists and top managers in the company. But the dinner came and went, and Beyster did not hand over as planned. The successor left. The board resolved the problem by engineering what was essentially a coup, to appoint a new CEO imported from outside. He brought in the paradigms of traditional, non-employee-owned companies, and the majority of the board were soon persuaded that being private and employee-owned was no longer viable. Within a short time the shares were floated and much of the ownership excitement and drive deflated. Board members who knew the value of entrepreneurial employee ownership soon left. In employee ownership the price of the company's ordinary shares had more or less doubled every five years. From the 2006 initial public offering (IPO) to summer 2010, it remained pretty well static.

Succession is manifestly a minefield. The way to make it work well seems to be to plan it overtly, discuss it regularly and ensure that it happens as planned. A great leader will have the self-denying ability not to cling to power. While it is the stories of dire outcomes that seize the headlines, most employee-owned companies find good successors for the top jobs. Succession has to be built into the brickwork. Steps which will reassure the retiring leader that the best of the old ways will be maintained may help: perhaps the constitution can be revised to incorporate them. Or perhaps the retiring individual can be funded to play a promotional role in the world of employee ownership.

The papermill where I started my employee ownership career has had four CEOs since the all-employee buyout was completed in 1994.

The people chosen have proved superbly good leaders. Each of them in turn 'got it' – they were energised and inspired by the vision of what employee ownership could do for their company and for all the people in it, and in turn they energised and inspired their fellow employee-owners.

13

Lining Up the Arrows

Employee-owned companies work better. They are more productive and the people in them have happier working lives. This chapter looks in greater depth at how that comes about.

Working this way appeals to people at a deeply natural level. There are many aspects to this appeal, and people are happiest and perform best when all the different facets are lined up, pointing the same way. If even a single important factor contradicts the others – for example, if a director just goes through the motions of consultation, without really listening – then that can undermine the effect of many other efforts aimed at working in partnership. A single raised eyebrow or ironic tone at the wrong moment can make people retire into their sceptical shells. These are not engineered systems but human beings, people who are easily turned off. But in a benign environment they can achieve extraordinary things when they are given their head, with each factor reinforcing the others, each arrow pointing in the same direction, each piece of feedback saying, 'Yesss!'

THE OWNERSHIP EFFECT

In all the interviews I conducted for this book, with people in large companies and in small, in many kinds of businesses, in various countries, with each country and each company having its own unique culture, the uniform message was that when you own the company, you feel different. Owning the company leads you to care more about the company, to think more, to try harder, to keep working at problems, to come up with more ideas. Quite simply, you are more committed. Ownership triggers a different part of the brain, and draws into the game another side of the human heart.

This should not be a surprise. The whole of capitalism is predicated on that effect. People who own businesses tend to make them more vital and entrepreneurial and successful than people who, for example, work for companies owned by the state. Good, basic, capitalist thinking.

The surprise is that this insight has been hijacked – held to apply to the small number of capitalists, but not to the ordinary working people who make up most of the population. Somehow nobody has noticed that the rationale for capitalism – the fact that people come alive as owners – has been distorted, to justify a system in which very few people own businesses and everyone else works for them. But there is no justification for this narrowing of focus. The idea has been hijacked and the wealth along with it, leaving most people poorer, which in turn has undermined the self-respect and happiness of the humiliated majority. Generation after generation, people are forced to accept servitude, when rightfully they should be partners sharing in the ownership of the businesses to which they devote their lives.

Owning a business together with fellow workers is an idea that appeals to most people. Everyone sees instinctively, intuitively, that a system where everyone has a stake will work better than a scheme where people work for a boss.

In a Waitrose supermarket in London, owned for decades by its employees, a middle-aged woman stacking shelves with bottles of wine – pretty basic work but essential to the running of daily life for all of us – struggled to articulate why she felt so good about working in the company, and eventually burst out with: 'Well . . . it's my company too!'

Fairness

One aspect of that intuitive appeal is the simple fairness of the system. This comes through again and again when you talk to employee-owners. In Los Angeles, for example, a young woman working as a design engineer in Arup wrote to the chairman of their employee ownership trust: 'How refreshing it is to know that I am working for a firm where the CEO and the shareholders aren't creaming off the profits.'

Near London, Marie Jarvis, the finance director of g3*, a firm specialising in engineering for the oil industry, says 'The fact that it's employee-owned is very important to people. I wouldn't enjoy it so much if I knew that my efforts were lining the pockets of three people, even if they were three good people who talked to me and listened to my ideas.'

Philip Baxendale, who together with his cousin sold their boiler manufacturing company into employee-ownership at a 90 per cent discount, says, 'How can you talk to someone about improving things if they're not going to get any benefit out of it?'

Of course you *can*, and much of management training is in how to do that. But all the best efforts of management are undermined by that basic unfairness, whereas in an employee-owned company good management finds its natural home. In Oregon it was expressed by Ricky Walsh, a supervisor in Woodfold, a door manufacturer owned by its employees for the last ten years: 'If we're saving a dollar for the company, we're saving a dollar for ourselves.'

That may sound as if it's purely financial – and the financial aspect is important – but in fact its effect is wider and deeper. He continued: 'We all feel like owners.'

Management initiatives to involve people in improving the way things are done become enormously more powerful when the results belong to all. Chris Parr the CEO of Tullis Russell (and a keen golfer) puts it like this: 'We have this massive club in our bag. We are able to say, "This is for everyone's benefit." That is the banner that people will march under.'

It's a good banner. We all create the wealth, and we all share in it.

---

* Formed by engineers who were inspired by the principles developed by Philip Baxendale and embodied in Baxi Partnership, the new company adopted the full name of g3baxi partnership. To avoid confusion, it is referred to in this book simply as g3, which is in any case common day-to-day practice. The essence of Philip Baxendale's thinking has three main elements: a strong trading enterprise, in employee ownership, with a partnership culture. The employee ownership is rendered stable by holding at least 50 per cent in a permanent trust.

That is fair. And fairness appeals to us at a deep level. Owning together the company where we work *feels* fair.

In control

A second facet of ownership, when it is spread among all the people who work in a company, is that it puts them in charge of their own destiny. The company will not be sold over their heads. They will not wake up to find a new set of bosses running the show.

You do not have to be a control freak to feel good about being in charge of your own future. Knowing that you are in control together just feels right. As long as the company is owned by outsiders, there is uncertainty in the air. You never know what they will do, and they don't have to bother asking you before they do it. They can sell the company, for example, without considering your situation or your views. They don't even have to go to the trouble of telling you once they've done it. This environment is completely different psychologically from one where everyone is a partner and has a say in the big decisions. People like being in charge.

Kate Hall, the Arup engineer running the team providing design services for the Olympics infrastructure in London, puts it this way: 'Understanding that the firm is owned by all of us allows us to do things in different ways. We have that flexibility.'

David Hodgkinson, a physicist in the field of nuclear waste, built a successful business as a division inside a large company; he then had that division sold over his head, a traumatic event over which even he as division CEO had no say. 'Two years later I resigned to start my own company. Life's too short to be in a miserable environment. You want to spring out of bed ready to go to work, not force yourself to go to work just because they give you a salary.' When he started his new company he decided this time to make it employee-owned – something his adviser gave him a solemn warning against doing. As the old business fell apart under its new owners, the best people came to join him in the employee-owned one, and a key part of the attraction was that they would share the ownership. *This* one would never be sold over their heads.

When Ken Shuttleworth and Barry Cooke left the Norman Foster architects' practice to set up an employee-owned company of architects

– called Make – their advisers too were very much against making it employee-owned. But once set up it attracted so many good people that it grew to a practice of well over 100 architects in three years. Every person working there is simply a 'partner'. Ken Shuttleworth says:

'There's this great feeling of ownership, the feeling that it's *our* company. To my mind that makes more sense than just employing people, beating them up and sending them home miserable. If someone wanted to buy us it would be a massive group decision. But at the end of the day I can't imagine doing it, to end up beholden to somebody else. The great thing is that we haven't got shareholders or investment banks telling us what to do.'

It doesn't take a high level of education to grasp the point – it is something fundamental to human life. In Manchester, Elaine Miller, the leader of an employee-owned company of carers looking after old people in their own homes, summed up the appeal for her fellow owners: 'There's no big fat cat sat at the top who can take everything from beneath you.'

In Spain I asked Mikel Lezamiz, head of the training college in Mondragón, why he had stayed for decades when he could have earned more by working for a conventional company. 'It is because we are the owners. Not to have to work for another person – working for ourselves together – that means more than anything to me.'

Being a fellow owner stimulates and satisfies the whole person, brain and heart together. To exclude people from that potential is to make working life akin to cruel and unusual punishment. It certainly fails to open up the space for initiative and drive and thoughtful engagement that is so satisfying to those involved and so productive for the business.

Profit-sharing

As co-owners, people in employee-owned companies share in the profits. This can be done as a dividend on the shares they hold. Or it can be done simply as a bonus. A third option is the Mondragón system: the profit share is the cash payment of 7.5 per cent interest on the personal capital accounts, together with the sums that are added to those accounts in every profitable year.

Usually, like the ownership, profit-sharing is carried out on a relatively egalitarian basis, and in some companies it can amount to large sums of money. The John Lewis system has been mentioned already: the same percentage of salary for every employee-partner, 15 per cent in 2010, up from the previous year but well below the peak of 24 per cent some years earlier. Whatever your salary, an extra two or three months' pay is a considerable sum, which, paid in early summer, it is very nice to receive.

In Make Architects, it can reach higher levels still. There is an annual profit share, most of which is allocated as a percentage of salary. But 20 per cent of the pot is allocated by the partners themselves (everyone being a partner). Each person is given six votes to assign: one each to six different people. Each vote carries the same sum of money. People whose contribution is appreciated by their peers thus share in the profit to a greater extent. If the total amount for profit-sharing is £150,000, the amount to be distributed through voting is £30,000; if there are 600 votes in total, then each vote is worth £50 to the recipient. So each person has £300 to give to others – when you assign your vote to someone, it is as if you are giving him or her a £50 note.

In 2008 Sam Evans had the job of storing documents and accessing them when required – an important role in an architects' practice, but still a relatively junior one. She was overwhelmed when she discovered the effect of the voting on her bonus. 'It is a phenomenal thing for me to work in a profit-sharing company. When I was paid my bonus this year I burst into tears.' She laughs. 'I just couldn't believe how much I was getting paid – it was more or less my whole salary again.'

The personal impact is also striking. 'It's not just about the money. The fact that they would give this money to me – it gave my self-esteem such a boost. "Wow! My colleagues actually value me this much!"'

Psychologically, the effect of profit-sharing is not the same as shared ownership. Cash bonuses trigger big smiles, but the smile effect probably declines over a period of a few weeks. Knowing that the profit share will be paid – having confidence in the system – tends to create a positive background feeling for longer than the 'smile' period. But this effect is separate from the ownership effect. Ownership breeds commitment through periods of profit and loss alike. It will motivate people to get through long difficult periods, when there is no expectation of profit. Profit-sharing spreads delight, and as long as there is an expectation of profit, it will provide strong motivation too. Both are good, and they are complementary in nature.

Profit-sharing has been shown also to have a direct effect on how people behave towards their fellow workers. One of the supposedly insoluble problems raised by ideologues hostile to employee owner-ship is the so called 'free rider' problem. Somehow employee-owners are supposed to breed shirkers – people who hitch a free ride on the back of the efforts of their colleagues. In their own inimitable way, economists add gravitas to this fantasy by turning it into algebra: it is called the 'one over N' or $1/N$, problem. A worker puts in 100 per cent of any discretionary effort, but, if the number of workers is N, only gets one Nth, $(1/N)$, of the benefit. Therefore people will shirk – so the thinking goes.

On the other hand, people will supposedly work hard in a conven-tional company. When we express in the economists' beloved algebra the incentive for an employee of a conventional company, it turns out to be $0/N$ – zero. They get *nothing* from any extra effort, except that they get tired.

Algebra can be useful. No matter how large the number N gets, $1/N$ is still infinitely greater than zero. So the effort to undermine employee ownership proves instead that it provides an infinitely better environment to encourage people to work hard.

There is another leg to the $1/N$ theory. It says that not sharing in profits doesn't matter: employees in conventional companies will work hard because they are supervised. But this ignores how people actu-ally react to being supervised – they are as likely to resent it and to respond with active efforts to shirk. In any case, in most businesses it is impossible to supervise in any sustained way. The extent to which this approach misses the point is seen from the fact that if employees wish to protest without going on strike, they work to rule – that is they make a special effort to meet the terms of their contracts. When they do that, the whole business grinds along so slowly and ineffec-tively that negotiations are usually arranged rapidly to return to normality, which is active cooperation beyond the terms of the contract. All businesses depend on the employment contract's terms being exceeded through voluntary cooperation. Without discretionary effort by the employees, businesses fail.

As we might expect from this look at the theory, the facts point in favour of employee ownership. A study carried out by Richard Freeman and others[68] showed that when a profit-sharing scheme is introduced, the employees are much more inclined to bring slackers into line. Supervision by all one's colleagues is a highly effective form of supervision. Recall that in employee-owned Schafer in Ohio, the employees did not pass the buck: they did not leave the discipline process to the supervisor – they would themselves talk to the slacker. And which is the more powerful message: 'You are wasting the boss's money' or 'You are wasting money that belongs to all of us'?

When you are all working for a boss who appropriates all the profit and will ultimately if possible get rid of you, why should you care if people are not pulling their weight? And why should you make extra effort yourself? Shirking seems an eminently understandable response in those circumstances. But when we all share in the ownership and the profits, of course we will do something about anyone trying to take us for a ride.

FEELING LIKE AN OWNER

Ownership itself is important: it is the base on which people start to act like owners. We have seen that people can feel and act like owners without actually having an ownership stake, but they are being fooled – it can all be taken off them in an instant, by the actual owners. The opposite is also true: people can own the company without feeling like owners, and as a result without behaving like owners.

Owners, when they feel like owners, have a highly developed sense of responsibility. They care about the things they own, and care for the things they own. This attitude is at the root of the way employee-owned companies perform. But you cannot just give people ownership and expect them to feel and behave like owners. Employees are bred all their lives to be employees, enticed into being employees, or coerced into being employees. Employment is usually their only option. When you make them owners they think that's a great idea, but it takes time for them to feel in their bones that they really are the owners. And only then do they plug in and start performing. Only then is the enormous energy released that comes with real, deeply felt ownership.

The behaviour of the managers is the key factor that spreads ownership's 'magic fairy dust', a phrase that came rather surprisingly from a finance director: Marie Jarvis of g3, the employee-owned company formed by engineers – designers of offshore and onshore oil and gas production facilities – who left Halliburton when their attempts to buy their unit were refused. One of their main aims was to develop a culture of partnership, in contrast to the top-down corporate culture within Halliburton. They saw that a genuine partnership had to be based on shared all-employee ownership, and that the shared ownership would feel real only if everyone in the company was treated as a true partner. The two elements, culture and ownership, interact. Their experience is that this approach enables them to do better for their clients as well as for themselves.

There are several aspects to management behaviour that spread and reinforce the feeling of ownership.

Telling it like it is

The first and most essential thing that the managers in an employee-owned company must do is *talk* to their fellow owner-employees. They must pass on information, tell people what is going on, what performance has been achieved, what the plans are and why decisions have been made the way they have. They have to keep pushing out information, whether the news is good or bad, certain or probable. If it feels to the managers like overkill – as if they are giving out too much information – then they may be close to giving out enough. If employee-owners are to contribute to the extent of their capability, it is essential that they understand what is going on and why.

When people know what is going on, they can respond intelligently and take useful initiatives. A cost-cutting exercise imposed without information by top-down management authority is experienced as an imposition against the interests of those on the receiving end. But if the situation has been explained regularly, if people have been kept up to date and have the relevant information, they will understand. And, on the basis of the fact that they own the business, they will work intelligently to contribute. Without information, they can do nothing positive – they will tend simply to feel resentment at being pushed around again. Talk of employee ownership will tend to seem like just another ruse to squeeze more work out of them.

Over time, if communication takes place regularly and reliably, there is a fundamental change in the relationship between the managers and the people they manage. Trust develops. Ricky Walsh, the supervisor in Woodfold, the door manufacturer in Oregon, spoke about the way that the employees had consistently been given a whole range of information: 'It's been a very honest thing. I've felt like they've been honest with me.'

What a difference that feeling makes to a person at work. The people above me tell me the truth – that is really something. It is the beginning of trust, the opening of a doorway into a world where it is possible to dream of behaving differently, the key to a life of joint action and shared results, the un-damming of energy.

For some people even the very fact that they are getting information is hard to absorb. Derek Hay, a team leader running a huge coating machine in Tullis Russell, speaks about the early days of the switch to employee ownership:

'They never hid anything. Everything was up front. That's what I couldn't believe. You were told everything as it happened. If we were making money you were told; if we weren't making money you were told too – but you were also told what they were doing to rectify that. And you had the opportunity at the end of the briefings: "Any questions? Anything you weren't sure about?" If the person giving the briefing didn't know the answers they went away and found out. It certainly was a shock to the system. I'd never worked for anybody that actually told you anything about the business.'

For some people among those responsible for managing what goes on, it can feel risky to open the books, to proffer information freely. But the information given out should not be limited. In the rather dated language of John Spedan Lewis, the early genius:

Modern teamwork is apt to mean monotony and boredom. To a really important extent this is diminished if workers of all grades are given interesting knowledge of the broad results of what they are doing. This can be done by constant publication of everything which will not be too useful to business competitors.

In the twenty-first century, that continues to be interpreted liberally in the John Lewis Partnership. For example, as we have seen, the results of each department are available to all each week. For some, that triggers a healthy competitive response. Gill Wright recalls the time when she worked in dress fabrics:

'I had evening wear and velvets. I wanted to know exactly how much money my section was taking. It was absolutely up to date. You could look at it by section so that you could say, "I sold more than you!" Very childish. But it gets people thinking about it.'

Mo Asif, working in the bistro, had the figures in his head. He knew that his department's results had over the year to date risen by more than the average department and he wanted to use some of the cash the bistro was creating to hire more people, so that it could give even better service. It is not surprising that this chain is rated top by customers – even relatively recent and relatively sceptical recruits like Mo enjoy the feeling of getting their business running well. It is equally unsurprising that it continued to do well through the recession – employee commitment of this kind breeds customer loyalty and trust.

Sharing the information in any company – if the Stock Exchange will allow it – can produce something of this effect. But sharing the information on the basis of shared ownership produces a different level of response. You are beginning to line up the different arrows, and as each one is added, the barriers weaken and more potential is released.

Listening, hearing, responding

Now there are three factors pointing in the same high-performance direction: shared ownership, shared profits and shared information. What more can a manager do?

The fourth factor is listening – consultation. Charlie Mayfield, the chairman of John Lewis, summarises the Partnership's approach: 'What partners think, matters.'

The employee-partners are given the information and over time become educated, and educate themselves, about the business. It is their business, and consequently they think about it. Thinking about it, they develop ideas and views. And those ideas and views are important.

It is not that management are setting out to be nice. There is no pretence. They recognise that what goes on inside the heads of the people in the business really does make a difference. What matters in a business is what people do when there is no supervision – which in most businesses is most of the time. And what people do is greatly influenced by what they think. What they think, matters.

It is worth recalling the John Lewis Partnership Letters Page in the weekly *Gazette*. In most companies the promise to publish all letters would be seen as a hollow boast: who would really express an honest opinion? The power of the managers would be turned on anyone who did, and the writer of a serious complaint would be for the high jump. The same danger exists in any institution, wherever there are people with different levels of power. But to foster the feeling of ownership they really do want to ensure that public opinion is expressed openly, and not suppressed. Opinions are not dangerous, because everyone is pretty well on the same side. This can be achieved only when people's actions are 'for real', when they really do behave in line with values officially espoused. In such an environment it is a valid act for a junior person to call to account a senior one for failing to behave properly. If the opinion of the junior person does not count, or if the response of a senior person is to pull rank or use power to get back at him or her, then any attempt at high performance will in the end fail. Human beings are highly sensitive to degrees of sincerity and insincerity: fakery waves a vivid flag, drawing attention to itself. We feel in our gut whether or not someone is to be trusted – or distrusted. There are powerful evolutionary reasons why we should have that sensitivity: those brothers and sisters of our ancestors who were too naïvely trusting were taken advantage of and tricked, so much so that they failed to pass on their genes to the same extent. But we all have the capability to trust and to distrust. The over-naïve are preyed on; the paranoid tend to drive people away. But most of us are designed to distrust people with power who are insincere.

In a sense, the whole trick of building participative employee-owned companies comes down to removing barriers. When employees do the work and owners get all the rewards, a barrier is created. Having no information, employees are excluded: that is another barrier to their behaving intelligently and with commitment. When their views are ignored, they are demoralised, and yet another barrier is created.

People have views on the company and its operations at many levels. On the shop floor, they will come up with ideas on how to improve the way things are done. As already mentioned, in Woollard and Henry, the Aberdeen engineering company, the views of a couple

of operatives opened up a whole new segment of the market at virtually no cost. In Loch Fyne Oysters they led to a drastic reduction in
the costs of packaging. In Schafer, in Iowa, persistent questioning from
the shop floor as to why a coating process had to be carried out on
some plastic rods resulted in savings of $40,000 a year.

But at the other end of the scale, in strategic planning, ordinary
employee-owners will also have views. In Mondragón the strategic
planning process starts with the senior people, but once a draft is
produced there is wide consultation, involving quite large numbers
of people drawn from different levels. Mikel Lezamiz said:

'When is the most important moment to participate? When you
are doing the strategic planning. For example, in businesses that have
300 or 400 people, maybe they start with only fifty or sixty people
doing the planning, but after that everybody participates in the second
step, to listen and have the opportunity to give their views. Then the
final decision is taken by the Governing Council. The second step –
wide consultation – is very important.'

In the specialist chemical manufacturer Scott Bader, employee-owned
since 1951, the CEO was slightly taken aback to be told during the recession of 2009 that normal communication procedures needed to be
speeded up. There is a general awareness in any company of how well
the business is doing, and how the senior people are behaving, and both
affect the general mood. Everyone was aware that things were tough.
At a consultation meeting where the CEO showed the latest plan to the
elected representatives, someone from the plant responded with: 'This
is just what we need. We need this out now, because heads are down,
everyone's nervous or unhappy. So something that says, "There is a future
here, this is where we're heading" – that is just what we want.'

The plan was put on the notice boards throughout the plant.
Without that consultation, and the manager's response to it,
momentum would have been lost, and performance would have
declined. A better decision was made.

In the area of consultation, it is vital that those who have power
behave consistently. In the case of National Freight Corporation, the
large transport company privatised by Margaret Thatcher in 1982, Peter
Thompson, the chairman, lined up these practices well, resulting in
a huge improvement in performance. One of the commitments he
made was to consult on all major decisions affecting people who

worked for the business. If they were going to sell a subsidiary, for example, they had to win agreement from the employees affected.

'We were very clear that if we sold a business we had to convince the employees that it was in their best interest to leave. In one case, the Waste Management Company, we offered each employee a considerable amount of money if they would agree to go, but it had to be their decision. They rejected it, so I said, "You've rejected it. Now it's up to you to improve your performance." And they did.'

After leading the company through years of superb performance on the basis of employee-ownership, Thompson handed over to his successor James Watson, the Finance Director. After a strategic review Watson decided to sell Pickfords, a subsidiary with some 1,200 employees, because it lay outside the mainstream of the business – road transport and logistics.

'I don't think that James Watson understood that by doing it without full consultation and agreement of the employees he had actually destroyed one of the fundamental NFC values, which was that people have a right to have an input into any business decision which affects them. His argument was, "We can get rid of those employees who are not part of the core business, and the others that remain will understand." But what the others understood was that they had just behaved like any other management: they had departed from the core value that made NFC special in the eyes of the employees.'

Owners want to have a say, they want to be heard. It is not that every suggestion has to be accepted and implemented: as a response to an impractical idea, an explanation as to why it is being rejected will do nicely. This basic respect shown in listening to a person who thinks about the business and puts forward ideas is another vital element in fostering the feeling of ownership. And, of course, it has the practical result that real improvements are made, throughout the whole business. People who are ignored and disparaged feel daunted and revert to being passive; but people who are heard become more active.

INVOLVEMENT

One step up from managers listening is active involvement of all the employee-partners. Here the most important thing to do is to make it easy – above all to stop preventing it. When people come to work, what drives them is primarily the need to obtain money to live. But they are people. They do not do anything for just one reason, with just one part of their personality. They carry their whole self to work – with all the complexity of motivations and responses that this implies. By far the majority will want to do something that makes them feel good for having done it. Everyone, except perhaps for a troubled few, wants to feel good about what he or she does. And one of the ways to get people to feel good about what they do is to allow them to make a difference. Don't take away their control over what they do. Give them what they need, to be able to improve the way things are done. The need might be for techniques of problem identification and analysis, it might be time to discuss with their team-mates what they do together, it might be an organised way to collect ideas – there are a thousand different techniques and processes that liberate people to make a difference.

But giving them instructions to do so is not one of them. This was brought home to me by Jean Newman, a tough-minded American consultant who gave us advice when I was running the Scottish paper-mill. I wanted to begin the process of generating a more participative style by calling together the managers to set targets for participation.

'It's no good, David,' she said. 'It won't work.'

I bristled. I was executive chairman and de facto chief executive. People did not contradict my ideas.

'If you tell them to participate, and they participate,' she said, 'they will not be participating.'

I began to think that we'd hired a very confused consultant. Then she said something that has seemed self-evident ever since.

'They'll just be obeying orders as usual.'

Instead, guided by Newman, we picked a group of people from every level, individuals with reputations for not holding back and for having the respect of their colleagues; we gave them a budget and time; and told them to do anything they liked to make things better. That was the beginning of an unending process of improvement after improvement after improvement.

Early on, one of the things they did was paint the toilets. Managers tend to look down on workers when they focus on apparently mundane things, instead of addressing business issues. But when they painted the toilets they weren't just painting the toilets. They were choosing what to do, and doing it; discovering that they could make a difference, and getting involved, and succeeding. With that behind them, they set about making more important and more adventurous decisions. Soon other groups were formed and one of them came up with a timed sequence for opening and closing valves each time their enormous machine was changing from producing one grade of paper to producing the next. They saved hundreds of thousands of pounds in materials that would otherwise have gone down the sewer. Of course, in theory, managers should have thought up that valve procedure years earlier. But managers don't have the intimate knowledge of every stage of every machine process, nor the time to think it through in detail. The people who really know the detail are the operatives. Given their heads (a happy phrase) – especially in an environment where they share the ownership and therefore have a common interest – they think and act together, and they make breakthroughs. To allow this to happen means, for the managers, unlearning the habits of top-down power. It is not easy, but it is hugely rewarding for all concerned.

In one of the papermill's subsidiaries, a plant employing just over 100 employee-owners, some figures show the progress made between 2007 and 2009 through an intensive process of involvement:

- For the first time ever, there was no 'lost time' accident at all during a three-year period.
- In 2009 the number of customers complaining that they had been sent bad paper was 80 per cent lower than two years earlier.
- The cost of putting right those errors fell from £157,000 to £29,000.
- The proportion of orders supplied on time and in full rose from 60 per cent to 96 per cent.

One result of the last achievement was that the machines did not need to run for so long. This in turn meant that the people were not fully occupied. In a normal company there would be a knee-jerk reaction: if they are not all needed then some of them should be sacked. A pity, but that's business. This approach is of course unfair: the progress has been made because the people involved have been working so well and so effectively that they don't need as much time to do the job; as a result some of them lose their jobs. It is not simply unfair: it penalises productive behaviour. 'If you make a difference, someone will get the sack' is the message to the people involved. That is a serious disincentive to being enthusiastic about making improvements.

Instead, the extra time available was used to train every single operative in the techniques of continuous improvement: how to identify and define a problem; how to measure it statistically; how to work together to come up with creative solutions; how to put them into practice. The training was designed to give them the skills to make an even greater contribution, and a self-reinforcing spiral of improvement resulted. The training was also designed to enable them to pass recognised national qualifications. This approach gave benefits to the business and also to the individuals. At the end of it they all had a share in the profit and the deep satisfaction of having contributed to making their company hum. When the profit share was paid out, they felt they had earned it, and they had.

One of the side effects of this process was a reduction in any sense of hierarchy. With the knowledge and skills shared out, rather than concentrated in the hands of supervisors, the feeling of teamwork was unmistakable. In every sense the teams of employees really owned the business.

This was brought about and reinforced in quite subtle ways. The process of managing maintenance tasks gave an illustration of the kind of thing that had this effect. On one of the production machines, which spread a fine coating of valuable chemicals on the paper, a range of about twenty tasks had to be carried out each week. Some, like lubrication, were to do with keeping the machine in good mechanical running order; others, such as cleaning tasks, were to ensure the quality of production. Yet others were aimed at keeping the workflows clear of obstructions and bottlenecks. And so on.

Previously, the teams had been given instructions by the supervisors as to what they should do and when they should do it. This took up time for the supervisors, and left the team hanging, uncertain about what would be required until the supervisor exercised the authority to instruct them. Now the team introduced a technique based on one originally invented by Toyota and called *Kamishibai*: a simple set of cards held in a slotted board, like those used in clocking-in systems. The slots were in columns headed with the days of the week, and each card, coloured red on one side and green on the other, was marked with a task. At the beginning of each week, the team selected the cards for the tasks to be done in the week, and placed them in the slots with the red side visible. The people in the team could see immediately what had to be done, without waiting for a supervisor to decide. They were in a position to choose which task to do and when to do it; having carried out the work they would turn the card round, green side out. This created a simple visual record of tasks outstanding – the red cards – and of tasks completed – the green cards. There was no need for anyone to exercise any authority: the team ran it themselves.

The beautiful simplicity of this solution disguises a really important psychological fact: people are genuinely placed in control of their own working lives. The word 'empower' is sprinkled through management texts and corporate pronouncements, often taking the form of pious PR, without substance. This production team had taken control of their own working environment; they were genuinely empowered, not because they had been given power, but because they had been placed in a position where they could take it. Meanwhile, the supervisors' time and attention had been freed, enabling them to contribute more usefully elsewhere.

Above all, the team members felt like owners, not simply because they were owners, but because they were able to behave like owners. They were making their co-owned business run sweetly, with enormous improvements in quality and efficiency, and that gave them huge satisfaction.

Baxi Partnership, now an employee-owned investment fund and consultancy that helps each client company structure its all-employee buyout and develop a partnership culture, has carried out attitude surveys in many of its client companies over several years. One of the strongest predictors of whether a person feels like an owner is how recently he or she has been involved in making an improvement. The more recent the involvement, the more positive the attitude. This is a correlation, not a proven cause–effect relationship, and it will almost certainly run both ways: the more you feel like an owner, the more you get involved in making improvements; and the more you make improvements, the more you feel that your ownership is real. That is statistical evidence for the positive upward spiral that employee ownership creates. Get involved and feel the reality of ownership; feel the reality of your ownership and do more to help the company improve. In employee-owned companies, business performance and happiness go hand in hand.

WORKING TOGETHER

This process of working together on a shared undertaking can release aspects of ourselves that are full of potential but are normally given hardly any room for expression. Margaret Elliott, the down-to-earth founder of Sunderland Home Care Associates, points towards this aspect of working in an employee-owned company:

'It's nice to earn money. It *is* nice, and it is nice to have nice things, but that's not the be-all and end-all. There's a much deeper thing to life than possessions and money. There's something about how we are human beings – how we interact, how we get on, how we can help each other – that's really, really deep-seated. It's profound, and it's worth much more than money.'

Fred Bowden, now chairman of employee-owned Tullis Russell, puts a similar point this way:

'Looking at the combining, the sharing of wealth, and really getting people involved and participating in the business – that gives me immense pride and immense joy. It's a much more pleasurable environment for me to come into – seeing people doing well for themselves and getting on in the business – than ever it would be to make millions of pounds just for myself.'

His successor as MD, Chris Parr, voices it in terms of a sporting analogy:

'We *are* one team. We play different positions and it doesn't mean that one position is more important than any other. Genuinely we respect each other. The question to ask is: "How can I help you play your position better?" And if I don't play my position properly that's going to have a negative impact on the team. If we get that collective philosophy we create a culture where high achievement is the norm and people really feel that they're valued and that they've made a difference. And if everybody feels like that we're creating something very special indeed. And it's passed on to the next generation.'

In Iowa, Victor Aspengren, the CEO until 2005 of Schafer Industries, which had 62 per cent ownership in an ESOP, summarises one
psychological effect of working together as owners: 'Shared ownership reduces stress. It's like in the military: I know somebody's covering
my back.'

A related impact was reported by the young oil industry engineers
in g3, who felt that they worked harder than they had ever done in
conventional firms, and helped each other more – yet they felt more
relaxed.

With this decreased emphasis on hierarchy there are still clear roles
and responsibilities, but the differences in power are much reduced.
Some companies convey this difference by reversing the traditional
organisation chart: instead of having the CEO at the top, the CEO is
at the bottom, with the wide base of the triangle sitting at the top;
the idea is to represent the role of the managers as *serving* the front-
line workers, rather than pushing them around. The purpose of the
hierarchy is to enable the front-line workers to be wholly effective.

In this mode it becomes much more likely that there will be a fairer
sharing of money as well as of power, and less abuse of power by
self-serving chief executives. A fairer distribution of wealth has healthy
effects in the local economy and in the lives of the people involved.
We will look further at that in the last section.

SUSTAINING EMPLOYEE OWNERSHIP

If we are going to pass it on, then employee ownership itself must
be maintained. Quite a large number of companies have been
employee-owned, often very successfully and for periods of many
years, but have ultimately reverted to the unholy arrangement of servitude to external 'owners'.

We know that employee-owners usually don't want to give up their
real partnership and come to regret it if they do. Why then do they
do it?

Sometimes the exit is forced by poor performance, almost always
caused, as in any business, by erroneous decisions by top management. In other cases it comes down to temptation pure and simple.
Performance has been so good that the shares are worth a previously

unimaginable fortune. Cashing them in proves irresistible. The regret that usually follows is tempered by healthy bank balances for those who make the biggest gains. Future generations are not so lucky. Gasforce, for example, was formed in 1996 by the employee buyout from British Gas of the loss-making maintenance operations serving industrial customers. Jack Fallow, the HR director of British Gas, had been given the task of closing down those operations. He realised that they could form a viable business, and instead of closing them he led the buyout. The advisers recommended an MBO, a management buyout, which would have concentrated the ownership in the hands of a few top managers, but at Fallow's insistence all 200 employees were included. The employees worked in small teams, on site at their clients' locations, which numbered many thousands. It was impossible to supervise the teams because they were so widely distributed. Discretionary effort would make all the difference: if the employees were switched on and committed, the business would boom. As Fallow expressed it: 'I felt that having everybody with a serious vested interest would be the secret of our success.'

And so it turned out. They bought the operations – which were losing about £1m a year – for £1.4m. The person with the largest stake – just 1 per cent of the shares – was Fallow himself, who became chairman. The ownership juice worked magnificently, and by 2002 the company was worth over £20m. Every £1 invested by the employees had increased to a value of about £15. In due course a suitor appeared in the form of a large company. Its managers dangled a mouth-watering prospect before the eyes of the Gasforce managers: as well as cashing in their shares, they would be allowed to operate the business with little change, and as part of a much larger group they would have more capital available to develop the Gasforce operations. The seduction worked. Against the advice of Fallow, the employees accepted £21.7m – and the managers quickly discovered the worthlessness of the blandishments to which they had succumbed. The acquirer put in new managers, the available capital did not reach the amounts they had anticipated and within a relatively short period most of them left or were forced to leave, deeply regretting having sold their company.

Good performance, when the share structure is vulnerable, can also force the company into an IPO – flotation on the Stock Exchange – even when nobody wants it. Wall Street and the City of London are well practised in the ways and means of making it more palatable for the top managers. The normal line is that the external investors will be much reassured if the leaders of the company are tied in by having large stakes. In the case of eaga, a British company with some 5,000 employees, which produced stellar growth after privatisation into employee ownership in 2000, the decision was taken to float the shares, in part to enable it to make acquisitions. In the process the senior managers were persuaded to accept share allocations that made them multimillionaires. One imagines that any questioning of the propriety of those allocations may not have been too challenging, nor the outcome much in doubt – a bit like the ritual in which each new emperor of China was required to refuse the throne twice before accepting it. It will be interesting to see whether the spirit of employee ownership in eaga can be sustained over the years. Competent and enthusiastic management during the period of employee ownership certainly made the most of it, and they have at least made a serious attempt to provide the basis for its continuance by retaining some 37 per cent of the shares in a trust for the employees. But the track record of such attempts by other companies does not bode well.

It can also happen that employee-owned companies are simply hijacked, as illustrated by one particular case in the UK. The family sold the company, at a discount, to a trust for the employees. Their motivations were the same as in the case of so many owners: an appreciation of the work that the employees had done to make the company successful; a desire to give them the chance to be partners in the business; recognition that if the company were sold the employees would be likely to suffer; and the belief that performance would probably improve when the employees became the owners. To ensure that their concern for the interests of *all* the employees would be unshakeably established as a principle, they wrote into the trust deed (its constitution) provisions that restricted the proportion of the shares that could be held by any one employee.

The business worked well in employee ownership. Some years later the chief executive persuaded the trustees to pass the shares into another trust. A point he did not emphasise was that this new trust did not have the same restrictions aimed at fairness. He then persuaded the directors, over a period of years, to give him large numbers of share options at a low share price – options which on exercise would buy the shares from the trust. All this was done over an extended period of time, by persuasion, in a legally correct way. Eventually he engineered the sale of the company, triggering the options and collaring tens of millions of pounds for himself. The employees averaged a few hundred pounds each and lost all the benefits of working in a company they owned together.

The structuring of the ownership is of crucial importance in ensuring longevity. When all the shares are held by the individual employees a substantial 'repurchase liability' – the need eventually to find the cash to buy back the shares – builds up. This has forced some companies to float their shares on the Stock Exchange, allowing outsiders to buy them, because in that way the company is not responsible for finding the funds. In contrast, the companies that have sustained their employee ownership over decades have mostly had some form of collective holding: a permanent trust, a foundation or a cooperative holding.

But even if the ownership is structured with the long term in mind, to be sustainable it is important for every company to solve two particular issues around power: how power is managed, and who gets to hold it – governance and succession. We must keep control of our leaders. Constitutional structures and procedures can achieve only so much in that direction: each employee-owner needs to get to grips with the issues and play a part in ensuring that the right decisions are made.

Employee-owned companies with sound leadership can last for decades, even centuries. The proportion of those that endure will steadily grow as we develop the insights and absorb the lessons of experience, incorporating them into the design of future employee-owned companies. Success will render the economy productive and working lives humane. There could hardly be a more worthwhile project.

In the USA, the project is now being picked up by some of the unions. The United Steelworkers (USW) has a distinguished history of putting ESOPs into companies that need rescuing. Several of them ran for many years before being acquired, closing down or losing employee control. However, the ESOP does not provide a stable base for employee ownership beyond the medium term: all the shares are eventually fed out into the accounts of the individual employees, and have to be sold.

In 2009 the USW announced a new approach: it has signed a framework agreement with Mondragón to work together on building up cooperatives on the Mondragón model. In the *USW News* for 27 October 2009 the union president, Leo Gerard, was quoted as saying:

We have lots of experience with ESOPs, but have found that it doesn't take long for the Wall Street types to push workers aside and take back control. We see Mondragón's cooperative model with 'one worker, one vote' ownership as a means to re-empower workers and make business accountable to Main Street instead of Wall Street.

This effort clearly recognises the issue of power – the subject of the next chapter.

14

Governance and Power

Our beloved democracy can degenerate into a dictatorship through the abuse of power by those at the top – but also through the failure of those at the bottom to use the power they have.
  José María Arizmendiarrieta

Like a stream in flood, the behaviour of powerful people is not easy to moderate: it goes where it wills. The nineteenth-century historian Lord Acton's famous dictum – 'Power tends to corrupt, and absolute power corrupts absolutely' – applies in companies as well as in politics. The chief executive must have power – the freedom to make decisions and to act in the interests of the business. The possibility of the abuse of power is therefore always present, whether the companies are owned by outside or inside shareholders, no matter what governance structures are in place.

Companies owned by their employees have developed and continue to develop a variety of ways to address this problem, most of them to a greater or lesser extent democratic. Whatever the structure, there exists an equally insidious temptation that can overcome the relatively powerful and the more humbly placed alike: the temptation of apathy. One of the wisest warnings about corporate governance was expressed by Father Arizmendi, the priest who inspired the building of the Mondragón group – which, it cannot be repeated too often, places power not at the apex of the organisation, but in the hands of the ordinary people who work in the individual business units. He recognised that structures and constitutions are important, but he emphasised, as in the epigraph above, that it is up to those involved to make them work. Even the best structures can be made effective only through the courage, energy and personal ethics of those involved.

Peter Beeby and his colleagues in School Trends, an employee-owned company that provides school uniforms and sportswear to schools and also designs school websites, have developed this idea with beautiful simplicity, emphasising their insight that every right has a corresponding responsibility. All employee-owners have the right to receive information, for example, but with that the corresponding duty to attend all communication events, and to make sure that they understand the information provided. They all have the right to express their opinions, and with that the duty to listen to others' opinions and to raise issues openly. And so on. These formulations provide a useful tool for those in the business to hold each other to account, regardless of seniority.

There is no obvious answer to the corporate governance problem. In looking at the solutions which have been proven to last, it is self-evidently necessary to focus on the longer-lived companies.

Arup, the global engineering consultancy with some 10,000 engineers, owned for forty years by trusts for the employees, does not have a democratic structure. Feedback seems to work in Arup by a form of osmosis. Power at the top is divided between the board, with its CEO, and the trustees, who are all insiders, including a large proportion of retired Arup engineers. In addition, the directors invite more or less senior people, who have what the directors judge to be the right attitudes and skills, to join an informal advisory body of some 500 people. This group is sounded out periodically by the board before decisions are taken on tricky issues or major policies. Like the unwritten British constitution (which in practice under Tony Blair was often ignored on important decisions) this system works by precedent and a shared understanding among those involved. In the past people tended to join Arup and stay for life; they are aware of the implications of the more rapid turnover of people that is the general trend in the business world. As tenure shortens, a system largely dependent on informal cultural understandings might be subject to rapid change and even abuse.

As we have seen, the John Lewis Partnership, employee-owned for eighty years, does have a democratic system: the top Partnership Council, elected by all the employee-partners, holds the directors to account and can sack the chairman. Everyone signs up to participate in the democratic system if chosen by their fellow workers in each department. The individual doesn't have to put his or her name forward – everyone's name is on the ballot. The result is that the people who are elected are generally trusted and recognised to know what they are talking about, but might not otherwise have stood in an election. The quality of the democracy has been improved by having everyone stand.

This system was first used by St Luke's, an employee-owned advertising agency in London. Its employees organised a buyout when their huge parent company was sold to an even more enormous corporation and they didn't want to be part of the deal. Their customers supported them, putting them in a very powerful negotiating position to get a good deal from their new parent. Andy Law, who led the buyout, tells the exciting story in his book *Open Minds*.[69]

In Mondragón, as among the Italian cooperatives, the system is also democratic, with an elected board that has essentially two roles: to appoint the general manager, who in turn appoints the managers and then runs the executive team; and to have the general manager account to the board periodically, usually every month.

Suppose the chief executive goes wrong – either abusing his or her power or failing to lead the business to success. Who can sack him or her, and how is it done? Those are key questions in corporate governance.

In Arup that power rests with the trustees of the two trusts, who have never in practice had to exercise it. In John Lewis it lies in the hands of the top elected council of sixty-seven representatives – and again it has never been exercised. In Mondragón in Spain, with 100,000 employees in over 100 businesses, the elected directors in each business can get rid of the general manager if things don't work out. In the opinion of one senior and long-serving member of the group, that system has resulted in a tendency to change the general manager perhaps a little too readily when a business hits a difficult patch. But it has also prevented runaway inflation in chief executive remuneration.

Furthermore this system has not damaged the performance of the businesses. During my first stay in Mondragón, in 1984, I heard a visiting banker produce an 'ah, but': these businesses had flourished because of the protection of import barriers – they would struggle when Spain's entry into the EU ended that protection. But actually that entry enabled Mondragón to continue its growth unabated. In the 1990s I heard another 'ah, but': they would flounder against global competition. In reality they competed very effectively, and they now have operations in every continent, with over seventy foreign subsidiaries. What is hard for outsiders to grasp is that the Mondragón structure is completely bottom-up. Each individual business is sovereign. The businesses have cooperated voluntarily to build a superstructure, but the people in that superstructure have no power other than the power of persuasion. The group looks like a corporation and calls itself a corporation, but each business remains part of the group only by voluntary decision. A simple two-thirds majority vote in any individual business would take it out of the group.

This is not an empty constitutional provision. A recent example was provided by Irizar, the second largest coach-manufacturing business in Europe. In the early 1990s this company was turned round under the leadership of a charismatic new chief executive. Methods were copied from the most advanced manufacturing companies, hierarchy was reduced, autonomous teams flourished, and the performance of the business rose steeply. It became internationally renowned as a beacon of successful operations management. Harvard Business School academics were impressed, and sent a team to write a case study about it (in which the fact that the business is owned by its employees is barely mentioned).

The recession from 2007 onwards triggered a reappraisal of Irizar's commitment to the contract signed by each business forming the Mondragón network. This was because the rules of the network are designed to give priority to workers who are full members of the businesses where they work, as opposed to being on temporary contracts as employees rather than members. Up to 20 per cent of a company's workforce can be non-members. If one company is doing well, and another is doing badly, the members of the one suffering a downturn will be passed on a temporary basis to work in the one that is doing well. If in the successful business there are temporary employees who are not yet members, that business will if necessary 'let go' their temporary workers in order to make way for the members of the other cooperative.

In the same geographical area as Irizar, a number of Mondragón cooperatives found themselves overstaffed because of the recession. This rule was now to be applied in Irizar: they would have to turn out employees on temporary contracts to make way for people who were members of the other businesses.

In Irizar, because of the importance of the high-performance culture, the recruitment process was always taken very seriously indeed: potential employees were vetted carefully for their attitudes and for their fit with the teams where they would work. The teams themselves did the recruiting. The people on temporary contracts had been selected through that process, and all were expected to become members in due course.

The same rigorous process could not be applied to the members being transferred in from the other cooperatives: Irizar would have to accept all the members, regardless of their attitudes or suitability for the culture. A great deal might be lost in terms of fit, attitudes, experience and the potential for the future. For this reason, Irizar refused to comply, rejecting the influx of members from the other cooperatives. This broke one of the fundamental tenets on which the network is built; as a consequence Irizar left the group. The decision was made at a general meeting of all the people working in the business. The hope on both sides, however, is that in time Irizar will return to being a member company of Mondragón.

This recent experience illustrates where power ultimately lies in Mondragón: with the individual member businesses, in each of which the sovereign body is the general assembly of all the members. This constitution is clear in placing 'hard' power in the hands of the shop floor members of each business – power that ultimately prevails. It is noticeable that this power has not been operated to take companies out of the group and sell them. There was one case of abuse: a cooperative in another part of Spain applied to join Mondragón, received a great deal of aid and support, then once it was functioning strongly took itself out of the system, so that the senior managers could sell the business. But that is not a typical story. Instead, the cooperatives choose to stay together in the group.

In the UK, some employee-owned companies have tried a different approach to corporate governance: their experiment has been to elect two directors from the employees to join the executive board. The UK board has a much more executive role than the supervisory boards widespread in continental Europe, or even than those of American companies, where it is unusual to have executives on the board, except for the CEO and perhaps the finance director. In general, when there are elected employee-directors on the board, communication tends to improve. It also tends to provide assurance that nothing is happening behind closed doors: employee representatives are present at all key decisions. However, the ability of the employee-directors to change the course of events in a crisis would be very limited, which means that the governance role is only weakly carried out. For the great majority of the time, the professional executive directors lead and the employee-directors of necessity listen. Because the employee-directors lack the experience and sometimes the education to play a full role in the regular meetings, they would find it hard to insist in the event of a showdown.

One response to this problem has been to separate the governance role from the board meeting itself. This involves having an elected body, separate from the board, but meeting with the board several times a year. In Tullis Russell, for example, a body of fourteen elected representatives meets with some or all of the directors four times a year, and twice a year separately with the non-executive directors alone. Having a larger number of elected people removes the understandable intimidation that characterises the position of a small number of elected people in a normal board meeting, and the fact that the purpose of the meeting is governance rather than strategic decision-making helps to ensure that the function is carried out. The CEO reports on the performance and plans of the company, reinforcing the recognition of accountability to the employee-owners, and there is an open agenda under which any question can be raised and discussed.

As identified previously, the big question in any governance system is: what if the CEO starts to abuse his or her power? Can the people with responsibility in the governance system recognise the abuse and then prevent it? Or, if it has already happened, can they deal with it rapidly so that the effects are minimised?

The existing governance structures in public corporations have shown that they cannot deal with it – the CEOs, rampant, are simply running away with the loot. However, there are enough examples of employee-owned companies in the US, the UK, Spain, Italy, France and Germany to give some hope that the problem can be better solved by the employees functioning as active citizens in a well-structured system.

There are also several examples where the governance systems in employee-owned companies have failed to control essentially self-interested behaviour in their leaders. It is not easy. But it can be done. The employee-owners certainly have a real incentive to do so. If they are to succeed, the constitution must set out to make it possible, by giving the power to the people who work in the company, and to their representatives; the people involved must be given the training, and finally, as in any system, they have to apply themselves actively to the task.

15

A Thousand and One Ways of Structuring Ownership

You can see a painting or play a computer game and enjoy it, without understanding the techniques by which it was created. But knowing about those techniques can add to the pleasure. Technicalities can be fun. Inevitably, in structuring ownership, there are technical ramifications. It is useful to have a general understanding of some of the main points.

Whether ownership is direct or indirect, in shares or in trust, or in any other of the myriad ways that people have invented to give employees their stakes, the good news is that we can transform the ownership of business gradually, piece by piece, company by company. We don't need to tear everything down and start from scratch: we simply need to use the strength of existing businesses to transfer them into the ownership of their employees. Eventually, no doubt, that will lead to better instruments of ownership, new inventions in how to embody it and better legislation. That, in turn, will lead to the transformation of the employment relationship itself.

But the process of change can start now. The people who can make in happen immediately are the people who own companies: they can simply decide to follow the example of John Spedan Lewis, and a great number of others since, by selling their company to an all-employee buyout. Employees can raise the idea with their employers. Journalists and advisers can bring themselves up to date; instead of remaining in thrall to the prejudices of the past, they can start to recommend employee-ownership as a way forward. Bankers can look at their loan books and ascertain – as the British bank Unity Trust did many years ago – that employee-owned companies are good clients: they survive better through bad times, and default at a lower rate than conventionally structured companies. We can all play a part in promoting this beneficial, exciting, transformative form of ownership, so good for the economy and for all the people involved.

FUNDING

There are two ways to fund employee ownership of companies. The first is achieved by the employees buying the company directly. Obvious benefits accrue where people make a personal investment. Arguably, they will care more about something they have paid for than about something that they have received free.

In Mondragón every person who becomes a member of the company where he or she works has to put in capital – at the time of writing some €14,000 each. This method is used in part because of Mondragón's particular history: all the businesses were started from scratch, without access to friendly capital. Even after they had set up the bank, the businesses really needed that capital injection from the employees. In the same country, many of the 'employee companies', or SALs, were set up through direct investment by the employees.

Elsewhere, in various ways, groups of employees have paid very significant amounts of money to win ownership of their companies.

In the US the pilots and machinists of United Airlines – helped by a big merchant bank – won control of 55 per cent of the company's shares in 1994 by agreeing to cost-reducing changes in working practices and pay valued at a total of nearly $5bn. And when Ford closed its Maumee Authority Stamping plant in September 2007, fifty employees each put in at least $16,000 to fund transfer into worker ownership.

In the UK the Thatcher government, after defeating the miners' union, closed all the deep coal mines. Two hundred miners at the Tower Colliery in Wales bought their mine by investing £8,000 each, mainly redundancy money, raising £1.93m – some of which came in the form of donations from local supporters. They also borrowed £1.5m. Subsequently they managed the coal mine successfully in employee ownership until the coal ran out twenty-two years later.

And in UBH, a plant manufacturing liquid transportation tanks, ninety-one blue-collar engineers invested £5,000 each – some using redundancy money, some personal borrowings – to buy the assets of the business, which they proceeded to make superbly successful.

It is clear, therefore, that one way of establishing employee ownership is personal investment by the employees.

The second way, however – the leveraged all-employee buyout – is more powerful. Most employees simply cannot afford to buy the companies where they work – but most companies can over time afford to pay for themselves. The reason why investors buy companies is because the companies eventually pay out more than the cost of buying them. It is possible to make use of this fact to fund the transfer of the ownership to the employees. It is, then, not necessary for employees to pay for ownership, except by working to make the company successful. The legacy of John Spedan Lewis and Louis Kelso shows how this can be done. In essence, the company borrows the money, pays the shareholders for their shares, and transfers the shares into some kind of holding mechanism on behalf of the employees: a trust or foundation, or an equivalent.

In the American ESOP, that trust is a pension fund. The pension fund borrows the money and the company guarantees to provide the funds to repay it. At first, when there is a high level of borrowing, the shares are held without being allocated to the individuals. As the borrowings are repaid, the shares are gradually allocated into the pension accounts of each individual employee. The more rapidly the company repays the borrowings, the more rapidly the value of the individual pension accounts rises. This gives a direct link between company performance and the personal wealth of all the employees involved. This is a hybrid system combining trust ownership and individual ownership: it starts with a company-funded trust and ends with the shares allocated out into each person's pension account.

In the UK, the trust is usually an Employee Benefit Trust. The shares do not have to be passed out to the individuals, except in the case of a highly restricted form of trust, a Share Incentive Plan or SIP. At the time of writing, the restrictions placed on this trust allow it to be used only to a small extent in employee buyouts.[70]

Normally a company is quite properly prevented from providing finance to fund the purchase of its own shares; otherwise companies could create unreal demand for them and in so doing keep the share price artificially high. But for these employee schemes the provision of finance is permitted.

REPURCHASE LIABILITY

The British companies with really long-lasting employee ownership, such as John Lewis (eighty years), Scott Bader (sixty years) and Arup (forty years), all have their shares permanently in trust, not allocated out to individuals. This means that those shares never have to be sold again.

In the US, the system is different: all the shares are eventually passed into individual ownership. Whether the shares are owned by the individual employees in the first place, or are passed into their hands over time, each individual owner will eventually want to sell his or her shares – to cash in the capital stake that has been built up. (In the case of the US ESOP, that happens only when the person leaves or retires.) Unless the employees want to see their ownership transferred to outsiders, these shares will have to be bought back by the employee ownership system; since the employees will not usually have enough cash, the company will have to provide funding to buy back those shares. This 'repurchase liability' can mean that in effect the company has to fund another complete buyout in each working generation. That is a high financial burden – and, since the share value rises with success, the more successful the company, the higher the burden becomes.

In the case of National Freight Corporation (NFC), where over 90 per cent of the shares were in the direct ownership of individuals, and where the company's performance was spectacularly good – driven in large part by that ownership – there was eventually no way to fund the repurchase of the employee shares. To solve that problem NFC floated its shares on the Stock Exchange, allowing the shares to be bought by outsiders. As the proportion held by employees fell, and as the pressure from the outside shareholders rose, the management approach changed back from participative to top-down. The psychology of ownership was lost, performance spiralled downwards, and eventually the company was taken over by a foreign competitor. In the US quite a number of ESOPs have ended in similar fashion. One solution for a company that wants to perpetuate ownership by its employees is to build up a cash fund over the years, eventually buying back the shares, rather than leaving the funding to the vagaries of the future.

Trust ownership is indirect: the shares are held by trustees on behalf of the employees, rather than the employees holding the shares directly. This means that the task of creating a genuine feeling of ownership is perhaps a little bit harder than if each person has a share certificate – legal proof of direct personal ownership. However, since a great part of the real feeling of ownership depends on how people are treated and how they learn to behave, with the actual ownership essentially a background factor, this is not as great a problem as it might appear. The evidence from John Lewis, Arup and Scott Bader, all owned wholly through trusts and all outstandingly successful over many decades, shows that indirect ownership does work psychologically, as it also works supremely well in promoting long-term sustainability.

We have seen that both in Arup and in John Lewis there are people who have the specific role of maintaining the spirit and vision of the shared ownership – in John Lewis the Registry, and in Arup the Trustees, who include among them people who have retired from executive work, but who are steeped in the vision and the practical ways of implementing it. In Mondragón, the people working at the group level, whose only power is the power of persuasion, also play that role.

However, if employees are *not* owners – not even indirectly, through trusts – then you cannot achieve the ownership effect by tricking them into feeling as if they are. There is good evidence that ownership itself is a vital part of the equation – ownership may be indirect, but it must be real.[71]

A group of UK companies, having understood these lessons, have used a hybrid solution: they have placed a significant block in trust, but less than 100 per cent. The larger that block, the more fully it addresses this problem of the repurchase liability, because those shares never have to be sold again. The rest of the shares, usually less than 50 per cent, can then be owned by the employees individually. They have chosen this solution in order to gain on the one hand the benefit of stable employee ownership through the trust holding – indirect employee ownership – and on the other the benefit of the direct psychological connection formed between the individual and the company when each employee has a personal stake. The system was first used by Philip Baxendale in 1983, and there is now a long list of such companies: Tullis Russell, Woollard and Henry, UBH International, Loch Fyne Oysters, Highland Home Carers, Stewartry Care, g3 and an ever-growing number following the same route. Many of them have been funded and advised by the Baxi Partnership, itself an employee-owned company, which runs both a £20m fund aiming at facilitating employee buyouts in the UK and a consultancy arm focused on helping employee-owned companies anywhere develop a true partnership culture.*

CONSEQUENCES

Employee-owners share the fruits of success. They also suffer the consequences of failure. This is no bad thing.

In Mondragón, when new members invest their money to buy their stakes, they instantly lose 20 per cent of their investment, which goes into the general reserves of the company. They receive interest of 7.5 per cent on the remainder, paid annually in cash, and in addition an allocation from the annual profit, which is added to the capital value of each member's account. In a successful business each person can build up over the years a considerable block of capital. If the business is unsuccessful then part of any loss is also attributed to the capital accounts of the members. In this way their personal wealth is directly connected with the fortunes of the business.

In the case of an ESOP, or if the shares are owned directly by the employees without using a trust, the value of the capital stake varies in a similar way: if the business does badly, the share price falls,

---

* I have worked in various capacities in Baxi Partnership since 1987, at first as a trustee, then as chairman, then director and at the time of writing non-executive director. As executive director from 2001 to 2007 I led its rebirth into its current form, with the mission of structuring and funding all-employee buyouts, and providing new employee-owners, including managers, with the understanding and skills required. See http://www.baxipartnership.co.uk/

lowering the value of each person's holding. If the business does well, the share price rises and each person becomes more wealthy. Again, there is a direct link between the fortunes of the business and the personal wealth of the employee.

Capital ownership by employees involves the possibility of gain and the possibility of loss; people share in the benefits of the success they obtain, and they suffer the consequences of any failure. This direct connection with the results of their joint actions is sometimes characterised purely in terms of risk, but it is much more than that: it is also reward. Furthermore it stimulates people to learn, to understand how things work, and to get stuck in, to make a difference. This is pure net gain for the employee where, as in the case of an ESOP or a leveraged employee buyout, it is by making the company successful that the employees 'pay' for the shares: it is the company (not the employee) that finances the transfer of ownership. Although this method does not require the investment of employees' savings, there is still a direct link between performance and personal wealth. If in year one there is a profit, which is allocated to the account of each individual, a loss in year two will then reduce the value of each person's holding. Another profit will increase the value again. This is the healthy dynamic that gives capitalism much of its positive creative power. But here it is applied to all, not just the privileged few.

Where the individuals have to pay for their shares out of personal savings or borrowings, those funds are put at risk. Where the company finances the transfer, the employees seem to receive the ownership for nothing, but in practice they have to make the company successful if they are to benefit. Payment is made through achieving company success.

When the ownership is 100 per cent in a permanent trust, as in Arup and John Lewis, success is shared with all the employees through profit-sharing, and there is no financial risk for the employees.

REINVESTMENT

If the employees do not own any shares personally, then there is in theory a conflict of interest between paying out profits and reinvesting profits. To the extent that the shares are held permanently in trust, any profit reinvested in the business is lost to the employees – they benefit during their working lives by the strengthening of their company, but they take nothing with them when they leave; they do not personally share in any of the capital invested. As we have seen, economists predict that employees will therefore never want to reinvest any profit, instead paying it all out to themselves. And as we have also seen, they are wrong. Nonetheless it is a reality that, for example, when John Lewis funds the building of a new department store, it uses profits that could otherwise be paid out to the partners. Once the money is invested, it cannot be paid out. Why then do John Lewis and similarly structured companies, like Arup (which has grown fast and consistently for decades through reinvesting, without ever having to borrow), reinvest their profits?

The answer seems to lie in the commitment of the people as human beings to their company and to future generations. They want to keep the company strong for their own sakes and they want to pass it on strong to the next generation. They are people with the privilege of making themselves wealthier than their employee equivalents in similar companies. They want to give the same good fortune to those who come after them. They have human aspirations which include elements of conscience and of generosity: they are much more than the immediate-money-grubbing automata of economists' models.

The Mondragón solution to this reinvestment problem has twice been invented independently – in the 1950s by the Mondragón cooperatives in Spain and in the 1970s by David Ellerman and his colleagues in the Industrial Cooperative Association in Cambridge, Massachusetts. This solution is the individual capital account. In some ways it is the best formula yet found.

We have seen that each Mondragón member invests nearly a year's salary in the business. That money is not given in exchange for shares: it is put into the member's capital account. The employee-owner-member used to be given a booklet in which the value of the account was tracked; now the tracking is done electronically. This account is as clear a proof of individual 'ownership' as a share certificate, but easier to understand, because like a bank statement it is expressed in terms of its current monetary value. The capital sum is increased every year by a distribution of profit (or reduced by a distribution from any loss), and it receives a cash yield through the interest payments

at the rate of 7.5 per cent. The capital can be withdrawn when the
person leaves the company or retires. Unlike a share, it does not carry
governance rights that can be traded, nor any right to the wealth that
will be created by future generations in the same company. The right
to vote, to participate in general meetings, and to appoint and dismiss
the general manager are rights that are held by each member as
personal rights. They cannot be sold. Even if the current generation
builds up the capacity of the company enormously, so that it is clear
that huge profits will be produced in future, they cannot appropriate
the value of those future profits as a financial payment. In this respect
the capital accounts are distinct from shares – shares in a company in
that position would rise dramatically in value, because they carry the
right to *future* profit. With capital accounts the value of future profits
is left to the people whose work will make it real, as autonomous
members in the future. They will be lucky. But so are today's
employees, who have inherited a successful business and will share in
building it further, in charge of their own destiny.

There is room here for innovation. The individual capital account
seems like an excellent solution, but no doubt it can be fine-tuned
and improved.

The fact that the US ESOP solution uses a pension fund can allow
problems to develop. The essence of employee ownership lies in asso-
ciating each individual employee with the rewards and the risks of
the specific enterprise in which he or she works. The rewards can be
great, but the risks are real: that is part of the reason why ownership
has such an energising effect on the owners. There is a direct connection between the individual and the ups and downs of the business.
But this direct connection with the vagaries of a business is in some
ways the opposite of what most people want in their long-term savings
aimed at funding retirement. It is right that pensions are generally
invested to spread risk, to diversify away as much risk as possible.
There is thus a contradiction between the pension's need for security
and the employee's need for direct connection with the specific
company.

In practice, and in most cases, this is much less of a problem than it
appears to be. There is sound evidence that companies with ESOPs
generally also have diversified pension fund investments: the ESOP is a
net addition to the wealth of employees, not a substitute for more secure

pension investment.[72] However, the risk is there, and employee pensions can suffer at the hands of ruthless individuals, as happened in Enron.

In the UK the Employee Benefit Trust also has its problems. Its design harks back to the time of the Crusades, when a wealthy landowner about to go to fight in the Holy Land would appoint a trusted individual to look after his estate in his absence. With that history, very wide discretion is given to the trustees over what they can do with the shares, and that discretion cannot be constrained significantly. This means that even principles of fairness can only with great difficulty be written into a trust deed: the interpretation will always be left to the trustees at the time. Trustees can select even a single employee to receive a benefit from the trust. In England, but not Scotland, there is also a problem with perpetuity: at the time of writing no trust is allowed to last longer than eighty years. At the end of that term the assets in the trust must be distributed to the beneficiaries. If that provision had applied to the John Lewis trust, which has existed for eighty-one years, the distribution of the assets would have occurred in 2009. However, that trust used a quaint variation of the perpetuity rule, also dating back to the era of the Crusades: the trust was set up to last until twenty-one years after the death of the last survivor of the descendants then living of the British monarch at the time – King George V. This means that twenty-one years after the death of the Queen or, if the seventh Earl of Harewood lives longer, twenty-one years after his death, the trust will have to be wound up. Fortunately, the lawyers involved believe that they have found a solution to continuing employee ownership, which has been crucial to the company's spectacularly outperforming its rivals.

In 2000 the Baxi Partnership went so far as to obtain the passing of its own Act of Parliament, in part to get round the perpetuity rule. Under the Act this trust, which holds the majority of the company's shares on behalf of its employees, will last as long as the company lasts. In the opinion of the legal officer in Parliament who supervised the passing of this Act, there was a gap in UK legislation: what Philip Baxendale was setting out to achieve – long-lasting employee ownership of his company – was so beneficial that it ought to be facilitated by law. Unfortunately, he was on the point of retirement and so was unable to pursue the question of implementing a general improvement in the law, to facilitate sustainable employee ownership.

Essentially, what this discussion of US ESOPs and UK trusts shows is that currently the methods employed to establish employee ownership have evolved – been cobbled together – using legal mechanisms that were originally formulated for other purposes. The nearest thing to a good solution is the capital account originally developed by the Mondragón cooperatives – which are acknowledged in the tax laws. The future may well see the spread of such a mechanism, suitably developed. It would also need to be protected from the punitive taxation rules currently applied in the US, the UK and probably elsewhere.

16

Culture

In the end, the ownership way of doing things becomes natural, second nature, normal. The employees are the owners, have the rights of owners, take the responsibilities of owners. The managers keep them informed, listen to them, involve them, challenge them, give a lead – help them perform to their best. At the end of the year, some of the directors stand in front of the employee-owners and put themselves forward for re-election.

However, it usually takes years for this to become normality. The old ways linger in the shadows, ready to rear their unproductive heads and slow things down or even reverse the progress that has been made. But with time the great happiness of working together, productively, to make *our* business successful, brings energy and even joy to the working day.

The power of ownership can be hard to credit when it is seen in action. Even those who believe that it can be done, and should be done, can be quite overcome when they meet it in practice.

Fred Freundlich, in Mondragón, tells the story of how he hosted a visit from a number of Canadians, experts in and enthusiasts for cooperatives, but coming from an environment where cooperatives were few in number and only a proportion of them were worker-owned. After seeing the Mondragón audiovisual presentation given to all visitors, being escorted round a business and having a number of discussions with members of cooperatives, one or two of the Canadians still could not quite believe that they were being shown the truth. Surely there must be a more disappointing reality behind the rosy glow? Aren't these people perhaps management stooges, chosen from an enthusiastic minority, and not telling the whole truth? In the evening they were walking across a square in town, on their way to have dinner. One of the visitors, seeing a young man coming towards them, stopped him and, with Freundlich's help, interrogated him. They were surprised and delighted to find that this man, chosen at random, was employed in a worker-cooperative; he described his job; and then with some trepidation the Canadians put the key questions:

'You all vote for the board of directors?'

'Yes.'

'It's one person, one vote in the general assembly?'

'Yes.'

'And you divide up the profits at the end of the year?'

'Yes.'

One of the Canadians, unable to contain himself, burst out with: 'Isn't that *amazing*?'

And the young man, with a puzzled shrug, replied, 'No . . . no. All the companies round here are like that.'

In Massachusetts, in the woodlands some distance south of Boston, there is a company, Litecontrol, that manufactures and sells lighting fixtures for office blocks and other workplaces. I was taken to visit this factory by Chris Mackin, an adviser to employee-owned companies and to the unions, and a member of the teaching faculty on the Harvard Trade Union Program. He has worked for decades to help establish and make a success of employee ownership in many companies, often working with the unions to do so. His motivation centres on the human growth that can take place.

'I'm interested in the human development, the effect on personality, the way employee ownership can build healthy non-intimidated human beings, people who have a place to stand, from where they can deal with the frictions and fears and roiling emotions that arise in hierarchical social life. A democratic firm properly structured has the best chance of being a community of equals, but only if you really understand power in organisations and the challenge of the relatively unpowerful and the less educated. Many of them, when confronting their superiors and betters, will fall back on just telling the boss to fuck off. But in a democratic firm you can create a culture where the less powerful can feel unintimidated and open.'

One of his key experiences was a negative one, in the United Airlines buyout in 1994. He worked with the unions and managers to try to make the most of the 55% ownership stake that the pilots and machinists unions had won through making concessions. Even though the unions had selected a new company CEO, Gerald Greenwald, as part of the deal, it was evident that resistance in senior management ranks to the idea of employee ownership was widespread. Soon after the historic ownership agreement had been negotiated, the unions voted in new leadership with different philosophical priorities. This combination of resistance from key sectors of management and a newly ambivalent union leadership proved fatal to the opportunity to create a committed ownership culture.

Some years later, Litecontrol proved more fertile ground. Veda Clark, the chief executive, is a friendly, professional woman who has worked there for over twenty years. She came into the company from a job as a consultant on Wall Street, helping to develop mutual funds for institutional investors. 'I wanted the feeling that I was helping along something worthwhile. I wanted to be contributing more. But Wall Street was all about the money, not the people, or building anything. I knew I didn't want *that!*' And she laughs ruefully.

Bob Danforth, the owner of Litecontrol, finding that none of his four daughters wanted to come into the business, recruited Veda as his potential successor. Gradually he developed a determination to sell the company to its employees. He used an ESOP, to ensure that it was the company, not the employees, paying for the ownership to be transferred into their hands. Veda was enchanted by the idea: it just felt naturally right – as it does for most people of any age in every country – and she was keen to make the most of it.

The first tranche of about a third of the shares was bought by the ESOP in 1999, with a plan to complete the $25m buyout by 2013. In fact under Veda's leadership – and with ever-improving understanding and commitment from the employee-owners – the performance climbed and climbed, allowing the completion of the buyout six years early, in 2007.

Employee-owners are very different from shareholders on the Stock Exchange. Wall Street traders like to talk about having skin in the game, but their skin is only in the form of money, and it can often be taken out of the game in an instant. Employee-owners cannot do that: their skin and their bones are unavoidably in the game. They are deeply entwined with the business, they spend a very large proportion of their waking hours in it, and of all the potential stakeholders, employee-owners have the most to gain by making the company successful, as well as the most to lose if it fails. Even without ownership, they are committed in the sense that their working lives are bound up with the company. The tragedy of the normal top-down system is that this de facto commitment is generally not recognised; instead of being treated as partners in the business, employees are treated as servants of little or no importance, or even as quasi-outsiders, not to be trusted, simply to be manipulated and controlled through their employment contracts, through supervision and surveillance, and through more or less manipulative PR.

As in most employee buyouts, the changes that were necessary in Litecontrol took time and hard work to achieve. And as in most such buyouts, it was the people at supervisor level who found it most difficult to trust and support the new participative way of running the company. To illustrate this at a practical level, here is a snippet from a rapid-fire conversation among a number of employees who are active on the Ownership Improvement Committee or OIC, one of the new governance bodies.

Paula, from sales: 'There was a lot of cynicism about the employee ownership, and it was coming from the supervisors. They weren't buying into the whole idea.'

Shaun, from the receiving department: 'They would directly contradict what we were trying to do. They would say openly, "It is a wa-a-aste of ti-i-ime" (he emphasises the insultingly drawn-out delivery).

Chris Mackin: 'So Veda told me to suit up and go into a room with these people.'

Shaun: 'Chris wore a helmet . . .'

Greg, from sales: '. . . and carried a whip.'

Paula: 'Chris spent a half day with them and the managers, talking about the message that we need to give out. And that really made a difference. The insidious stuff stopped.'

Me: 'And do you think they get it now?'

Paula: 'They really do.'

Chris Mackin: 'The reason they get it now is not just that meeting, it's because you guys have some skills and know what you're talking about.'

Brian, from new-product development: 'And they see us making it work.'

These employee-owners recognise that, after some ten years working at it, they are still in the early stages of developing an active ownership culture and effective governance structures. They were starting from behind. The old paternalistic approach – which had eventually resulted in the transfer of ownership to the employees (a very positive thing), but without involving them in the decision (not a good start to their lives as responsible owners) – had generated over the years before the buyout a feeling that everyone would be looked after, that they were entitled to their jobs and to bonuses, regardless of how the business was doing. No information was made available: not even the senior managers saw the figures. People without information are simply not in a good position to improve how things are done. It is a passive life – doing your job, carrying out the instructions of the supervisors, being paid and going home. Brian summarised the effect: 'You come in, do your job, and somebody else makes the money. You have a salary and that's it, that's what you get paid. If you do better, well, you might get a raise. But now, the better we all do, the more goes straight to *our* bottom line.'

At the beginning, in 1999, few people believed that last sentence. Faced with this situation, supported strongly by Veda and with Mackin's guidance, the committee responded by handing out information. Everyone gets the figures now, every month, with a major review every quarter led by Veda. As mentioned before, she opens each meeting by saying, 'I'm the president of the company. I work for the 200-some people that work here.'

And the relationships are changing. In the middle of the 2009 recession Paula was walking behind Veda as the factory people were coming out towards them. A woman from the factory stopped the CEO and asked how they were doing.

'Fine,' said Veda.

'No, I mean how are we *really* doing,' said the employee-owner. And she insisted that Veda give her numbers.

The other members of the committee joined in with comments:

'They care not only about their jobs, but what it means in terms of revenue.'

'And they're not scared to talk to Veda. They call the CEO by her first name.'

From someone who works in the factory: 'You don't just skulk off down the hallway . . .' (and, to laughter, he mimes a skulking employee).

'The quick answer wasn't enough – she wanted the whole story.'

'I can't even imagine doing that to the CEO in my old company. It'd be like "Howdy!" and I'd just keep walking.' He imitates a stiff, awkward walk. 'And if I ever did manage to ask him the question and he said, "Fine", then that would be it. I'd just keep walking.'

'He would say, "My door is always open."'

'Only he wouldn't mean it.' Loud laughter.

Actually, that CEO might feel that he means it. But he probably has no appreciation of what it would take in courage for an ordinary worker to come into the office, let alone go to the top floor, brave the CEO's personal assistant, and knock on the door. It wouldn't happen. It doesn't happen. The 'my door is always open' line is like the 'market forces' line: it is simply unreal, part of the ideological fantasy that justifies the current system of ownership and control. What is really pulling the strings is the power that runs down the hierarchy.

With employee ownership, that top-down power is closed into a circle, a feedback loop: the CEO, who during the year has the responsibility and authority to run the company, is accountable at the end of the year to the owners, the employees. It is thus in the interests of that CEO to make sure from month to month that the employee-owners understand what is going on, and why decisions are made. The incentive structure has changed. The CEO has just as much autonomy as before, has the same right to manage and the duty to manage. But instead of being able to use PR to bury the bodies and to persuade ignorant shareholders that all is well, the CEO is visible all the time to the owners, who know him or her personally. Better to come clean and invite people to get involved. It means being more humble and more honest. And it means listening.

The first Litecontrol committee, back in 1999, worked on ways of getting everyone involved, now that they were owners. Given the history, there was a slow start, but over the years, with hard work and in fits and starts, they have made progress. The method they chose was the approach known as 'Lean Manufacturing', an accumulation of improvement techniques developed mainly by the Japanese automobile manufacturer Toyota. By 2009 pretty well every single employee had been trained in methods for identifying problems and solving them. This spread the feeling that they really were owners – or for some just that they really might be (which was still progress). A few could not yet quite bring themselves to suspect the best. But the out-and-out sceptics were pretty well silenced.

The most difficult question is how they would respond if the CEO went bad, either failing strategically or abusing her power. The Ownership Improvement Committee members are realistic: 'We don't have an official process set up; we're just starting to figure this out and put some structure to it. At the moment we would be able to go to Veda and say, "Look, we think we're on the wrong track and here's what everybody is saying . . . "'

This, of course, is not yet secure governance. But the potential inherent in this development carries infinitely more promise than the bankrupt pretence that non-executive directors will genuinely stop CEOs from cashing in on their power. To the democratic purist, this is still a long way from democratic governance, from genuine accountability to the employee-owners. But there is great good faith on all sides, and a genuine wish to get things right, including the design of the governance structures.

In some ways the desire to ensure good progress has meant postponing the implementation of democracy, to give time to develop an effective method. Before the committee was established, very few people would have stood in an election to join it. So Veda tapped on the shoulder people recognised as movers and shakers among the employees. They have already been through a learning process: the first committee was beginning to drift into organising social activities, but some members felt that this would detract from the seriousness of the question of ownership. They passed the social activities to another group, made up of fun people, so that the OIC could concentrate on the serious business of ownership and making their company succeed. Now that the committee has visibly brought about an open culture and real participation in improving how things are done, they believe that a normal democratic election may bring forward good people. Their goal is to move to elections in the near future.

These people are committed to building their business, to solving all its problems. These are the people who will, together, expand the economy and have a good chance of making corporate governance work. They are employee-owners.

One big difference between an ownership culture and a traditional, top-down culture is the attitude to training. For traditional companies training is often seen primarily as a cost. Moreover, it is a cost that has no sure return, because the employee who is trained may not be very committed to the company: he or she may simply be taking the opportunity, at company expense, to improve his or her CV.

In a company owned by its employees, it is simply self-evident that if someone wants to develop a useful skill and is capable of doing so, the opportunity should be provided.

We have seen how the paper-coating company in England, when the improvements in efficiency meant that people were underemployed, instead of reducing the number of people through layoffs decided to train every single employee in the techniques of lean manufacturing – the same system used by the employee-owners of Litecontrol. Over time, as people retire or leave, the number of people employed will reduce, but without destroying the trust and confidence that is inherent in a well-functioning ownership culture.

We have also seen how the managers in John Lewis operate with a wide range of people-oriented behavioural targets, as well as the normal business targets addressing sales, operations and finance. In this area too there is the opportunity to deepen the understanding and improve the skills of everyone involved.

Some companies go further than others. In Parametrix, an environmental engineering company headquartered in Oregon, the nearly 600 employee-owners have moved away from thinking in terms of the rights of owners to an approach that recognises each employee-owner primarily as a human being. An important step on the way was an intensive week-long training course. When I talked to her in April 2009, Darlene Brown, the chief financial officer, put it like this:

'We'd gone through some yuk stuff in the industry and we'd had to shut part of the company. There was a lack of trust between employees and management. We were struggling with the rights and responsibilities of employee-owners: "What are my rights? What do I get to vote on? What do I get involved in?" We decided to change the discussion to: "How do we interact with our fellow employee-owners as people?" The aim was that Darlene Brown, the CFO, could interact with anybody – it was just Darlene and whoever: "You be up front with me and I'll be up front with you." I believe the course changed our company, because it broke that mistrust. We took seventy people through it in the first year. They said, "Hey, we don't trust you!" and the managers said, "Yeah, we understand you don't trust us. Let's talk about this. How did we lose that trust? Help us to earn it back!" Our CEO at the time, now retired, joined in.'

The course was evidently quite a rich brew.

'This class is like no other I've ever been in. It's the heart of leadership, how we communicate with people and respect them. With complete confidentiality people bare their souls in a class of thirty people, and it just changes how they feel about their fellow employee-owners. I was in a class with some of my direct reports, the receptionist, and some from other departments. We went through it for seven days, and we've had over 300 employees go through it.'

The managers have discovered a useful pointer that highlights how well they are walking their talk. 'When trust slips or is lost between management and employees, the question of rights surfaces again.'

No matter how useful a course is, however, a culture is built and shaped over periods of years, not weeks or months. It is shaped at every moment by the actions of every person in the company. Over time Mackin's dream, harking back to the ideals of the Founding Fathers, can be realised: a community of equals, of healthy, non-intimidated, open human beings.

We have seen that sound constitutions are essential; and also that they depend for success on the active participation of those involved. It is the culture that encourages everyone to participate actively, to be brave and confident in dealing with the many issues that inevitably arise when they are dealing with people and with wealth. It is possible, by doing these things well, to achieve something rarely dreamt of under the current system: a combination of excellent economic performance and superb personal fulfilment, not just for the few but for all involved. Mondragón has adopted the tag-line 'Humanity at

Work' to express its vision. By bringing into the corporation the insights and values that are already the foundation of democratic politics, we can transform our working lives, transfigure the corporation and let humanity work.

PART FOUR

HUMANITY FLOURISHING

More equal societies work better for everyone.
Richard Wilkinson and Kate Pickett, 2009

17

Hunters and Gatherers
Go to Market

ECONOMIC MAN

In thinking through economics and the design and operation of our businesses, we need to recognise more fully the complexity of human nature. It is unhelpful to use an impoverished caricature of what it means to be human: we can hope to make progress only if our models come closer to reflecting reality. Traditional economics, driven by the need to fit the target of 'scientific' mathematical model-building, has operated with one such caricature – so-called 'economic man'. By this hypothesis, human nature is driven by a psychotic focus on marginal self-interest: if we can make a few pennies by doing something we will do it, regardless of considerations of fairness, or commitment, or integrity.

In this book we have seen that the thinking based on this attenuated picture of human nature is incapable even of recognising the very simple reality before our eyes: that compared with how corporations operate today, shared enterprise makes us richer and happier. This fact should be trumpeted from the rooftops.

However, many obstacles stand in the way. Most pernicious is the pretence that the impersonal Market, rather than the exercise of power by our leaders, is shaping the world around us. According to this ideology, it is the Market that relieves us of the wealth that we create together, whereas actually it is a legal system shaped over two centuries by the people in power, precisely to give them the right to extract that wealth and maintain that power for themselves. It is worth recalling Lord Wensleydale, the judge who in 1830 reminded his fellow judges that they could execute protesters reacting against the squeezing of wages down to starvation levels: 'If that law ceases to be administered with due firmness . . . our wealth and power will soon be at an end.'

He was not talking about the wealth of the human race, but of the landowning aristocracy that dominated Parliament and the judiciary. Today the equivalent is often to be found in the City of London or on Wall Street. However, the ideology of today, refined over the nearly two centuries since, has it that the wealth of the whole human race is under threat if we point out that the invisible hand/Market ideology has no clothes, and that the Market's puppet-masters are simply people in power backed up by a legal system that they and their forebears have designed.

According to the prevailing theory, just as in the time of Lord Wensleydale, it is the Market that increasingly drives wages to poverty levels. And if the Market does it, then it must be right. It is not that for centuries the wage-earners have been deprived by the powerful of their right to participate in the wealth they help create. No, it is the Market, whose invisible hand forever guides us to the best of all possible outcomes and justifies irrefutably the way things are – on the one hand the enormous wealth of the chief executives and financiers, as well as funding for academic tenure for their servant economists, and on the other people who work full-time and don't earn enough to buy groceries if they are forced by illness to have a day off.

In the 2008–9 banking collapse we saw the end result of that approach. Greed, deception, utter irresponsibility and blinkered self-centredness ended in the destruction of so many jobs, ruining the futures of so many youngsters and the livelihoods of so many people round the world.

However, it is not simply the *consequences* of that approach that should give us pause. It is the fact that the *thinking itself* is inadequate. A distorted picture of human nature is at the root of it. If we believe that we are selfish *and nothing else*, and if we invent the idea of an all-powerful invisible hand to relieve us of any responsibility for the consequences of our actions, then we are free to use all our talents ruthlessly to get rich. We should simply exploit the legal structures that we inherit, and use them to our personal advantage, regardless of the consequences. If we run up against others who stand in our way, then we are justified in using whatever means we can to push them aside. If the workers object to having their rights removed, then although in most countries we are not able to execute them any more, we do have every right to use all possible means to defeat them. For we represent the Market at work. And the Market tells us to use our power to take from the employees all that we can. Employees have no rights; they are not the Market-appointed winners – we are. The Market like a machine gun sweeps them aside, and we, the leaders, must wield it. Otherwise we will all end up poorer.

There are two main flaws in this approach. Firstly, the legal system is not the Market: it is a system of power that deprives the employees of their autonomy and hands control to the 'owners'. In denying the worker a stake in what he or she helps create the law relies on a conception of rights that is without any firm basis in reason or nature. Secondly, to the extent that a market is operating, there is no guiding invisible hand which relieves us of our responsibility to think about the consequences of what we do, and to shape them so that we make things better rather than worse. For example, Goldman Sachs, the most successful investment bank on Wall Street, sold derivatives designed to help the Greek government disguise the scale of its borrowings. At the time the transaction was legal. At the same time, knowing because of their involvement that the debt of Greece was publicly understated, people in Goldman Sachs effectively shorted Greek debt. That was ostensibly a normal risk-covering transaction. But in the case of massive transactions there is a complication: such bets may *shape* the market – they can make the situation worse by triggering a run against a company or country, which can make default more likely. This therefore placed at risk the interests of Goldman Sachs's client, the Greek government, but worked in the interests of the bank itself. In theory all banks have a fiduciary duty to work in the interest of their clients, but when the Market ideology operates it is not clear that your bankers will feel they have to act in your interests. In Senate hearings held in April 2010 on the role of Wall Street in the mortgage securities debacle, Senator Susan Collins asked of Daniel Sparks, formerly a top manager in Goldman Sachs: 'Do you have a duty to act in the best interests of your clients?' In response there was a significant hesitation before Sparks avoided saying yes, to the audible shock of many listening. 'I believe we have a duty to serve our clients well,' he eventually replied.

To this ideology morality is not seen as a strong constraint, partly because the invisible hand will make everything all right. But should the fact that market transactions are involved justify irresponsibility? 'We have a situation in which major financial institutions are amplifying a public crisis for what would appear to be private gain,' said the chairman of the banking committee, Senator Christopher Dodd, in February 2010.[73] The consequences of this transaction were severe: they helped bring Europe and the euro closer to financial meltdown. It would be argued that such actions were justified on the basis that it was the Market at work. But the fact that Market transactions were involved justifies nothing.

It is true that when we operate in a broadly competitive market, with transparent information, regulated to ensure honest behaviour and with a balance of power between many competitors in that market, then generally good things follow – much better than the alternative of control and direction by authorities. Under those conditions, markets do work. Unfortunately those conditions are often absent. And the ideology built on the recognition of markets is generalised to justify a system of corporate power that has nothing to do with markets: it is about power in the hands of a few people over the many.

What have the bankers done with their political influence? When their hubris destroyed their businesses, to avoid suffering the consequences they pressured and frightened the politicians into giving them truly gargantuan sums of taxpayers' cash – which they would have fought hard against being done for any other business. The governments did this by buying huge quantities of debt – transactions that were mightily profitable for the banks. So they paid themselves huge bonuses. What of the non-banking people and businesses who, due to the crisis, need support? To hell with them. Let the banks bankrupt them and repossess their homes. It's the market at work.

IN ALL OUR GLORIOUS COMPLEXITY

Human nature is far more complex than the caricature of economic man allows.

Yes, we are self-interested, and it is a good thing we are. If we were not driven to look after our own interests, then we would end up in a very bad way indeed: filthy and starving and quite useless to those around us. We must look after ourselves or others will have to look after us – as if we were forever children.

But we are not purely selfish. We are not crazedly selfish. We have fellow feelings. Even in dealing with strangers, we are sensitive to fairness and to unfairness. We can see when someone is being abused and we react against that – especially when it is someone that we care about – unless we have been so inoculated by ideology that we feel we should suppress this natural response.

As mentioned before, the economist Robert Frank and his colleagues investigated the effect over time of studying the traditional economic model.[74] They showed that first-year students of economics give the same amounts to charity as do first-year students of astronomy. But final-year economics students give significantly less than final-year astronomy students. It is not that studying the stars encourages generosity, but that studying economics involves being told month after month that you are nothing but a self-interested automaton, with the implication that it is stupid to behave generously. This ends up making you less inclined to act on the essentially moral and generous impulses that we all share, and that you did in fact act on only three or four years earlier.* We have all been subjected to the ideas of the Market model, remorselessly and continuously, for almost all our lives. Somewhere in our schooling the ideas that we should share and cooperate and be good and responsible citizens are morphed into the notion that 'really' we are all selfish and it is right to be selfish and we have to compete against each other ruthlessly and the Market will make it come out all right.

When we recognise that we are not only capable of sharing, but that sharing satisfies something deep within our nature, then the framework changes, and we are enabled to perceive at last the facts of employee-owned companies, their economic success and the happiness that they provide for their partner-employee-owner members.

Michael Jensen of the Harvard Business School, for a whole lifetime a great theoretician of the capital market, and joint author of the academic paper that has done so much to block the recognition that employee-owned companies perform well, has acknowledged late in life that there is more to it than he thought. It is not quite an Alan Greenspan 'there is a flaw' moment, but it is close. He now recognises that there is 'a hidden yet critical factor of production – equivalent in importance to labor, capital, technology, knowledge,

---

* It is worth adding that the shift was statistically significant, but that many economics students still gave generously. That is the point, really: the model does not capture the reality of our nature, just twists it against the grain.

and strategy and one that is invisible to economists and to most businesses.'[75]

This unrecognised factor is integrity. Integrity in his model is a unity or wholeness: the term is used in a descriptive rather than in a moral sense. For a person, it is achieved by honouring one's word.

In my own view, applying that concept to the corporation, it is self-evident that the conventional corporation cannot have integrity – cannot be a unified whole – because the leaders are required to manipulate the employees to perform, without treating them as partners in the enterprise. In view of this recent work by Jensen, there is some hope that he will eventually come to withdraw his earlier predictions of poor performance by employee-owned companies. Those predictions were extended to include simply nightmare fantasies. For example, the German corporate system, which had a supervisory board made up in part by representatives of the shareholders and in part by representatives of the employees, would inevitably end with 'fairly complete, if not total, state ownership of the productive assets in the economy.'[76]

During the thirty years following the publication of that paper, this prediction, like the predictions about employee-owned companies, has proved untrue. In contrast, the banks in capital-market-dominated America and Britain *have* ended up depending on government support and partial state ownership. There could have been no more dramatic contradiction of capital market theory than the necessary rescue of the banks by governments in 2008-9. Jensen was wrong to say that employee ownership would not work well. He is right to identify the role of integrity – which employee ownership tends to foster.

THE HUMAN RESPONSE TO SHARING

In contrast to the 'economic man' theory that lies behind traditional economic thinking, there is a natural fit between people and a sharing system. Sometimes, when individuals realise that they really are involved in a genuine sharing system, they go through a considerable psychological upheaval – a really positive change in their view of the world, of their place in it and their feelings about it. Enormous energy can be released: there is a transformation from suspicion to trust; from lack of commitment to strong commitment; from holding back to plunging in; from disappointed wariness to confident hope. In the 1980s I saw this happen to three individuals as we developed employee ownership and participation in the papermaking company where I started. They had been elected to the top representative body, which met with the board four times a year. At first they were intensely suspicious – they had been elected because they of all people would be able to see through what seemed likely to be no more than the latest trick by management. But after about three years they realised that the move to shared ownership and involvement was for real, at which point they were personally transformed into active enthusiasts. Amazed at the power of their responses, I felt that this would be worth further investigation. What is it about human nature that makes us so positively responsive to shared ownership with minimal hierarchy and high participation? I made the decision to study the psychology of sharing.

The most secure intellectual perspective for approaching the human animal seemed to be to acknowledge that we evolved. As an intellectual starting point this would create a tough test of the sharing hypothesis: the caricature version of the 'selfish gene' operating in evolution did not readily suggest that our nature should respond particularly well to sharing. And yet we human animals had found ways to cooperate to an extraordinary extent. Had our evolution in some way primed us to take so enthusiastically to shared ownership?

I was lucky to be able to do a part-time Ph.D. at the University of St Andrews, supervised by Professor Andrew Whiten, an evolutionary psychologist and one of the leading primatologists in the world.

I started by looking at the environment in which we evolved. To the extent that our psychology was shaped by evolution, it would be adapted to that environment – not to the environment of today, marvellous and barely recognisable as it would be to people from just a century or two ago. Even over the last 10,000 years, the period since the first crops were grown and the first animals domesticated, not enough time has elapsed for evolution to have brought about a change in human nature through change at the level of the genes.

In thinking through the evolutionary pressures that shaped our psychology, the relevant environment is the social environment rather than the physical one. Our deepest human psychology has been shaped not by companies and businesses and governments and armies, but by the time until 10,000 years ago that we spent living as hunter-gatherers in small bands of family and friends, a way of life that obtained for hundreds of thousands and possibly millions of years.

Since this was the social environment that shaped our instincts and feelings, the first question to investigate was: how did we live when we were hunter-gatherers – what sort of society did we live in?

The evidence shows that, for all that time, making a living was a shared undertaking. From the time some six million years ago when our ancestors developed the first distinctively human features, right through to now, very few people survived for long alone. Thomas Hobbes, the influential seventeenth-century philosopher, could not have been more wrong when he fantasised that life before civilisation had been a 'warre of all against all', with the lives of individuals being 'solitary, poore, nasty, brutish, and short'.[77]

The lives of hunter-gatherers were in fact intensely sociable, egalitarian and generally free from war. Those who argue that hunters used to fight wars take their evidence often from tribes that in modern times cultivated fields and were in constrained geographical areas. Neither of these circumstances applied in the case of our early ancestors, who cultivated nothing and so were free to move wherever they wished, across vast spaces of unspoiled land.*

A fascinating world opens up in the reports of the people who had early contacts with hunter-gatherers. I gathered every report I could find, analysing them for common features. To be eligible as a possible evolved characteristic in human nature, or as a social characteristic likely to have shaped human nature, any trait would have to be found universally. Out of the seventeen possible characteristics considered, just two proved to be universal among the hunter-gatherers described in the last 400 years. Every hunter-gatherer group shared meat among all its members – not just with kin and not just with those who were capable of reciprocating. When the hunt was successful, if you had a mouth you got fed. And no hunter-gatherer group had a permanent leader – there seem to have been no chiefs at all, appointed, elected or imposed, prior to contact with the 'civilised' world.

Meat was a key resource in human evolution and sharing it carried several benefits. Its concentrated protein and food value were vital. But it was unpredictable: even the best hunters had only a small chance of

* With no policing, there was, however, a high rate of homicide compared to the rates seen today, even in the worst American cities.

coming back with meat on any particular day. When they did succeed, they might come back with the meat of an antelope, or something even bigger – enough to feed the whole group for several days. Sharing the meat evened out the supply across time, making sure that everyone had the best chance of survival. Even the best hunters might go for days without success; through sharing, everyone would survive and have the chance to thrive. Sharing was the economically efficient solution.

Most of the calories were provided not by hunting, a predominately male undertaking, but by gathering, which was primarily carried out by groups of women and children. The fruits of gathering were not shared so widely – in most groups mainly just with kin and close friends. The difference has been interpreted in two ways: firstly, in terms of unpredictability – dealing with risk. In hunting, with the outcome highly unpredictable, someone might try extremely hard for long periods, but still have to return to camp with nothing to show for it. In these circumstances, where there is inherently great uncertainty about the outcome, sharing just seems natural. Today, a lottery-winner will often share the proceeds widely. Sharing things that come by a stroke of good fortune just naturally seems right.

In the gathering of wild fruit and vegetables, however, where the outcome is achieved mainly by hard work and can be forecast with reasonable confidence, the person who ends up with none has probably been lazy rather than unlucky. No share for them, then – unless we know them well, and like them and so forgive them their foibles. In contrast to lottery winnings, we would be very surprised if people shared out their salaries.

The second explanation for the ubiquity of sharing is in terms of mating. The good hunters were widely respected. They tended to have the pick of the girls to marry – characteristically preferring the competent to the merely pretty. And when anthropologists asked women about extramarital affairs, the good hunters featured as lovers more often than the bad. Having a reputation for successfully providing meat for the group made a man attractive as a mate, whether as a husband or a lover.

Sharing meat thus contributed to survival and to reproduction, the two key factors in evolution. Sharing could reasonably be expected to be sustained over the long term, and psychological traits that tended to support it would both survive and be reproduced. These are good grounds for suggesting that sharing has played a significant part in our evolved human nature.

Sharing has certainly been around long enough to affect our evolved nature. In Germany, along with the bones of wild horses from 400,000 years ago (at that time all animals were of course wild), archaeologists have found sophisticated throwing-spears.[78] These ancestors of humans, who hunted horses, would almost certainly have been sharing the meat: otherwise much of it would have rotted – even two or three hunters could not eat a horse. Furthermore, if they refused to share the meat the hunters would have had to defend the carcass against hungry group members, a very risky thing to do when there were throwing-spears around. In the face of a spear launched from some distance away, even the strongest hunter would be at risk. Better to share.

Moving from the subject of food-sharing to the second universal characteristic, that of leadership, the reports showed that no hunter-gatherer group had a permanent leader. This was unexpected. People occupying positions of leadership seem to be such natural parts of our social and political landscape that it is hard to conceive of a society without them. Yet at the point when the hunter-gatherer groups on all continents first had contact with outsiders, they simply did not have individuals designated as leaders. Moreover, where groups were studied in depth, anthropologists found that there seemed to be stable ways in which the groups actively prevented leaders from arising.

Normally, if a decision was to be made by a group – Should we move camp today? Where is the best chance of finding game? Is it time to have a ritual dance? – there would be a discussion. Charac-teristically everyone had the right to have a say, usually even the young-sters, and if there is one characteristic that shines through the often academic use of language in the anthropological reports, it is the will-ingness of people in hunter-gatherer groups to express their minds. The experienced Cambridge-based consultant Chris Mackin's ideal of 'healthy, non-intimidated human beings . . . in a community of equals' accurately describes many a hunter-gatherer group. As a result the discussions could go on for a long time. In the end, usually the group would listen to the person or people acknowledged to be expert in the particular field under discussion. But if anyone became too assertive – 'I'm the best hunter, you should listen to me!' – then the group would make sure that he or she was brought back down to earth,

often with a bump. Andrew Whiten and I came to call that reaction
'counter-dominance'. It seems to be instinctive – nobody likes being
dominated or pushed around; at the very least we bristle and feel
resentment. Among the hunter-gatherers, if an individual became
insistent, demanding the right to be heard in preference to others, the
group would escalate the counter-dominant response. They would at
first just take the mickey out of the arrogant individual, which by
itself could be highly effective. For example, one anthropologist
describes an occasion when everyone except for the would-be leader
ended up rolling on the ground, helpless with laughter, as a grand-
mother with a lively tongue recounted humiliating stories, suitably
embroidered, about his youth. If ridicule proved insufficient, then the
group could be more direct, agreeing among themselves to do the
opposite of what the upstart was proposing, or simply walking away.
In extreme cases they could banish the person from the group, or even
kill him (it was usually a 'him').

We know that among primates life is stressful for the individuals
placed lower in the hierarchy;[79] we know too that government bureau-
crats, although they are educated and well off, die younger if they are
lower in the hierarchy at work.[80] All of this evidence suggests that a
social environment with reduced hierarchy, and one in which key
resources are shared, will fit our evolved minds and hearts more naturally than one in which there is no sharing, whether of money or
influence. My conclusion, based on this research, is that we are primed
by our evolved nature to be natural partners in businesses that we
own together. The system fits us well. That is why we can feel so
intensely liberated and enthused as fellow owners.[81]

It followed from this work that people who live today in relatively
egalitarian communities should have a more natural fit with their
society than those of us who live where there is a large gap between
rich and poor. To test that idea, I therefore set about measuring as
best I could the wider effects of employee ownership on a community in Italy.[82] The earliest employee-owned company discussed in this
book was the one founded in Imola by Giuseppe Bucci. His example
was inspirational, and by 1920 the area had many similarly structured
businesses. This has remained the case: Imola has ever since then been
the site of one of the largest concentrations of worker-cooperatives
anywhere in the world. The nearby town of Faenza has about half

the proportion of employee-owned businesses, and a little further away the town of Sassuolo has none.

In these three towns I compared public data on mortality and a number of other measures – voting, blood donation, car ownership, household wealth and others – and carried out a random survey of households in each town asking about such things as the gap they perceived between rich and poor, their own social networks, their attitude to the authorities, their educational experience, and their perceptions of crime, including domestic violence.

The overall pattern of results showed that the towns with a greater proportion of businesses owned by their employees had healthier communities.

They perceived a smaller gap between rich and poor.

They had larger and more supportive social networks – more friends to call on if they needed help.

They saw the political authorities as being more on their side.

They believed that domestic violence was less prevalent.*

They gave more blood – blood is a pure gift in Italy; no payment is made.

Their children stayed at school longer, and did better.

They continued being trained and educated all their lives, to a radically greater extent.

More of them voted in elections.

Moreover, they didn't bother buying big cars to show off their wealth to each other – Imola had the second-lowest proportion of large cars in all the towns of Italy surveyed by the government. And that was not because they didn't have the money to buy larger cars: Imola was at the time of my research, and remains today, a highly prosperous town, as were the two other local towns where my comparisons were made. In fact the Imola people had higher disposable incomes than average, as you would expect since one in four of them

---

* Except for domestic violence, crime rates were so low that I could not generate useful statistics on crime. I did not ask them how often they beat their wives, but how often they thought their neighbours beat *their* wives. The people in Imola thought their neighbours generally didn't beat their wives; the people in the other towns had a less rosy view, the town with no worker-cooperatives being the worst. Across all the people sampled, women thought there was domestic violence to a greater extent than men did.

worked in a business where, as co-owners, they shared in the profits. They were therefore better able to afford big cars, but they didn't actually buy them. This indicated a different mind-set: it is possible that because they themselves were not dominated at work, they didn't need to try to dominate each other; or perhaps because they were all similarly prosperous, they did not feel the need to make a public display of their wealth.

And they lived longer. Quite a lot longer. People who spent their lives in Imola died two and a half years later than equivalent people in Sassuolo, the equally prosperous town in the same area, but with no employee-owned businesses at all. Its businesses were owned by rich people; most of the population were employed by the rich owners, and subjected to the authority of the managers serving the owners. In other words, Sassuolo was like any prosperous town anywhere in the world. And the Imola people, who lived in a community where one in four worked in an employee-owned business, outlived them by two and a half years.

Why should they live longer? For the reasons that this book has set out already. In each employee-owned business the employee-owners vote their colleagues on to the board, which chooses and supervises the boss. Together they are in control of their destiny. They share the profits they create together through their work. They are full partners in their businesses. They live lives in which they are respected, active participants, engaged players, and nobody has authority over them that they cannot together remove if it is abused, or if the person in authority does not perform.

As a result, like the employee-owners of g3 and of Schafer and of so many other companies we have seen, they relax. They work harder, but they are less stressed.

The difference in the mortality rates between the towns was explained above all by differing rates of cardiovascular problems: heart attacks and strokes. The cardiovascular system is the one most sensitive to prolonged stress. The people in the cooperative town were simply less stressed.

In short, they were happier. Happiness is not just a subjective feeling – it is a physiological state. It is good for you. And for them. Happiness is fostered by the sense of fairness, by the knowledge that the gap between the rich and the poor in the town was actually not great, by the knowledge that the political authorities were on their side and would listen and respond, by the sense of being in it together. That feeling led them to give blood at more than twice the rate of the people living in the town which, in international terms, is normal. The normal system made people die younger than they had to. The more equal and involved community gave people longer, happier lives. There is every reason to believe that if the world were more like Imola – characterised by employee-owned businesses – then similar outcomes would spread.

THE IMPORTANCE OF RELATIVE EQUALITY

Happiness runs very deep and has many effects. A key driver of it seems to be the gap between rich and poor, so salient in the town with no employee-owned businesses, so inconspicuous in Imola. The work of Richard Wilkinson and Kate Pickett[83] shows just how important it is. These two epidemiologists have demonstrated that across all the developed countries the smaller the gap between rich and poor, the better is life expectancy. In countries with greater equality of income, such as Sweden and Japan, people can expect to live longer than in countries with large inequalities of income, such as Britain and the US. Inside the US, the same relationship holds: the inhabitants of states with a relatively equal distribution of income, such as Utah, Vermont and New Hampshire, can expect to live longer than people in states with greater inequality, such as Alabama and California, particularly in the latter case Los Angeles.

Wilkinson and Pickett show that this does not apply just to length of life. A wide range of social problems has a similar pattern: the problems are worse where the gap between rich and poor is greater. This is true of levels of trust, mental illness (including drug and alcohol addiction), infant mortality, obesity, educational performance, teenage births, homicides, rates of imprisonment and social mobility. There is a painful irony in that last fact: social mobility in the land of the American Dream is significantly worse than it is in the Scandinavian countries that are often characterised as having less fluid social structures. American citizens believe they live in a country where anything can be achieved by anyone; but in America in fact it is more difficult than in any other developed country for anyone actually to achieve a better income than their parents had.*

In companies co-owned by their employees, each person shares in the profits, and in many of them individuals also build up capital. Moreover, the incomes at the top tend to be somewhat more moderate than in 'normal' companies. The net effect is to reduce the gap between rich and poor. As this system spreads, the effects on our societies can only be positive across a wide spectrum of important characteristics. It matters when we lock up large numbers of young people. It matters that girls have babies when they are barely out of childhood them-selves. It matters when young people become addicted to drugs. It matters when lives are ruined through mental distress. It matters that young men kill each other. It matters that through living under stress people die early.

And all these social failings will respond to a key aspect of employee ownership: a better, fairer distribution of wealth.

One of the claims made in support of inequality is that without it societies will be less innovative. That view is widely held – it is part of the standard ideology supporting the way things are done now. But it is mistaken. When you plot the patents per head against degree of inequality, the same pattern emerges as with the other social prob-lems listed above: the more unequal the society, the *fewer* patents per head. The US is *less* innovative than Sweden.†

Wilkinson and Pickett point out that relative equality can be achieved in more than one way. Internationally, Japan has the lowest govern-ment spend – that is, proportionally the smallest government – of any developed nation, while Sweden has one of the highest. But both have

---

* This measure is available for eight countries. USA is worst, a little behind the UK. Germany is significantly better, followed in order of improvement by Finland, the trio of Canada, Denmark and Sweden, and best of all Norway. The latter five form a cluster at the top, the USA and UK sit together at the bottom. Germany is in the middle, but closer to the good than the bad end.

† This work has also been done by Wilkinson and Pickett. The following is an extract from their website, http://www.equalitytrust.org.uk/why/evidence/frequently-asked-questions: 'As a check on how inequality might affect creativeness and inno-vation, we have now looked at the relationship between inequality and the number of patents granted per head of population. There is a weak but statistically signifi-cant tendency for more equal societies to gain more patents per head than less equal ones.'

a low gap between rich and poor and both do well on the various measures of social health listed above. Sweden distributes wealth evenly by means of a highly redistributive tax system; Japan achieves its low gap by not having huge differentials of pay in the first place. Within America, neighbouring Vermont and New Hampshire both have a relatively small gap between rich and poor, but Vermont takes the Swedish route – it has the highest tax burden of all the states – and New Hampshire takes the Japanese one: it has the second-lowest. Both do well on the list of social problems, apparently because both have a low gap between top and bottom net incomes.

One of the attractions of employee ownership is that it lowers the gap between rich and poor not by taxation (which is painful and can be reversed by the next administration), but by a more even distribution of wealth in the course of creating it. In the very process of creating wealth, employee-owned companies distribute wealth more evenly. This fact holds out the hope that it is a sustainable, long-lasting process. We will be able to pass on to our children a better way of doing things than we ourselves received from our parents' generation, and our descendants will be in a position to sustain it by making their own businesses successful. They will not depend on politicians. Nor will they depend on the grace and favour of enlightened owners, who if they do not reverse their paternalism themselves will likely see it reversed by the large corporations or the private equity investors to whom they eventually sell their businesses.

Employee ownership runs with the grain of human nature. That is why it works so well, and that is why it is so satisfying.

Epilogue:
What is to be Done?

Through spreading the employee ownership of businesses, we can all help to spread prosperity, health and happiness.

The people who can act most easily are the people who own companies: they can sell them to their employees, in well-structured, sustainable all-employee buyouts. Employees buying the companies where they work have to be vigilant: if the owner persuades them to pay too high a price, then the company will be overburdened with debt. But the vendor who acts in good faith leaves with a fair price and with the satisfaction that he or she has done a good thing, has made things better, has not betrayed the employees by selling them out, but has set them up with the best possible chance of achieving wealthier and happier lives.

Where the state owns businesses – operations that can be structured as companies – it too can sell them to their employees. Again the employees have to watch out for bad faith: politicians will be attracted by the idea of removing costs from the national accounts, and may be tempted to cut corners and the rights of employees. In the privatisations in the former Soviet bloc, the promise of employee ownership was used to make that development more palatable politically, but in practice the way the buyouts were structured made it inevitable that the businesses would fall into the hands of the politicians and senior managers. And in the process the employees were persuaded to accept a reduction in their rights, such as pensions. Employees would do well to be careful and to obtain help from experienced advisers.

Where the owner, whether private or state, is acting in good faith, it will probably be possible to borrow the money required not from a bank but from the vendor – in other words, to pay the ex-owner not all at once but in instalments. A vendor can help a great deal by agreeing to be paid over time. This method has been widely used, ever since the first instance, the John Lewis Partnership.

The managers of larger companies, with their shares traded on the Stock Exchange, can take them private in all-employee buyouts. Investment bankers can help them do it, educating themselves about the workings of the legal structures and financing that can be used, and perhaps coming up with creative solutions in the process.

If financial innovation were used for the benefit of wide employee ownership rather than the self-enrichment of a few, what a difference it would make. The temptation will be to skew the ownership and power radically towards the senior people, the chief executives and directors who already do so well out of the current system. That has to be resisted. The powerful need a change of heart, to recognise that this is worth doing. Most senior managers will have to make do with a smaller proportion of the wealth created by the enterprise. In a competitive system some preside over companies that achieve overwhelming success in their markets and will benefit accordingly. But the collaboration between finance and senior management that currently skews rewards in favour of management regardless of their contribution will come to an end. And managers will certainly have to learn how to exercise their power differently – they will be accountable at the AGM to the people they manage during the year. But the satisfactions to be gained from doing it are real and deep.

Company advisers such as corporate lawyers, accountants and business consultants have an enormous role to play. They are usually the first port of call when the owner or owners of a company decide that it is time to sell. Uniformly, the advisers recommend a trade sale or, if the business is large, an IPO, selling shares on the Stock Exchange. The advisers need a change of outlook. The first recommendation should be a sale to a vendor-financed all-employee buyout; the second, and perhaps the third too, should be a sale to a leveraged all-employee buyout.

Time and again, owners are attracted to the idea of selling their company to the employees. When they ask for advice on how to do it the advisers try to put them off the idea, sometimes in the starkest terms. This has to stop. Stopping it will often make the advisers feel somewhat exposed, because what they sell is expertise, but in the field of employee buyouts many of them don't know what they are talking about. But they can learn, and this is a growing field, in which at least in the UK there are very few competitors. The advisers who prepare themselves properly will find many takers. Again, the employees doing the buyout have to be careful: Baxi Partnership has seen several companies who had paid very large sums for what had proved to be inadequate advice, where advisers were trying to educate themselves about employee buyouts and charging their clients for the privilege.

Traditional economists can stop passing out the old nonsense, and start spreading the word about what is really happening in employee-owned businesses.

Business managers can acknowledge what they have always known in their hearts: there has to be a better way. Now they know. There is. Particularly in know-how businesses, from home care to engineering design, from advertising to software, if the owners refuse to sell to the employees then the employees can simply walk out and start up their own company. There are complex legal ramifications, but many groups have done it. A good example is provided by the oil industry engineers who walked out of Halliburton and started g3. The main attraction was the idea of building a company with a genuine culture of partnership. And in *Open Minds* Andy Law wrote up the enthralling story of St Luke's advertising agency, where, using – politely – the threat of a walk-out, they negotiated a very good deal in their all-employee buyout.

Journalists, steeling themselves against the thing they fear most in all the world – the risk of seeming naïve to their cynical fellow journalists – can start to investigate and tell the truth about the productivity of employee-owned businesses and the happiness of their employee-owners.

And the great mass of us can start to agitate. We need to persuade our politicians that the capital provided by companies for their own all-employee buyouts should not be subject to tax – in America this is largely the situation already. People who sell their companies to the employees should pay less in capital gains tax. Earnings by banks and investors from capital that helps finance all-employee buyouts should be recognised in the tax system. We should require our governments to give preference in awarding contracts to companies owned by their employees – a similar provision in Italy has led to a proliferation of successful workers' cooperatives in the construction industry. Employee ownership is something which will increase prosperity, and therefore taxes, and at the same time will reduce the impact of social problems, thereby reducing the cost of social expenditure. Purely in self-interested governmental terms it is worth promoting, even without giving any weight to the happiness and education and participation in communities that it brings. It makes good citizens, the 'healthy non-intimidated human beings' identified by Chris Mackin as a key outcome of employee ownership.

Furthermore we need to make a serious attempt to formulate a variation on corporate statutes, to create a legal corporate form that is suited to sustained employee ownership. The current enterprise forms have been cobbled together from pre-existing structures designed for other purposes. We can do so much better. As the parliamentary legal officer said in 1999, and as the judge Lord Eustace Percy recognised in 1944, there is a gap in the legislation: employee ownership ought to be facilitated. There is now a crying need for the political parties to pick that up, as also for the governing bodies of the legal profession and the industry organisations.

If we are members of trade unions then we need to persuade the union leaders to recognise the importance of gaining the rights of ownership and the opportunities that they create to enhance both the earnings of working people and their rights to information and influence. Well-structured ownership, because it places the employees genuinely in control, also gives them the power to sustain those rights and those shared benefits over generations. It means getting to grips with the responsibilities of ownership as well as the rights – including the responsibility for losses, to the normal extent for shareholders in limited-liability companies. This is a considerable change of perspective for most trade unions, but the benefits of doing so are huge. In America the United Steelworkers' Union's framework agreement with Mondragón, aimed at developing workers' cooperatives in the US, is a hugely encouraging initiative.

As we have seen, a major problem in any governance system is the tendency of the powerful and the competent to arrogate power and privilege to themselves, overriding the interests of the less powerful. Trade unions could play a useful role in spreading the skills and confidence so that elected representatives of the employees as owners can play an effective role in guiding companies to shared success. And in any large human organisation there needs to be a process for individuals and groups to defend themselves if they are rolled over, inadvertently or not. Rick Dubinski, the leader of the union in United Airlines, the man who led the 1994 employee buyout which obtained 55 per cent of the stock in the company, believed that he had achieved more for his union members through employee ownership than he had done in a lifetime of negotiations within the prevailing ownership structure.

If we are not members of unions, then as would-be employee-owners we can make enquiries. Express enthusiasm. Prepare the case. Contact advisers. Approach the owners of the businesses where we work. And the consequences of not being allowed such a buyout can again be hinted at, politely. Demoralised employees do not build good businesses. Much better to sell to us, and retire not only rich but happy at the happiness you have given us, Mr or Ms Owner. We helped you build the business: now help us into the next stage, in which you will get your money and we will take it further and make it perform better. This outcome will be so much better than if you just sell out and place our destinies in the hands of probably ruthless owners who don't care one whit about us and, given the present sorry state of the legal system, don't need to. Sell to us, retire happy, and we will take things further than any of us has dreamed of. We will transform the corporation and get humanity working, bringing prosperity and happiness to all involved.

Can we do it?

Yes we can.

Acknowledgements

It is customary to wait until the end of the list before thanking one's spouse, but mine deserves first mention. Jennie devoted acres of time to detailed, editorial, hard-graft reading, making countless suggestions for improving the quality and flow of the language, particularly. To do this, she put her own writing in abeyance for many weeks. I am deeply grateful.

My next editor, Dan Hind, was in many ways the midwife to the book: he commissioned it, and then painstakingly helped structure and shape it into a better form, and I am grateful.

The third editor was Kay Peddle, who helped craft it into publishable shape and worked tirelessly to do so. And finally Will Sulkin had overall editorial responsibility for the book in Bodley Head. Kay and he proved a highly supportive team, and I am grateful.

A number of long-standing friends in the world of employee-ownership made particular contributions. In America, David Ellerman, Richard Freeman, John Logue, Chris Mackin, Loren Rodgers and Corey Rosen helped hugely. In the UK, Patrick Burns, Abdi, Robert Oakeshott and Ken Temple deserve special mention. In Mondragón Fred Freundlich and Mikel Lezamiz made possible what I could not have done myself. To all of them, I am grateful.

The School of Management in the University of St Andrews provided a much appreciated academic home. The views expressed are of course not in any way to be associated with the school (or anyone else for that matter, except where specifically expressed as such). But the school did a perfect job of providing access to academic resources, and I am grateful.

My colleagues in Baxi Partnership proved understanding and supportive through the times when I was sometimes absorbed in the book. Special mention goes to John Alexander and Carole Leslie. Their insights into and enthusiasm for employee-ownership have constantly fed into this book.

Most fundamentally, I am grateful to the many people who willingly gave up their time to be taped in interviews, some of them more than once. The list that follows includes I hope all of them, grouped by the name of the company in which they work. In some cases, it was not an interview but a presentation that they gave. My deepest apology if anyone has been left off. Not all have been named in the text, but all contributed their stories, insights and enthusiasm. I could not have written the book without them. Sadly, as explained in the text, the lawyers have advised that some names cannot be mentioned. Those individuals know who they are. I am particularly grateful to them.

In the UK, in Arup, Pat Dallard, Kate Hall, Terry Hill, and Mike Shears; in Childbase, Alison Beard and Mike Thompson; in Debenhams, Ingrid Elliott; in g3, Tarik Al-Rikabi, Dave Bennet, Simon Beresford, Ros Broomfield, Marie Jarvie and Bobby Lau; in Greenwich Leisure, Ben Dixon, Spencer Pession, Holly Popham and Mark Sesnan; in Inveresk, Stefan Kay; in Make Architects, Barry Cooke, Sam Evans, Ken Shuttleworth, James Taylor and Jamie Wilkins; from NFC, Sir Peter Thompson; in Quintessa, David Hodgkinson; from SAIC, Peter Stocks; in Scott Bader, Luke Alger, Philip Bruce, Andrew Gunn, Sara Henderson, Carol Kennedy, Jamie Newall, Roy Phillipps, Pete Spriggs and Richard Stilwell; in Sunderland Home Care, Margaret Elliott, Joan Hutchinson and Sean Jackson; in St Lukes, Neil Henderson, Rajeena Holland, Andy Law and Natalya; in the Baxi Partnership, Philip Baxendale; in the John Lewis Partnership, Mo Asif, Shazia Chaudhry, Peter Cox, Kim Lowe, Charlie Mayfield, Jenny Ridley and Gill Wright; in Tullis Russell, Fred Bowden (Sen.), Derek Hay and Chris Parr; in Woollard and Henry, Fred Bowden (Jnr), Kenny Harris and Peter MacDougal.

In the USA, in ALG, John King; in Cooperative Home Care Associates, Stu Schneider; in Claremont Flock, Peter Pacquette; in Clima-Tech, Pat Ihli, Debbie Johnson, Darwin Roy and Kevin Speer; in CTL Engineering, Ali Jamshidimehr; in Davey Tree, Sandra Reid and Karl

Warnke; in ESOP Services, Ron Gilbert; in Fastener Industries, Forrest Franklin and Karen; in Gardeners' Guild, Michael Davidson; in Lite-control, Greg Banks, Anthony Caruso, Veda Clark, Brian Golden, Shaun Haskell, Brian Henry, Paula Shragge and Chris Wanawitz; in Litehouse, Charity Hegel and Kelly Prior; from Maryland Brush Company, Mary Landry; in Mediasource, Josh Platt; in Meier, Denise Sweeden; from Northwest Pump, Shawna Knutson; in Nypro, Chris Hurd and Gordon Lankton; from the Organically Grown Company, Josh Hinerfeld; in Parametrix, Darlene Brown and Waite Dalrymple; from RJ Martin, Marie Shankell; from Schafer, Victor Aspengren; from Southwest Airlines, Colleen Barrett; from Thomson Store, Tammy Pepper and Erin Walker; from Wilbur, Jeff Evans; and from Wood-fold, Ricky Walsh and Tim Wolfe. In addition to these interviews, I also drew on the 2009 conferences organised in Oregon by the NCEO and in Ohio by the OEOC. Presentations by people from Namaste Solar, Norcal, Praxis and Ruhlin proved particularly apt.

In Italy, Benito Benati and Anna Benati gave invaluable help, and Catherine Urch's interpreting skills were vital. On the use of employee ownership in China, Chris Ruffle was hugely helpful, and on the Polish situation, Ryszard Stocki.

My agent, Isobel Dixon provided an ideal mix of stimulation and support throughout the long gestation, as well as the prolonged process of writing. Without her encouragement I would never have started writing, and I am deeply grateful.

And finally, Jennie deserves a second mention. I simply could not have done it without her.

Notes

1. Frank, Gilovich and Regan, 'Does Studying Economics Inhibit Cooperation?'
2. When I joined the mill there were about forty paper mills in Scotland: thirty-two years later only four survived.
3. I would like to believe that my interviewees had encountered only the rougher end of the private equity trade. But I fear that the stories distilled here are typical of many. Certainly, the rights of the people involved are as described, no matter how those powers are exercised in practice.
4. See the PBS television programme *The Warning* in the *Frontline* series, at http://video.pbs.org/video/1302794657/ telling the terrible story of how Greenspan and his supporters blocked the regulation of derivative markets by Brooksley Born in 1998.
5. See the numerous experiments using the Ultimatum Game, e.g. Cameron, 'Raising the Stakes in the Ultimatum Game'.
6. Kruse, Blasi and Park, 'Shared Capitalism in America'.
7. Presentation to the Congreso Internacional CIRIEC, Seville, September 2008.
8. Ehrenreich, *Nickel and Dimed*.
9. Ortega, *In Sam We Trust*.
10. Kruse, Freeman and Blasi, *Shared Capitalism at Work*.
11. Conyon and Freeman, *Shared Modes of Compensation and Firm Performance*.
12. Jensen and Meckling, 'Rights and Production Functions'.
13. Faleye, Mehrotra, and Morck, 'When Labor Has a Voice in Corporate Governance'.
14. Writings held at the Mondragón Professional School, vol. 1, p. 68. Quoted in Arizmendiarrieta, *Reflections*.
15. *Writings on Cooperative Education*, vol. II, p. 31. Quoted in Arizmendiarrieta, *Reflections*.
16. Potter, *The Co-operative Movement in Great Britain*, Chapter V, pp. 117ff.
17. Corey Rosen, Employee Ownership Update, 17 November 2006.

18. See the website of the National Center for Employee Ownership, the most reputable source of accurate information, http://www.nceo.org/main/article.php/id/3/

19. Jensen and Meckling, 'Rights and Production Functions'.

20. Hansmann, *The Ownership of Enterprise*, p. 83.

21. Furubotn, 'The Long-Run Analysis of the Labor-Managed Firm'.

22. Boatright, 'Employee Governance and the Ownership of the Firm'.

23. Alchian and Demsetz, 'Production, Information Costs, and Economic Organization'.

24. http://www.nceo.org/

25. The latest manifestation is Kruse, Freeman and Blasi, *Shared Capitalism at Work*.

26. Bonin, Jones and Putterman, 'Theoretical and Empirical Studies of Producer Cooperatives'.

27. Jensen and Meckling, 'Rights and Production Functions', p. 489, emphasis added.

28. http://www.saic.com/about/history.html accessed 10 August 2009. See also Beyster and Economy, *The SAIC Solution*.

29. The '401k' scheme.

30. Jensen and Meckling, 'Rights and Production Functions', p. 483.

31. Ibid., p. 504.

32. Jensen, *Spain Pioneers Sustainable Democratic Corporate Governance*.

33. O'Sullivan, *Contests for Corporate Control*. She produces good support for her thesis that healthy economies are built by investing in organic growth, achieved through committed investment in research and in people. The American approach is shown to have produced more doubtful results.

34. Hansmann, *The Ownership of Enterprise*, pp. 90 and 119.

35. 'Floturn Forgoes Fat Profits to Boost Its Market Share', *Wall Street Journal*, 18 January 2000.

36. The Ohio Employee Ownership Top 50, *Owners at Work*, Winter 2007. Ohio Employee Ownership Center, www.oeockent.org/index.php/library/doc/132/raw

37. Bradley and Taylor, *Business Performance in the Retail Sector*.

38. Saxenian, *Regional Advantage*.

39. See the excellent exposition in Blasi, Kruse and Bernstein, *In the Company of Owners*.

40. Porter, *Competitive Strategy*, p. 4.

41. Jensen and Meckling, 'Rights and Production Functions', p. 485.

42. Article by F. John Reh posted on About.com, accessed on 28 February 2010, http://management.about.com/cs/generalmanagement/a/CEOsOverpaid.htm

43. http://www.aflcio.org/corporatewatch/paywatch/ accessed 29 December 2009.

44. *Forbes* Special Report on Executive Compensation, dated 22 April 2009.

45. Heather Landy, 'Behind the Big Paydays', *The Washington Post*, 15 November 2008.

46. See 'Learning from the Past: Trends in Executive Compensation over the 20th Century', at http://cesifo.oxfordjournals.org/cgi/reprint/ifp021vi

47. I am grateful to David Ellerman for drawing my attention to this, in Ellerman, 'The Two Institutional Logics'.

48. Keynes, *The General Theory of Employment, Interest and Money*, p. 151.

49. This chapter owes a great deal to the work of J. L. and Barbara Hammond, whose books on the history of the enclosures and the later consequences – *The Village Labourer* and *The Town Labourer* – I cannot recommend too highly.

50. Hammond and Hammond, *The Village Labourer*.

51. For clarity, the language has been slightly edited.

52. Hammond and Hammond, *The Village Labourer*, p. 223.

53. *The Times*, 8 January 1831.

54. Quoted in Hammond and Hammond, *The Town Labourer*, pp. 199–200.

55. Quoted in Engels, *The Condition of the Working Class in England*, p. 186.

56. Brown, *A Memoir of Robert Blincoe*, p. 36.

57. Oastler, 'Yorkshire Slavery', reprinted in Freedgood, *Factory Production in Nineteenth-century Britain*. Author's emphases removed.

58. Hammond and Hammond, *The Town Labourer*, p. 120.

59. Smith, *The Wealth of Nations*, Chapter VIII.

60. See for example Chang, *Factory Girls*.

61. Ellerman, *Helping People Help Themselves*. See also http://www.ellerman.org/

62. Frankl, *Man's Search for Meaning*, p. 75.

63. Oakeshott, *Jobs and Fairness*, p. 33. Quotation taken from Percy's Riddell lecture of 1944, quoted in Goyder, *The Just Enterprise*.

64. The story of their founder is told in chapter 2.

65. In John Lewis, the interviews with people other than Mo Asif were arranged with the help of the Registry, which is not part of the management hierarchy, but is an official section of the company set up to check up on managers, to make sure that the principles in the constitution are being practised. I had to go through the Registry because Mo Asif, the sole individual who agreed to talk without involving anyone else, had only two years'

experience. To obtain a longer-term view I had to get permission, as well as help in picking people. To avoid the possibility that I might be being fed specially selected people, management stooges, I rejected the whole list of people that the Registry prepared and asked instead to interview the person in exactly the same job as the manager I had interviewed in Debenhams, and one more chosen at random on a walkabout. I believe that this procedure gave a fair comparison.

66. The 'Dryden' text of Plutarch's *Lives of the Noble Greeks and Romans*, http://www.bostonleadershipbuilders.com/plutarch/alexander.htm accessed 29 June 2010.

67. 'Marines Do Heavy Lifting as Afghan Army Lags in Battle', *New York Times*, 20 February 2010. The other Afghan army is of course proving highly effective (at the time of writing), as previously the Afghans did against occupation by the Soviet army.

68. Kruse, Freeman and Blasi, *Shared Capitalism at Work*.

69. Law, *Open Minds*.

70. Note for UK legislators: with minor alterations the SIP trust could become a highly effective vehicle for employee buyouts, with little risk of its being abused by tax dodgers. The main adjustment needed is to allow it to hold shares over the long term.

71. See e.g. Dube and Freeman, 'Complementarity of Shared Compensation and Decision-Making Systems'.

72. Kruse, Freeman and Blasi, 'Do Workers Gain by Sharing?'.

73. www.usatoday.com/money/economy/2010-02-25-bernanke-fed-greece_N.htm accessed 8 May 2010.

74. Frank, Gilovich and Regan, 'Does Studying Economics Inhibit Cooperation?'

75. Jensen, Granger and Erhard, 'A New Model of Integrity'.

76. Jensen and Meckling, 'Rights and Production Functions', p. 504.

77. Hobbes, *Leviathan*.

78. Thieme, 'Lower Palaeolithic Hunting Spears from Germany'.

79. For example, Sapolsky, 'Stress in the Wild'.

80. For example, Marmot, 'Health Inequalities among British Civil Servants'.

81. This part of our research was written up in Erdal and Whiten, 'Egalitarianism and Machiavellian Intelligence in Human Evolution'.

82. I will always be grateful to Robert Oakeshott for the discussions that led to this study, and for pointing to the community of Imola as a town with an unusually high proportion of cooperatives. Also to Benito Benati, then MD of SACMI, and his daughter Anna for their help in carrying out this research.

83. Wilkinson and Pickett, *The Spirit Level*.

Bibliography

Alchian, Armen A. and Harold Demsetz, 'Production, Information Costs, and Economic Organization', *American Economic Review*, Vol. 62, No. 5, Dec. 1972, pp. 777–95

Arrizmendiarrieta, José-María. *Reflections*, Mondragón: Otalora (undated)

Bageant, Joe, *Deer Hunting with Jesus*, London: Random House, 2007

Beyster, Bob with Peter Economy, *The SAIC Solution: How We Built an $8 Billion Employee-Owned Technology Company*, Hoboken: John Wiley, 2007

Blair, Margaret M., *Ownership and Control: Rethinking Corporate Governance for the Twenty-First Century*, Washington DC: The Brookings Institution, 1995

Blasi, Joseph, Douglas Kruse and Aaron Bernstein, *In the Company of Owners*, New York: Basic Books, 2003

Boatright, John, 'Employee Governance and the Ownership of the Firm', *Business Ethics Quarterly*, Vol. 14, 2004, pp. 1–21

Boehm, Christopher, *Hierarchy in the Forest: the Evolution of Egalitarian Behavior*, Cambridge, Mass.: Harvard University Press, 1999

Bonin, John P., Derek C. Jones and Louis Putterman, 'Theoretical and Empirical Studies of Producer Cooperatives: Will Ever the Twain Meet?', *Journal of Economic Literature*, Vol. XXXI, Sept. 1993, pp. 1290–1320

Bowe, John, Marisa Bowe and Sabin Streeter, *Gig: Americans Talk about Their Jobs*, New York: Random House, 2000

Bradley, Keith and Simon Taylor, *Business Performance in the Retail Sector*, Oxford: Clarendon Press, 1993

Brown, John, *A Memoir of Robert Blincoe*, Sussex: Caliban Books, 1977 (1828)

Calvin, Joseph W., *A Piece of the Pie: the Story of Customer Service in Publix*, Kearney: Morris, 2005

Cameron, Lisa, 'Raising the Stakes in the Ultimatum Game: Experimental Evidence from Indonesia', *Economic Inquiry*, Vol. 37, 1999, pp. 47–59

Chang, Leslie T., *Factory Girls: Voices from the Heart of Modern China*, London: Picador, 2009

Conyon, Martin and Richard Freeman, *Shared Modes of Compensation and Firm Performance: UK Evidence*, NBER (National Bureau of Economic Research) Working Paper No. 8448, 2001. See http://www.nber.org/

Cooke, C. A., *Corporation, Trust and Company: an Essay in Legal History*, Manchester: Manchester University Press, 1950

Davies, William, *Reinventing the Firm*, London: Demos, 2009

Dow, Gregory K., *Governing the Firm: Workers' Control in Theory and in Practice*, Cambridge: Cambridge University Press, 2003

Dube, Arindrajit and Richard Freeman, 'Complementarity of Shared Compensation and Decision-Making Systems: Evidence from the American Labor Market', in Kruse, Freeman and Blasi (eds), *Shared Capitalism at Work*. Available as an NBER working paper at http://www.nber.org/books/kruso8-1

Ehrenreich, Barbara, *Nickel and Dimed: Undercover in Low-Wage USA*, London: Granta, 2001

Ellerman, David, *The Democratic Worker-Owned Firm: A New Model for the East and West*, London: Unwin Hyman, 1990

——, *Property and Contract in Economics: Democratic Alternatives to Capitalism and Socialism*, Cambridge, Mass.: Basil Blackwell Inc., 1992

——, Ellerman, David, *Helping People Help Themselves*, Ann Arbor: University of Michigan Press, 2005

——, Ellerman, David, 'The Two Institutional Logics: Exit-Oriented Versus Commitment-Oriented Institutional Designs', *International Economic Journal*, Vol. 19, No. 2, June 2005, pp. 147–68

——, http://www.ellerman.org/ makes available without charge the texts of most of Ellerman's papers and books

Engels, Friedrich, *The Condition of the Working Class in England*, London: Granada (Panther), 1979 (1892)

Erdal, David, *Local Heroes: How Loch Fyne Oysters Embraced Employee Ownership and Business Success*, London: Viking, 2008

Erdal, David and Andrew Whiten, 'Egalitarianism and Machiavellian Intelligence in Human Evolution', in Paul Mellars and Kathleen Gibson (eds), *Modelling the Ancient Human Mind*, Cambridge: McDonald Institute for Archaeological Research, 1996, pp. 139–50

Faleye, Olubunmi, Vikas Mehrotra and Randall Morck, 'When Labor Has a Voice in Corporate Governance', *Journal of Financial and Quantitative Analysis*, Vol. 41, No. 3, 2006

Frank, Robert H., Thomas Gilovich and Dennis T. Regan, 'Does Studying Economics Inhibit Cooperation?', *Journal of Economic Perspectives*, Vol. 7, No. 2, 1993, pp. 159–71

Frankl, Viktor, *Man's Search for Meaning*, London: Simon and Schuster, 1984 (1959)

Freedgood, Elaine (ed.), *Factory Production in Nineteenth-Century Britain*, Oxford: Oxford University Press, 2003

Furubotn, Eirek, 'The Long-Run Analysis of the Labor-Managed Firm: an

Alternative Interpretation', *American Economic Review*, 66 (1), March 1976, pp. 104–24

Gates, Jeff, *The Ownership Solution: Toward a Shared Capitalism for the Twenty-First Century*, London: Penguin, 1998

Goyder, George, *The Just Enterprise*, London: André Deutsch, 1987

Hammond, J. L. and Barbara Hammond, *The Town Labourer: 1760–1832: The New Civilisation*, London: Longmans, Green, 1995 (1917)

——, *The Village Labourer*, Stroud: Nonsuch, 2005 (1911)

Hansmann Henry, *The Ownership of Enterprise*, Cambridge Mass.: Harvard University Press, 1996

Hobbes, Thomas, *Leviathan* (1651), Project Gutenberg 3207

Hoe, Susanna, *The Man Who Gave His Company Away: a Biography of Ernest Bader, Founder of the Scott Bader Commonwealth*, Wollaston: Scott Bader, 1978

Hovencamp, Herbert, *Enterprise and American Law, 1836–1937*, Cambridge, Mass.: Harvard University Press, 1991

Jensen, Anthony, *Spain Pioneers Sustainable Democratic Corporate Governance Business Model with Sociedades Laborales*, Sydney: University Faculty of Economics and Business, 2006

Jensen, Michael C., Kari L. Granger and Werner Erhard, *A New Model of Integrity: The Missing Factor Of Production*, Harvard NOM Research Paper No. 10-087; Barbados Group Working Paper No. 10-03, 2010

Jensen, Michael C. and William H. Meckling, 'Rights and Production Functions: An Application to Labor Managed Firms and Codetermination', *Journal of Business*, Vol. 52, No. 4 (October), 1979, pp. 469–506

Kelly, Marjorie, *The Divine Right of Capital: Dethroning the Corporate Aristocracy*, San Francisco: Berrett-Koehler, 2001

Kelso, Louis O. and Mortimer J. Adler, *The Capitalist Manifesto*, New York: Random House, 1958

Keynes, John Maynard, *The General Theory of Employment, Interest and Money*, London: Macmillan, 1967 (1936)

Kruse, Douglas L., Richard B. Freeman and Joseph R. Blasi (eds), *Shared Capitalism at Work: Employee Ownership, Profit and Gain Sharing, and Broad-Based Stock Options*, Chicago: University of Chicago Press, 2010

——, 'Do Workers Gain by Sharing?', in Kruse, Freeman and Blasi, *Shared Capitalism at Work*.

Kruse, Douglas L., Joseph R. Blasi and Rhokeun Park, 'Shared Capitalism in America', in Kruse, Freeman and Blasi, (eds), *Shared Capitalism at Work*.

Landy, Heather, 'Behind the Big Payday', *The Washington Post*, 15 November 2008

Law, Andy, *Open Minds*, London: Orion Books, 1998

Lewis, John Spedan, *Partnership for All*, London: Kerr-Cros, 1948

——, *Fairer Shares*, London: Staples, 1954

Lieber, James B., *Friendly Takeover: How an Employee Buyout Saved a Steel Town*, London: Penguin, 1995

Logue, John and Jacquelyn Yates, *The Real World of Employee Ownership*, Ithaca: Cornell University Press, 2001

Mao, Tse-tung, *Quotations from Chairman Mao Tse-tung*, Beijing: Sinolingua, 1990

Marmot, M. G., 'Health Inequalities among British Civil Servants: the Whitehall II study', *Lancet*, 337, 1991, pp. 1387–93

McLachlan, Sandy, *The National Freight Buyout: the Inside Story*, London: Macmillan, 1983

Mill, John Stuart, *Principles of Political Economy*, London: John W. Parker, 1848

Oakeshott, Robert, *The Case for Workers' Co-ops*, London: Macmillan, 1990 (1978)

——, *Jobs and Fairness: the Logic and Experience of Employee Ownership*, Norwich: Michael Russell, 2000

Oastler, Richard, 'Yorkshire Slavery', *Mercury* (Leeds), 29 September 1830. Text reprinted in Elaine Freedgood (ed.), *Factory Production in Nineteenth-Century Britain*, Oxford: Oxford University Press, 2003

OEOC: Ohio Employee Ownership Center, 'The Ohio Employee Ownership Top 50', *Owners at Work*, Winter 2007

Ortega, Bob, *In Sam We Trust*, New York: Times Books, 1998

O'Sullivan, Mary A., *Contests for Corporate Control: Corporate Governance and Economic Performance in the United States and in Germany*, Oxford: Oxford University Press, 2001

Plutarch, *Lives of the Noble Greeks and Romans*, http://www.bostonleadershipbuilders.com/plutarch/alexander.htm

Porter, Michael E., *Competitive Strategy: Techniques for Analyzing Industries and Competitors*, New York: The Free Press, 1980

Potter, Beatrice, *The Co-operative Movement in Great Britain*, Swan Sonnenschein, 1899 (1891)

Rosen, Corey, *An Ownership Tale*, Oakland: NCEO, 2008

Rosen, Corey and Loren Rodgers, *The Ownership Edge*, Oakland: NCEO, 2007

Sapolsky, Robert, 'Stress in the Wild', *Scientific American*, 262: 1990, pp. 106–113

Saxenian, AnnaLee, *Regional Advantage*, Cambridge, Mass.: Harvard University Press, 1994

Schlosser, Eric, *Fast Food Nation*, London: Penguin, 2002

Smith, Adam, *An Inquiry into the Nature and Causes of the Wealth of Nations*, London: Strahan, Cadell and Creech, 1776

Stiglitz, Joseph, presentation to the Congreso Internacional CIRIEC, Seville, September 2008. See http://www.congresociriec.es/en

Thieme, H., 'Lower Palaeolithic Hunting Spears from Germany', *Nature*, 385, 1997, pp. 807–10

Toynbee, Polly, *Hard Work: Life in Low-Pay Britain*, London: Bloomsbury, 2003

Toynbee, Polly and David Walker, *Unjust Rewards: Exposing Greed and Inequality in Britain Today*, London: Granta, 2008

Tse, K. K., *Marks and Spencer*, Oxford: Pergamon Press, 1985

Voltaire, *Candide*, London: Penguin Classics, 2007 (1759)

Wearmouth, Robert F, *Some Working-Class Movements of the Nineteenth Century*, London: The Epworth Press, 1948

Webb, Sidney and Beatrice Webb, *The History of Trade Unionism*, London: Longmans, Green and Co., 1894

Whyte, William Foote and Kathleen King Whyte, *Making Mondragón: the Growth and Dynamics of the Worker Cooperative Complex*, Ithaca: ILR Press, 1988

Wilkinson, Richard and Kate Pickett, *The Spirit Level*, London: Allen Lane, 2009

——, data and writings available at http://www.equalitytrust.org.uk/

Index